THE
Epics of
Celtic *Ireland*

THE
Epics of
Celtic *Ireland*

Ancient Tales of Mystery and Magic

JEAN MARKALE

TRANSLATED BY JODY GLADDING

INNER TRADITIONS
ROCHESTER, VERMONT

Inner Traditions International
One Park Street
Rochester, Vermont 05767
www.InnerTraditions.com

First U.S. edition published by Inner Traditions in 2000

Originally published in French under the title *L'Epopée celtique en Irlande* by Éditions Payot 1984, 1992

Copyright © 1984, 1992 by Éditions Payot
English translation copyright © 2000 by Inner Traditions International

All rights reserved. No part of this book may be reproduced or utilized in any form or by any means, electronic or mechanical, including photocopying, recording, or by any information storage and retrieval system, without permission in writing from the publisher.

Library of Congress Cataloging-in-Publication Data

Markale, Jean.
    [Epopée celtique d'Irlande]
    The epics of Celtic Ireland : ancient tales of mystery and magic / Jean Markale ; translated by Jody Gladding.
        p. cm.
    Includes index.
    ISBN 0-89281-815-8 (alk. paper)
    1. Epic literature, Irish—History and criticism. 2. Mythology, Celtic, in literature. 3. Ireland—In literature. 4. Celts in literature. I. Gladding, Jody, 1955– II. Title.

PB1327 .M313 2000
891.6'2103209—dc21

                            00-026792

Printed and bound in Canada

10 9 8 7 6 5 4 3 2 1

Text design and layout by Priscilla Baker
This book was typeset in Caslon, with Barbara as a display face

Inner Traditions wishes to express its appreciation for assistance given by the government of France through the ministère de la Culture in the preparation of this translation.

Nous tenons à exprimer nos plus vifs remerciements au government de la France et le ministère de la Culture pour leur aide dans le préparation de cette traduction.

Contents

Foreword

More than twenty years have passed since this work first appeared, and for the public, Ireland is no longer a complete unknown. Tourism, the European Community, and various other ties have all helped open the door to this strange island lost in the Atlantic, at the farthest western limits of the Old World. But isn't this a somewhat superficial vision of a country that retains its mystery—and especially of a people whose behavior runs the risk of seeming as disconcerting as it is paradoxical? Heirs to a very ancient civilization, engaged now more than ever in rebuilding a modern society, the Irish find themselves at the juncture of two universes. And they convey this perfectly in their traditional narratives, in which they speak about the constant interpenetration of the visible and the invisible, the real and the imaginary, that which can be communicated and that which remains ineffable. Converted to Christianity at the very beginning of the Middle Ages under conditions that remain astonishing, they made their country into the crucible in which a new civilization was spawned. This civilization they helped disperse and establish over a whole continent letting itself be devoured by its own violence. Ireland reconverted Europe to Christianity; that is a historical reality. But Ireland is also where the culture of classical antiquity has been preserved, and, not the least of its merits, it has salvaged the great oral tradition of the Celts—thanks to its monks, who were careful to preserve the memory of all that had been their ancestors' special treasure.

And this extraordinary work of seventh- to fifteenth-century monks was not in vain. Because of it, Ireland has been able to survive so many centuries of oppression and, it must be said, colonization. And it is especially because of its myths, reverently compiled and distributed at the right moment, that Ireland was able to rise out of its ashes to become a modern state. Even as part of an intransigent Catholic Church, the Irish have never forgotten their ancient gods and the heroes of their fantastic epics. The Irish revolution that took place at the beginning of this century was carried out in their name. A statue of Cuchulainn is found in Dublin's major post office, the scene of the "Bloody Easter" of 1916. And in front of Trinity College, that venerable university, near a large modern store on a discreet little square that goes by the name of Setana (Cuchulainn's true name), a huge fresco illustrates the exploits of the greatest hero of the Gaelic epic. The Irish not only have a long memory, but they know how to graft their contemporary life onto the gnarled trunk of a history rich with teachings. They have not been content to relegate the vestiges of their past to the museums (which are well filled nonetheless). They have also wanted to reinvest the myths of another time with present-day significance. They set an example that deserves to be studied and taken to heart.

What is more, if we think about it, their myths are our own, the myths of all western Europe. They have had the wisdom to keep them alive, as opposed to what has happened in other countries. That is why, after more than twenty years, it was important to take up this *Epics of Celtic Ireland* once again, reconsider it, correct its flaws, and, especially, enrich it with new texts and new reflections. It is a matter, pure and simple, of exploring the very special universe of the Irish Gaelic epic, and adding commentaries when necessary—literary as much as mythological and philosophical—on these precious works, which are part of our birthright as well. It is important to know these masterpieces drawn from our European heritage.

Thus, this work simultaneously rejuvenates a tradition unjustly underrated and occasionally scorned, and contributes to the knowledge of European culture.

Poul Fetan

Introduction

The Irish Epic

There was a time when Celtic literature was considered nonexistent. Besides, why should we be concerned with the literary productions of these barbaric peoples who never had the good fortune of being conquered, occupied, and Latinized like the Gauls? All light emanated, necessarily, from Rome, or just possibly from Greece, and it would have been inconceivable to make any comparisons between a work from classical antiquity and a Celtic or Germanic work.

Then, with the development of sensibility and taste at the end of the eighteenth century, while Diderot was demanding for poetry "something enormous and barbaric" and asking poets to go find their inspiration in the depths of the forests, a voice was raised in the northernmost regions of the Celtic isles. It was the voice of a Scottish poet by the name of Mac Pherson, who claimed to have rediscovered the traces of an ancient Gaelic poetry and who published about fifteen poems in prose in 1760, so-called translations from the Gaelic in which the heroes were Ossian the poet and Fingal the old king of the Fiana. Mac Pherson persisted. He then published many collections in the same vein, and sooner or later all of Europe began to take an interest in the adventures of these more or less superhuman, more or less divine heroes who appeared in the shadows of old ruined castles, in the fog, or during a storm, like wailing ghosts in search of paradise.

These were fakes. This became apparent very quickly, because Mac Pherson was unable to produce for his critics the originals of the poems that he had supposedly translated. But Europe couldn't have cared less. And Ossian caused an explosion in the sensibility and soul of his readers, shaking the dust from a dead literature and giving the signal for the romantic revolution. That says something about

1

the importance of such a work, even if we know it to be a literary hoax, because, though there was clear proof of forgery, where there's smoke, there's fire. And when things calmed down it became clear that tenacious folklore traditions, on which popular storytellers were raised, actually existed in Scotland, the Hebrides, and Ireland. Mac Pherson *had invented nothing.* He had let himself be inspired by the themes of these popular stories and had adapted them to present-day tastes—in an artificial literary context, to be sure, but one that touched the public, because the feelings expressed were those the public itself was waiting for.

These discoveries would lead to others. Just as occurred in Armorican Brittany, where Hersart de la Villemarqué reproduced Mac Pherson's forgery—and his feat—a systematic search began not only for the oral traditions still widespread among Celtic-speaking populations, but also for the earliest manuscripts, which had preserved the texts from those specifically Celtic periods. And some of them were found. Beginning in the ninth century, Irish monks had transcribed in Gaelic most of the pagan Celtic legends that had been transmitted to them orally, or through even earlier manuscripts. Then more of them were found. One whole school of Celtic scholars, English, Irish, and German, began to study the ancient Gaelic language and to translate the texts.

Of course, it was primarily a passion for archaeology that drove these respectable scholars. They took hardly any interest in what they translated. All that mattered to them was the pleasure of translating, studying, and then classifying ancient relics. Let us listen to Georges Dottin, who at the beginning of the twentieth century began to feel some affection for the works themselves: "The value . . . of Irish literature . . . has been much debated. In the preface to the *Yellow Book of Lecan*, one of the scholars who has contributed the most to Gaelic studies, Robert Atkinson, declares it poor and unvaried, irrelevant to classical and medieval cultures, lacking in elevated thought or dignity. Echoing him, J. P. Mahaffy states in 1899 that when it wasn't inane, it was indecent." Moreover, we find no judgments of a literary nature coming from Withley Stokes, or Kuno Meyer, or any of those who were the best and most passionate translators of Celtic epics into English at that time. And the same is true for d'Arbois de Jubainville, the originator of Celtic studies in France, who was content to simply translate, classify, and comment upon the historical value of those works he nevertheless rescued from oblivion.

This disregard, not to say hostility, for Irish epic literature in academic circles should not be cause for astonishment, however. First of all, this literature is so totally different from the romantic eloquence of Mac Pherson, so totally different from the Mediterranean epics, that it surprises, it *shocks*, and it is sometimes even incomprehensible to a person raised exclusively on classical culture. Second, it is a literature deeply rooted in the distant past of Celtic civilization. To fully appreciate it, all romanticism must be swept aside, and it must be placed in its own cultural framework. And that can only be done in conjunction with the discovery of the great stages of civilization of the various Celtic peoples, on the Continent as well as in the so-called British Isles.

Finally—and this is the most important thing—the general public of the nineteenth and early twentieth centuries was still so imbued with Aristotelian logic, so enclosed within the strict framework of reason (arbitrarily defined), so used to an aesthetic inherited from Greco-Roman culture that it was impossible for them to be truly interested in a literature that constantly defied *good sense* and the familiar routine.

Since that period, we have experienced Hegel, Marxism, Freud, and surrealism. Good old logic, which had its hour and proved its usefulness, is beginning to give way to something else. The aesthetic has been disrupted. The development of new means of distribution and even of new art forms like the cinema has completely changed our way of seeing things. There is as much difference between a Mediterranean epic and an Irish epic as there is between a film from 1930–1935, logically constructed, respecting classical chronology and sequence of events, and a film from 1960–1970—at least among the experimental films, which use methods resulting from other demands and another kind of logic.

That is to say, then, that Irish epic literature is singularly *modern* in the strict sense of the word—which does not mean that the ancient Irish were many centuries ahead of themselves, but simply that their works belong to a certain way of thinking that we have currently rediscovered and that we exploit. The seventeenth century recognized itself in the great works of antiquity. The twentieth and twenty-first centuries recognize themselves elsewhere, and among the sources from which they like to drink, the Irish spring can quench its thirst for novelty and even heal certain ills that afflict it.

No one has ever invented anything. Civilizations, with their various phases, succeed one another. These phases are more or less long, more or less fruitful. And their fruitfulness is sometimes apparent only after a great lapse of time. Everything lies in knowing what we want, what we find interesting. Contemporary modern art is close to megalithic and Gallic art, because the classical Mediterranean source has been exhausted. A novel or a film by Alain Robbe-Grillet, (all reservations about content aside) is very close to an epic like *The Courtship of Etaine* or *Finn's Childhood.* Basically, we find in Irish epic literature the myths that interest us; we locate our own myths there. And this is what makes it so fertile.

Thus, it is necessary to assess and to judge these works rising out of the dim past, not only considering the archaeological references but also reading them with a *modern* eye, open to the discoveries of psychology and even of psychoanalysis, open to all forms of aesthetics but not forgetting that, as Michel Bréal said, "in the same instant when a myth reveals itself, it vanishes: you could say that it only exists on the condition of not being understood."[1] In all work, the part of dream and poetry is a *sacred* part. And to touch the sacred is an act of sacrilege that amounts to saying that any study of a text, especially a traditional text, contains in itself the destruction of that text. "It is necessary to try to live!" wrote Paul Valéry, searching for the fundamental myth of man within himself. This attempt the authors of Irish epics have embraced wholeheartedly. But it is not "on that peaceful roof where the doves walk" that they discovered beauty. It is in the depths of their heart, in the deep abyss of the mind, in the volcanic crater of their dreams. For them, as for André Breton, "Beauty will be convulsive or will not be."

Like the Welsh epic, the primitive Irish epic must have been composed from a series of poems, learned by heart and transmitted orally from *fili* to *fili*, those poets and keepers of the druidic tradition. Around these poems, which might be considered the fixed skeleton, the epic must have developed in prose according to each storyteller's whim as he improvised on the themes, adding or omitting episodes according to his audience. This is the system known in France as the *chante-fable,* and the model for it is the story of *Aucassin et Nicolette.* The subjects were either mythological or historical, but given the antihistorical Celtic nature, the two very often merged. It is more than likely that such works existed since the earliest times, for Greek and Latin writers described Celtic bards singing of their ancestors' exploits during battles in order to inspire courage in their warriors.

But we know that the Celts distrusted the written word, and that the druids forbade anything involving their tradition to be put in writing. Thus, it is not surprising that in Ireland, as in Brittany and Gaul, we find no written trace of these epics from the period when druidism still permeated all levels of society. It was only in the Christian period, and only in the British Isles, that, out of commendable concern for preserving cultural heritage, the decision was made to commit to paper everything that constituted the oral tradition. And it is no less surprising that these scribes, Christian monks, did not hesitate to occasionally alter what they no longer understood or what, in their Christian zeal, they found shocking. Thus, we have a profusion of texts, but they are sometimes incomplete or deliberately edited, often from a very different age with a very different language. Indeed, the earliest manuscripts go back to the ninth century and were recopied over the course of the following centuries. Each time, the language was modernized, in keeping with its development. The texts in old Irish were succeeded by texts in middle Irish up until the eighteenth century, when we find manuscripts that are transpositions of sometimes very ancient works into modern Irish.

Thus it is quite difficult to date works, since the age of the manuscript is often irrelevant.[2] The story's theme, evidence of characteristic customs, and linguistic archaisms form the primary basis upon which such an assessment can be made. Moreover, in the most ancient texts, the verse stanzas remain intact. But as these verses became more and more obscure, more and more difficult to understand, they soon disappeared, although we cannot conclude from this that the legend is more recent.

Thus it would be futile to sketch out a chronology of the Irish epic texts. Suffice it to say that they cover a period going back to the arrival of the Gaels in Ireland, that is, the sixth or fifth century B.C., up to the Scandinavian period, during the Norse invasions of the ninth century (the question of the manuscripts aside).

On the other hand, it is possible to make distinctions among this multitude of works, clearly very variable in worth and interest. The fili themselves classified them. So it was that, in order to be accepted into the brotherhood, each file had to know seventeen series of stories—which were, in fact, seventeen kinds of narratives varying according to subject. As the twelve principal series we find the *Togla* (destructions), the *Tana* (cattle raids), the *Tochmarca* (courtships), the *Catha* (battles), the *Uatha* (hideouts), the *Imrama* (navigations), the *Oitta* (violent deaths), the *Flessa* (feasts), the *Forbossa* (sieges), the *Echtrai* (adventures), the *Aithid* (abductions of women), and the *Oirgne* (murders). The five secondary stories were the *Tomadma* (floods), the *Fisi* (visions), the *Serca* (love affairs), the *Sluaigida* (military expeditions), and the *Tochomlada* (emigrations).

In our day there has been an attempt to classify these different texts according to their center of interest, either a province or a hero. Thus, we can identify four great cycles: the Mythological cycle, containing the narratives—not necessarily the most ancient—on the ancient Irish gods, the famous Tuatha de Danann; the Ulster cycle, the largest, revolving around Conchobar the king and the hero Cuchulainn, and to which is almost inevitably added all that concerns Connaught, Ulster's rival province; the Leinster cycle, which is also called the Finn cycle (Mac Pherson's Fingal) or Ossianic cycle, and which gathers together very diverse original narratives; and finally the Historical cycle, or the Cycle of the Kings, which begins with characters who really lived but also involves the most archaic traditions relating to mythology, druidism, magic, and the belief in fairy creatures.

In their work published in London in 1961, *Celtic Heritage: Ancient Tradition in Ireland and Wales*, Alwyn and Brindley Rees stress the parallels between Welsh and Irish epics as a way to try to define the thinking that animates the different cycles. And in fact, they find in them "the classic triad of mental faculties." The Mythological cycle supposedly corresponds to the intellect, the Ulster cycle to the will, and the Finn cycle to the emotions. As for the Cycle of the Kings, it is supposed to illustrate the nature of the monarchy as a marriage between the king and his realm.

Clearly, most of the narratives in the Cycle of the Kings treat the relations between the king and his people—the Celts—and, in particular, the Irish—being chiefly concerned with defining the role and the function of the sovereign, although a state, in the modern sense of the word, never actually evolved. But perhaps we must be careful about drawing any hasty conclusions with regard to the other cycles because they assemble works not only drawn from very different inspirations, but sometimes—even within the same cycle—from distinctly opposing ideas.

Thus, everything is linked. The adventure of a hero and warrior necessarily entails elements we'd call emotional. A *quest*, in the medieval sense of the word, is not only an instinctive search for answers to the great human metaphysical problems but also a palpable, if not sensual, experience. The world of the Irish epic has little use for too neatly defined categories because the Celtic mind is loath to lock itself into narrow frameworks offering no means of escape. And that is the great difference between the Irish and the Hellenic epics, much more than their subjects or their psychological depths, which some scholars consider unevolved or nonexistent in the Irish texts. We must note that in all epic works, whatever culture they belong to, the psychological element is secondary. We couldn't say that the character of Ulysses, for instance, is drawn with much finesse in the Homeric poems. No matter what adventures he has, Ulysses is always the same, imprisoned once and for all in those somehow *ritual* characteristics that have been attributed to him and that form part of the myth. If an author ever allowed himself to change the traditional epithets reserved for one hero or another, he would change the myth itself and distort the original weave. So why reproach the Gaels for paying so little attention to the psychological makeup of their epic figures?

This does not stop the storytellers from sometimes lingering over the complex feelings that can assail a character's soul. But for them, this is not a matter of launching into abstract considerations. They are addressing an audience that needs to believe them, that needs facts, gestures, words that are simple and direct. Out of this comes the importance of the concrete. Everything moves and everything lives in these epics. The animals talk, weapons and stones have the gift of speech: All of nature participates in this grandiose game that brings opposing forces face to face. Everything takes place as if we were the referees of a battle forever just beginning, because it is never decisive. If it were decisive, the universe would no longer exist.

It would also be futile to contrast Irish and Greek epics and to say that the Gaels followed the example of antiquity, that the *Iliad*'s influence can be felt in certain descriptions of combat. That is what all commentators who don't know what else to say feel obliged to do.

If there were some Greek influence, no one would consider this a problem, and it would not diminish the Irish storytellers' value—but there is no evidence whatever for such a claim. And if there are analogies, perhaps it is necessary to look to the shared Indo-European roots rather than arbitrarily championing the Greek model's primacy. After all, the Hellenes, especially the Acheans, broke away from the Aryans in about the same period as the Celtic Gaels, but the first wave headed toward the southeast while the second went northwest. In addition to the language, both took with them traditions, beliefs, and also a certain way of seeing things.

Ireland is said to have been the melting pot where two traditions merged, the Celtic and the classic, the latter brought there by Christianity. It is easy to respond that Celtic Christianity is so singular that it is really more Western than Mediterranean, and that the Latin culture was primarily a monastic one, limited to a few initiates—whereas epic literature was intended for a public completely ignorant of it and asking primarily for reminders of the lost golden age. It doesn't even seem that Chateaubriand's remarks regarding the superior attitude of Christian writers treating pagan subjects can be applied here. The Christian monks worked diligently to water down certain texts that struck them as too contrary to Christian dogma, but they hardly touched the texts' characters, morals, and customs, which often seem to us to spring directly from a very distant past, a past that, even in relatively late periods, they could not grasp at all.

In fact, the originality of Irish epic literature is absolute. It is perfectly explained by the isolation of the Irish isle at the western extremities of Europe. Ireland was never occupied by the Romans. Up until the Scandinavian invasions of the ninth century, it remained truly Celtic. And because all the great epic works were already composed by this period, it is absolutely certain that they represent an authentic Celtic tradition that Welsh literature, although just as fascinating from various points of view, never achieved with so much purity.

The influence of Irish pagan epic literature has been immense, not only on the British isle but on the Continent as well, usually indirectly, either through Welsh or the Anglo-Normand intermediaries. It is significant that one of the most widely known legends, that of Tristan and Iseult, is clearly and chronologically of Irish origin, and that it later acquired Welsh, Cornish, and Armorican characteristics before penetrating the depths of European culture.

Neither can we deny the influence of the Ossianic cycle, even as revised and corrected by that brilliant falsifier Mac Pherson. Without considering the themes that served as inspiration, Ossian created havoc in romantic Europe, and we are still subject to the fallout, even today. "The enigma of human destiny," said Madame de Staël, "is nothing for most men; for the poet, it is always present in his imagination. The idea of death, which discourages common minds, makes the genius more audacious, and the mixture of the beauties of nature and the terrors of destruction excite I don't know what frenzy of happiness and dread, without which one could neither understand nor describe the spectacle of this world." Would the baroness of Léman have written these lines without that essential contribution from Celtic culture, even in disguise?

And if an impartial observer opened a book by Chateaubriand and the Ossianic poems at the same time, wouldn't he be astonished to note that the most impressive stylistic strokes of genius by the Enchanter of Combourg are only plagiarisms—sometimes of entire quotations—from the work of the pseudobard of Temora?

> Rapturously, I entered the months of storms. Sometimes I would wish to be one of those errant warriors in the midst of the winds, clouds, and ghosts; sometimes I wanted only to be the kind of shepherd that I would see warming his hands before a humble fire that he had lit on a dark night. I listened to his melancholy songs, which reminded me that in every country, the natural song of man is sad, even when it expresses joy. The human heart is an incomplete instrument, a lyre which lacks strings, on which we are forced to render the accents of joy in the tones consecrated to sighs.

Life and death, joy and sadness, peace and destruction. All the Celtic epics of pagan Ireland are contained in these words. But as Lucan reminds us in an often-quoted passage from the *Pharsalia*, "death for you [the Celts] is only the middle of a long life." The shores are not sinister in the land of death. The evil-smelling river of Styx doesn't cross through it. There is the sea, or a river, where skin-covered boats navigate, taking those who believe in the value of humans and human destiny wherever they wish. "Rise, you desired storms, which must carry René toward the spaces of another life!" cries Chateaubriand, who adds, "So saying, I marched forward, my face aflame, the wind blowing in my hair, feeling neither rain nor cold, enchanted, tormented, and as if possessed by the demon of my heart."

Isn't this deep longing of the soul just what those heroes experience setting off in search of the Marvelous Land where the fairies reign, those smiling images of death and destiny?

> Bran finds that it is so marvelous to cross the bright sea by boat, while for me, around my chariot, in the distance, it is a blossoming field over which he rides. That bright sea for the boat with Bran at its prow, for me, in my two-wheeled chariot, it is a pleasant plain with many flowers. . . . The horses of the sea gleam in the summer, as far as Bran extends his gaze. Rivers pour forth waves of honey in the land of Mananann, son of Lir. . . . It is in the tops of the trees that your boat swims, crossing the heights. There is a woods filled with very beautiful fruit under the prow of your little boat, a woods with flowers and fruits, out of which rises the good odor of wine, a woods which neither fades nor fails, where the leaves are the color of gold. [3]

It's a long way from these idyllic descriptions to the dark caverns of the *Nekuia* where Ulysses sees the fleeting shade of Tiresias, or where Aeneas slips through the thick and gloomy grove that Dido, prisoner of her ghosts, can no longer leave. Only Orpheus understood that the infernal world lacked song and poetry: He succeeded in vanquishing death by *charming* the Underworld with his golden voice, which changed ugliness into beauty, sadness into happiness, and death itself into life. But the rational Mediterranean mind takes vengeance on him. Being unable to let one live who knew that the realm of the dead was not, after all, so terrible, he was condemned, first by having Eurydice snatched away from him, and second by being torn apart by the Bacchae.

But Celtic culture is an Orpheus, and an Orpheus who successfully completes the mission assigned to him. Chateaubriand again: "At night, when the north wind shook my cottage, when the rain fell in torrents on my roof, when through my window I saw the moon cutting through the banked clouds like a pale vessel plowing through the waves, it seemed to me that life intensified in the depth of my heart, that I would have the power to create worlds."

Finally, it is this power to create worlds that matters. "Under the guise of civilization, under the pretext of progress, we have managed to banish from the mind all that is called, rightly or wrongly, superstition, imaginings; to prohibit any kind of inquiry into truth which doesn't conform to common practice" said the *Manifesto of Surrealism* in 1924. Irish epic literature is one of those modes of inquiry into truth that has been systematically excluded from our culture, toward the undeclared goal of keeping people confined within those convenient strictures that make it possible to exploit them with impunity. To read, to understand, and to comment on an Irish epic is a revolutionary experience of the same caliber as studying *Phenomenology*, for example, or whichever Red (or Yellow or Blue) Book (the color being simply the result of an emotional drive taking precedence over a clear idea). Are we up to this task? Haven't we lost that sense of the "marvelous" that is necessary for penetrating the druidic forest? Baudelaire wrote :

Nature is a temple where living pillars
sometimes let out confused words:
There man passes through forests of symbols
which observe him with friendly regard.

We would need the "golden bough" to enter and decipher the messages there. But it is no longer Aeneas's golden bough we would find useful. Again from the *Manifesto of Surrealism:*

The marvelous is not the same in all periods; it participates obscurely in a kind of general revelation of which only the details reach us. . . . Within these frameworks, which make us smile, incurable human disquiet is nonetheless always portrayed, and that is why I consider them, why I judge them to be so many works of geniuses, who are, more than others, painfully affected by it.

11

However, we do possess this golden bough. Our reasoning faculty and our unorthodox knowledge of human nature, acquired recently thanks to surrealism, psychoanalysis, Marxism, and even structuralism, allow us to fully appreciate the productions of a way of thinking that coincides with our own contemporary one in so many ways. The *ex nihilo* creation is an impossibility. If we wish to *create worlds*, we must have the materials. Now, Irish epic literature—with all the problems it poses, all the solutions it suggests, all its frank and direct responses—constitutes new, virgin, material, unused for nearly a thousand years except by a few poets who were accused of illuminism. Modern Ireland is rich with writers who have been able to draw from the Gaelic source, but this spring is far from running dry. One Jonathan Swift, one James Joyce, one George Russell, one Yeats and one Beckett (both Nobel Prize winners), one Flaherty, and one unjustly unknown Pagraig Pearse have been able to drink no more than a mouthful of all its water.

Should we fear the imagination? *Manifesto of Surrealism:*

> The imagination may be on the verge of reclaiming its rights. If the depths of our mind harbor strange forces capable of augmenting those at the surface, or of struggling victoriously against them, there is every reason to capture them, to capture them first, in order to later subject them, if it is necessary, to the control of our reason.

It is in this spirit that we ought to approach the study of a few texts from the age of the Irish epic.[4] We must rid ourselves of any preconceived ideas, of all mistrust for an ethic and aesthetic entirely different from what we've been inculcated with—which doesn't in the least forbid us from pushing comparisons as far as we like or expressing reservations if the occasion arises. To be objective supposes a certain lucidity that we can only acquire by becoming familiar with the ancient human myths, which, moreover, reveal themselves to be the same today as in the past, although assuming different masks. Finally, we must rediscover a certain *faith*, a certain trust, much like the fili's listeners must have had when they listened to the exploits of Lugh or Cuchulainn, when they were told the tragic love story of Diarmaid and Grainne, when their eyes shone with wonder at the splendors of the Fairy Island. But *faith* does not mean *naïveté*. "I accustomed myself to the simple hallucination: I saw very clearly a mosque in the place of a factory, a school of drums made by the angels, carriages along the roads of the sky, a sitting room at the bottom of a lake," said Arthur Rimbaud.

Let us discover the Sunken City sleeping at the bottom of some lake or inlet protected from inquisitive eyes. In this city is found the princess who must be awakened.

Bieuzy-Lanvaux, Paris

1

The Mythological Cycle

Like all other Celts, the Irish Gaels have conceived of their history mythically. That is to say, they have tried to place the events they remember into a very supple sort of framework that uses the great myths as its reference points. These myths are primarily concerned with the arrival of the first inhabitants to Ireland and constitute a *de causis ad fines* explanation of the actual state of things during a specific historical period, generally from the beginning of the Christian era to the Scandinavian invasions.

It goes without saying that metaphysical preoccupations, which the Gallic druids shared (we know this thanks to Caesar's accounts), are not absent from these narratives. Even the form of the mythological epic lends itself easily to symbolism, even if this symbolism, interpreted in a later period, only imperfectly conveys the intellectual speculations of an elite generally considered intelligent and innovative.

Beginning from the twelfth century, there was an attempt, moreover, to bring some order to the muddle of mythological traditions, most of which had fallen into a fragmentary state. Clerics imagined a sort of corpus of all the traditions concerning the early ages of Ireland, and this work resulted in the great *Leabhar Gabala*, or *Book of Conquests*. This book is invaluable to us because it constitutes a framework in which the different mythological epics are joined.

An original race established itself in Ireland in the most ancient times, but it disappeared with the flood. Then came the land clearers under the leadership of Partholon. This race, which practiced animal breeding and began to cultivate the island, had to fight against some very mysterious peoples, the giants of the sea who, it seems, were the Fomor. One year Partholon's race disappeared, the victims of an epidemic. It was then that a new race appeared, the Nemed, but they also clashed with the Fomor, and disappeared in their turn, to be superseded by three peoples, the Fir Bolg, the Fir Gallian, and the Fir Domnainn.

There is clearly some confusion and chronological inversion here. Actually, the Fir (the word means "men") Bolg, the Fir Gallian, and the Fir Domnainn are none other than the Belgians, Gauls, and Domnonaens, or the Bretons. These are all the Celtic peoples belonging to the Britonic branch. Now, we know that the Gaelic people established themselves on the British Isles earlier than the Britons. Moreover, there had been invasions by Bretons, Gauls, and Belgians into Ireland. That is incontestable and proven by numerous texts and toponymic evidence. But they took place in the second and first centuries B.C. It is even more indicative that the *Leabhar Gabala* has them introducing iron tools and agriculture to Ireland, which means that they belonged to an iron dependent civilization and clearly to the second Iron Age, otherwise known as the Tène epoch.

The *Leabhar Gabala* maintains that this civilization disappeared before another invasion, this one by the Tuatha de Danann. In fact, these were people who predated the Celts and thus the Fir Bolg. These were the races that constructed the megaliths, who lived in Ireland during the second millennium B.C. and during a part of the Bronze Age until the dawn of the first iron civilization, called the Hallstatt. These Tuatha de Danann were organized into a religious and warrior aristocracy and seemed, in fact, to have a decisive influence not only upon druidic religion but also over the political institutions of the Gaels. And it is precisely the Gaels, called the Sons of Mile, who succeed them. At one point the Tuatha had fought against the immortal Fomor and been forced to join up with them. At the Second Battle of Mag Tured they had succeeded in establishing their dominance over all of Ireland. But the Sons of Mile then defeated them at Tailtiu. An agreement was reached. The Gaels would have the territory of Ireland, while the Tuatha would have the underground realm of burial mounds and megaliths as well as supremacy over the remote islands. However, this agreement would not stand in the way of relations, sometimes friendly, sometimes hostile, between the two races because, like all epics, the *Leabhar Gabala* reveals to us the coexistence of two worlds, the real world of the Gaels and the magical world of the Tuatha, the ancient deposed gods who retained all their magic powers and their supernatural nature.

Thus, the Irish Mythological cycle is the reflection of these deeply rooted beliefs. Taking into account the role of dream and imagination, it is the distillation of diverse traditions, not all Celtic, into which are mixed speculations on the universe, on life and death, on fate, and also on love. This last point is the most important of all, because during this period few European civilizations attach so much importance to love, whether it be true passion or simply amorous feelings.

The Story of Tuan Mac Carill

This narrative,[1] which may not be very ancient, perfectly illustrates the tone of the epics in the Irish Mythological cycle. Here we have a kind of testimony given by a supernatural being, a sort of demi-god who, having been reincarnated many times, has witnessed the various invasions of Ireland. An argument has been drawn from this in favor of a Celtic belief in metempsychosis, which seems unwarranted. As with the example of Taliesin in Welsh literature, the case of Tuan Mac Carill is primarily symbolic, and the fact that he has lived many lives is only explained by the author's need to present a short version of the legendary history of Ireland. This is, in fact, only a summary of the *Leabhar Gabala*, in a half-poetic, half-didactic form. And it is not without charm. Here is the complete translation:[2]

> There were five invasions of Ireland. No one came there before the flood. After the flood, no one came there before the year three hundred and twelve. Partholon, the son of Sera, arrived in Ireland, as an exile, with twenty-four men and their wives.
>
> They settled in Ireland and their race lived there for five thousand years. Between two Sundays, a great mortality struck them and they all died. But there is

no disaster without a survivor to tell the story. I am that man. So I went from hill to hill and from cliff to cliff, protecting myself from the wolves for thirty-two years during which Ireland was uninhabited. Finally, old age came upon me. I wandered in the deserts and along the cliffs. Then it became difficult for me to move and I lived in the caves.

Then came Nemed, son of Agnoman, who took possession of Ireland. His father was my brother. I saw them from the high rocks, but I did not want to be seen. I had long hair, long nails. I was decrepit, naked, and gray, miserable and suffering. One night I went to sleep and I awoke in the form of a deer. I was young and my spirit rejoiced.

Then I sang these words:

> *Strength today for the son of Senba.*
> *Vigor he has been granted*
> *not without celebrated beauty in his young strength.*
> *The son of Senba was an old brave.*
> *The men who come from the east*
> *with their spears which give them all their courage,*
> *I had no more strength in my hands and feet*
> *to drive them away.*
>
> *Near to me has come*
> *the race of Nemed, son of Agnoman.*
> *Ardent are their strikes against me*
> *to inflict upon me my first wound.*
> *So upon my head grew*
> *two horns and three score points.*

When Nemed came to Ireland with his fleet, he had thirty-four boats. For a year and a half, they wandered about the Caspian Sea. They sank and died of hunger and thirst, except for four couples surrounding Nemed. After that, his race increased and there were as many as four thousand and thirty couples. However they all died. Then old age came upon me. I fled men and wolves.

Then I took on yet another aspect, with a rough gray coat.

> *One morning when I was at Dun Bre,*
> *fighting against the old males,*
> *beautiful was my band crossing through the marshes,*
> *beautiful army following me.*
> *My band was swift*
> *among the armies of vengeance.*
> *They threw all their spears*
> *against the warriors of Ireland.*
> *Once, we were all gathered together*
> *to decide on the judgment of Partholon.*
> *What I sang to all was sweet.*
> *These were words of welcome.*

When I had taken this animal form, I became the head of the Irish herds. Great herds of deer raced around me, no matter what path I was on. Such was my life at the time of Nemed.

I was in the habit of returning in Ulster in the period of my old age and my decrepitude, because it was in this place that I had always changed my aspect, and that was why I always came there to wait for my body to rejuvenate. It was then that Senion, son of Stariath, took the island. From him came the Fir Domnainn, the Fir Bolg and the Gallian, and they possessed the island for a certain time.

Now I was at the mouth of my cave, I still remember. I know that the aspect of my body changed and I was a wild boar. Then I made up some verses about this wonder:

> *Today I am a wild boar,*
> *I am king, strong and victorious.*
> *My song and my words were agreeable*
> *in days gone by at gatherings,*
> *pleasant to the young and pretty women.*

My flesh was beautiful and majestic,
my voice had low and gentle tones,
I was swift in battle,
I had a lovely face,
today I am a black boar.

Beothach, son of Iarbanel the prophet, took possession of this island after having vanquished the races occupying it. It was from them that the Tuatha de Danann came, whose origin, they say, is unknown. But it is likely they came from the skies, so intelligent they were, so astonishing their knowledge.

Then I once again reached old age and I was sad at heart; I could no longer do what I had done before. I lived in the dark caves, the lonely rocks; I was all by myself. I went back into my dwelling place. I remembered all my earlier forms. I fasted for three days. At the end of three days, I had no more strength. I was changed into a great vulture, an enormous sea eagle. My spirit was joyous once again. I could do anything. I became curious and adventuresome. I traveled all over Ireland and I knew what was happening there. Then I sang some verses:

Today a vulture,
I was once a wild boar.
First I lived with a band of pigs,
now here I am with a band of birds.

That is how I survived all the races which invaded Ireland. There were the Sons of Mile who took the island by force from the Tuatha de Danann. At that time, I was in the form of a vulture, in a hollow tree near a river.

I grew heavy with sleep for nine days. I was changed into a salmon. Then I was in the river. I was fine there, I was active and happy. I knew how to swim very well, and for a long time, I escaped all danger from the hands of fishermen armed with nets, from the talons of vultures, from javelins that hunters threw at me. . . . But a fisherman caught me and took me to the wife of Carill, king of this country. I remember that very well. The man put me on the grill. The woman wanted me and ate me whole. And I was in her belly. I remember the time when I was in the belly of the wife of Carill. I also remember that after that, I began to speak as humans do. I knew all that had taken place in Ireland. I was a prophet and I was given a name. They called me Tuan, son of Carill.

The Battle of Mag Tured

With *The Battle of Mag Tured*,[3] we are dealing with one of the oldest traditions in Ireland, but it is a tradition that was revised and corrected somewhat throughout the Middle Ages by the storytellers and especially by actual mythographers who worked hard to bring a little order to the muddle of primitive mythology. But in so doing, they often altered the ancient narratives, interpreting them a little too much according to their own points of view and, especially, introducing into them elements that must have belonged to other legends.

Whatever the case, such a narrative holds prime interest for us. It shows us what the Gaels of the Middle Ages thought about the ancient inhabitants of Ireland. It also adds to our knowledge of those strange peoples like the Fomor and the Fir Bolg and the famous Tuatha de Danann, the ancient gods who, after their defeat at Tailtiu by the Sons of Mile (the Gaels), became the inhabitants of the underground world of the sidh (fairy mounds), that is, the tumuli and the other megalithic monuments scattered throughout Ireland, as well as those Marvelous Islands where there is neither death nor disease.

The Tuatha de Danann (people of the goddess Dana) came from the islands to the north of the world, which puts them in the category of the famous and mysterious Hyperboreans. They were scientists,[4] artists, magicians, and "druids," and this fact probably indicates that druidism might have been the religion handed down to the Celts from the people of the Megalithic period.

Now, one day the Tuatha de Danann landed in Ireland. They brought with them the "Stone of Fal which cried out under each king who ruled over Ireland," as well as "the lance which had been Lugh's (whoever held it in his or her hand could not be defeated in battle), Nuada's sword (no one could escape it when it was drawn from its sheath), and the cauldron of Dagda (no company went away without being grateful for it)." And the Tuatha de Danann formed an alliance with the mysterious people of the Fomor, monstrous warriors who strongly resembled the giants of the Scandanavian-Germanic tradition. What is more, it was a limited and unnatural alliance, but it was sealed with the marriage of the Fomor king's daughter, Balor with the Evil Eye, to Cian, the son of Diancecht, the physician-god of the Tuatha. It is from this union that Lugh the Manifold Artisan is born, who, apart from his functions, is equivalent to the Gallic god Mercury. Julius Caesar speaks of this god, and his name appears throughout in toponyms in the whole Celtic region. Then the Tuatha and the Fomor waged battle against the Fir Bolg who held Ireland in their sway. We must wonder who these people could have been whose name, supposedly, meant "bag men"—certainly not a justifiable description. Is this the memory of an invasion by the Continental Celts—in particular, the Belgians, whose name might be related to *bolg*, a term that literally means "bag"? Indeed, in other narratives we very often find the Fir Bolg in the company of the Fir Domnainn (Dumnonii—that is the Bretons) and the Fir Gallian (Welsh). But it is infinitely more likely that the Fir Bolg, the fourth people to invade Ireland according to its mythic history, were the "lightning men," warriors and metallurgists, inventors of the arts of fire. Because *bolg* actually comes from an Indo-European root that became the Latin *fulgur*, "lightning" (*foudre* in French). This explanation has the advantage of being much more logical than the other.

Briefly, the Tuatha and the Fomor enter into battle against the Fir Bolg on the plain of Tured (MagTured).[5] One hundred thousand Bolg men are killed, but the losses suffered by the Tuatha are equally severe. The king of the Tuatha, Nuada (in whom we can recognize the Gallo-Roman Nodens, and Nudd of the Welsh tradition), loses his right hand during the battle. Diancecht, the expert in the art of medicine, makes him a golden hand with the help of the smith Credne, and ever after

21

he will no longer be called anything but Nuada Argatlam (with the golden hand).[6] Thus the Tuatha and the Fomor are the victors, but Nuada can no longer reign because he has lost his right hand—which means that he has lost his power.[7] Then it is decided that the Irish realm should be entrusted to Bress, the son of Elatha, half Tuatha and half Fomor. But Bress favors the Fomor and imposes heavy taxes for their benefit. He imposes a tax on chimneys that smoke. He forces Ogma to carry heavy firewood for his palace, and makes the Dagda work for almost nothing building the fortifications for his castle. He aggravates all his subjects with his greed, and the Tuatha call for his abdication. Bress accepts, on the condition that he be allowed a grace period, which he is granted. Then Bress decides to ask for help from the Fomor. His mother, Eriu (Ireland), gives him the ring that Elatha gave to her; it is the token that will allow him to be received among the Fomor. Thus he is recognized by his father, Elatha, king of the Fomor, who takes him to Balor, king of the isles, and to Indech, another Fomor king. They promise to help Bress, and soon a formidable army prepares to invade Ireland.

But while Bress is away from the island seeking the Fomor, Nuada repossesses the throne, because a magician has succeeded in creating a new flesh-and-blood arm for him. One day while he is giving a feast, Lugh, the son of Cian and Ethne and thus the grandson of the Fomor Balor, presents himself at the door of the fortress and demands to be admitted. Because the porter refuses to let him enter unless he demonstrates his talents, Lugh declares that he is a warrior, harp player, poet, historian, magician, doctor, cupbearer, bronzesmith—in short, that he knows all the arts,[8] and it is for this reason that he is admitted to the last competition, a game of chess. He wins the game. Nuada receives Lugh the Manifold Artist and gives him the place of honor. Thus Lugh can show off his skill, and when someone asks him to play the harp, he lulls the audience to sleep with the tune of sleep, he makes the audience cry with the tune of sadness, and he makes everyone laugh with the tune of gaiety—which attests to the knowledge the ancient storytellers had of rhythm and music's ritual and magic functions.

But warned of the Fomor expedition, the Tuatha de Danann prepare to defend themselves. Nuada entrusts the army's command to Lugh, and preparations last seven years, which is obviously a symbolic number. Lugh and his brothers Dagda and Ogma divide up responsibilities. As the Fomor arrive, Dagda presents himself to the enemy camp and amuses them with his incredible gluttony. He swallows the entire contents of an enormous cauldron and returns to report to Lugh on the state in which he has found the Fomor.

Lugh holds council with the principal chiefs of the Tuatha. Each finds himself defining his role. Goibniu the blacksmith promises to immediately replace all damaged weapons and continually make new ones. Diancecht promises to heal wounds, Credne the bronzesmith to furnish swords, Ogma to win a third of the battle, Morrigan not to miss her mark, and Dagda to strike unerringly with his club.

And the Battle of Mag Tured—the Second Battle of Mag Tured, we should say—takes place on a date that the ancient chroniclers do not hesitate to specify as the year 3303 of the world. Every day fighting takes place. When a Tuatha de Danann warrior is killed, his body is thrown into the Fountain of Health, incantations are spoken, and the warrior regains life and strength.

We can compare this Fountain of Health to the famous cauldron of resurrection that we find in many Welsh texts, *Branwen* and *Peredur* in particular. When a corpse is thrown into this cauldron, a living being reemerges a little later.[9] The cauldron, like the fountain, is nothing other than an archetype for the Grail, which also restores life, but a larger spiritual life, a kind of immortality.

The Fomor send one of their men, Ruadan, son of Bress, to spy on the Tuatha. But Ruadan throws a javelin and wounds Goibniu. The blacksmith throws himself into the fountain and is healed. Then the Fomor begin to put stones into the fountain to fill it up. They launch a brutal attack against the enemy. Fighting rages. Nuada is killed. Lugh comes face to face with Balor, who, let us recall, is his grandfather. Balor has one peculiarity: "He had an evil eye which only opened in battle. Four men held the eyelid up with a well-polished hook. . . . The army which looked into this eye could not resist."

Balor's evil eye signifies the cyclopean aspect of this character. The same detail is found in the Welsh narrative of *Kulhwch and Olwen*, where it takes two pitchforks to raise the eyebrows of Yspaddaden Penkawr. Balor is a one-eyed god, but also a visionary like the Germanic Odin or the Latin Horatius Cocles. His blazing eye is powerful enough to set his enemies on fire or, at the very least, to terrify them and make them beat a hasty retreat.

But the encounter between Lugh and Balor deserves a pause. The two divinities—because this is a matter of a conflict between divinities—begin with an absolutely incomprehensible dialogue. Since all the rest of the narrative is very clear, we must conclude that this is a remnant from an ancient epic that was included without anyone knowing what it meant. That would prove—if proof were needed—the antiquity of the tradition involving the Fomor and Tuatha de Danann struggle. Balor asks that someone raise his eyelid so that he can see—or strike down—"the blabbermouth who is speaking to him." Balor's eyelid is raised, and Lugh launches a stone from a slingshot that makes his eye drop out of his head. And the eye falls on the Fomor, who are killed in great numbers.

Here is the theme of the cyclops blinded and reduced to powerlessness. This theme, developed in one way in the *Odyssey,* is presented in the Irish narratives as a family affair. Lugh kills his grandfather to take his place. In the same way the Welsh hero Kulhwch blinds Yspaddaden Penkawr to take his daughter, that is to say, to replace him. This is more than a generational conflict. We get the impression that we are witnessing a priest killing his predecessor to establish a new religion. This is, in fact, the substitution of a chthonic or maritime religion (Balor is "king of the islands") with an celestial or solar one (Lugh is a solar hero).

The end of Balor clearly marks the rout of the Fomor. The Tuatha Ogma is killed, but so is the Fomor Indech. Lugh grants pardon to the Fomor poet Loch the Half Green, because he hopes that Loch will make his art available to the victors. It is Loch who, with his song, signals the end of the war. Bress's life is spared because he promises, through his magic powers, to guarantee that the cows in Ireland will always have milk, a detail that shows us the first inhabitants of Ireland were primarily herders. But in addition Bress promises to teach the Tuatha de Danann how to plow and to harvest, which places the characters and the events just considered at the beginning of the Neolithic period, the time of the invention of agriculture, probably in the second millennium B.C. in Ireland.

But the conquerors reorganize themselves. Ogma is revived and, in the company of Lugh and Dagda, goes to reclaim Dagda's harp, carried off by the Fomor. It is a marvelous harp that plays the tunes of sorrow, of laughter, and of sleep. Finally Morrigan, the daughter of Ernmas, a strange half-erotic, half-warrior goddess (although one aspect never appears without the other) and archetype of the fairy Morgan, goes to spread the news of the victory of Mag Tured and to prophesy a somewhat dark future for a world permeated by the pessimism of humanity continually struggling against disease, war, and death.

The Fate of the Sons of Tuirenn

Among the Tuatha de Danann, the sons of Diancecht are the enemies of the sons of Tuirenn,[10] son of the god Ogma (Ogmios). Each time they meet, there is fighting. Now, one day Cian, son of Diancecht and father of the god Lugh, is killed through the treachery of the sons of Tuirenn.

Returning victorious from a battle against the Fomor, Lugh goes off in search of his father. He discovers the place where Cian has been assassinated. His father's shade speaks to him and reveals to him the names of his murderers. Lugh vows to avenge Cian. He takes part in the assembly of Tara, and when he sees the sons of Tuirenn in the audience, he publicly demands the price of blood. According to the laws in force, the sons of Tuirenn must accept. Lugh then demands some apparently very simple things: "three apples, the skin of a pig, a lance, a cart drawn by two horses, seven hogs, a young female dog, a brooch, three cries on a hilltop."

The sons of Tuirenn pledge to fulfill their promise. Lugh explains what this will entail: The three apples are those in the garden of the Hesperides; the pigskin is that of the king of Greece, which can heal all illnesses; the lance is the famous Luinn, which belongs to the king of Persia and which must be plunged into a vat of water to keep it from burning anyone with its heat; the cart is the marvelous chariot of the king of Siogar, faster than the wind or fire; the seven hogs are those marvelous animals that can be killed each night and come back to life each morning, a food of immortality; the dog is Fail-Inis (Isle of Fal), who can scare off any wild beast and who belongs to the king of Norway; the brooch is that of the women of the Isle of Caer. As for the cries, they must be emitted on the hill of Miohainn, in the country of the Fomor; whereas Miohainn and his sons are held by a *geis* (ban, taboo) to never let out a cry on this hill. And Lugh adds that if by chance the sons of Tuirenn accomplish all these feats, they will not come out of this last trial alive, because his father, Cian, was Miohainn's student, and Miohainn will take revenge.

Thus we have the sons of Tuirenn grappling with their fate. They go to ask their father for advice. The latter sends a request to Mananann for his boat. They obtain the boat and go off to sea in search of these mysterious objects. This "quest" obviously recalls many other legends, in particular the Welsh narrative of *Kulhwch and Olwen* in which Kulhwch must bring marvelous objects back to Yspaddaden Penkawr, Olwen's father, in order to win her hand. And Kulhwch cannot succeed in this quest without the help of King Arthur and his companions.

However, thanks to their intelligence and their magic powers, the sons of Tuirenn are able to get out of the worst situations and, through some extraordinary adventures, gain possession of all the objects demanded by Lugh. Now, Lugh, who possesses the visionary's gift, knows that the sons of Tuirenn are returning victorious. He sends them a magic wind that makes them forget the last demands, the brooch and the three cries. And when they present themselves before him in the presence of the king and the chiefs, he takes stock of all the objects and demands the brooch and the three cries.

So the sons of Tuirenn take off once more. They easily obtain the brooch and land on Miohainn's island. He rushes at them but is killed. Then the sons of Miohainn engage in battle against the sons of Tuirenn. The sons of Tuirenn are victorious, but wounded and so weakened that they have only enough strength to go to the hill to let out the three cries. Then they lie down in the boat, which returns them, dying, to the house of Tuirenn. Tuirenn goes to Lugh to take him the brooch and asks him, out of pity, to lend him the healing pigskin. Lugh remains uncompromising, arguing that this is not their custom. The sons of Tuirenn die, and Tuirenn dies of sorrow. And that is how Lugh avenges this father's death.

There is something harsh and painful in this narrative. Lugh's cruelty, even if it is justified in one sense, throws a heavy cloud over a universe where there is no pity, no pardon. Humans are entirely responsible for each of their acts. There can be no question of extenuating circumstances or of atonement. Certainly this conforms to the ancient Celtic law: The guilty party must pay a compensation, and it is the victim or the victim's family who decides how great it will be and what form it will take.

But then the characters of this drama are not like other men. These are the Tuatha de Danann, supernatural beings, and thus they do not have to have the same feelings as humans.

The Voyage of Bran

Bran,[11] the son of Febal, is walking by himself in front of his fortress one day and hears music so haunting that he goes to sleep. When he awakens, he sees a golden bough with white flowers beside him. He enters the fortress and joins the assembly gathered there. A woman approaches then and sings fifty quatrains praising the merits of Emain Ablach, the Land of the Fairies: "Here is a bough from the apple tree of Emain which I bring to you, the same as the others: it has branches of white gold and eyelids of crystal with flowers." After singing, the woman disappears, taking the bough with her.

The next day Bran leaves with three times nine men to journey across the sea in search of the Land of the Fairies. After two days and two nights of sailing, they meet a man in a chariot on the sea who makes it known that he is Mananann, son of Lir. He sings thirty quatrains inviting Bran to come with him to the Marvelous Land. Following this an island comes into view, which Bran and his companions sail around. On the island are people who can't stop laughing. Bran sends one of his own men onto the island, but as soon as he sets foot on it, he also begins to laugh, and despite Bran's cries, he no longer recognizes his companions. They are obliged to abandon him on this Island of Laughers.

Soon they discover the Island of Fairies, where they are received by the queen. She throws Bran a ball of string that is attached to her palm, allowing her to pull the vessel toward shore. They are shown to a large house and there they lead a marvelous life, each with his own woman-fairy, eating delicious foods that endlessly renew themselves.

But one day homesickness seizes Bran's companions, who ask to take off again toward Ireland. The queen tries to stop them and gives them warning: Not a single one of them must touch land. With this, Bran and his men embark and reach the shores of Ireland, upon which the men ask where they are. Bran tells them, but no one recognizes it. Then one of his companions hurries onto dry land, but he no sooner touches the

27

ground than he falls away to ashes. Bran realizes that they have already lived in Emain for hundreds of years, and that time does not exist in that marvelous country. He recounts his adventures to the men along the shore, and then "he bade them adieu, and no one knows where he went from that time on."

This text demonstrates both the attraction of those mysterious islands where beings live free of mortality and death, and the penchant for the quest—that is, that patient search for the treasures of the Other World through various kinds of trials. The quest was developed by the Greeks in the *Argonauts* when Jason sets out in search of the Golden Fleece. But *The Voyage of Bran*, as it has come down to us, seems truncated. Christianized, this legend will soon become the voyage of Saint Brendan in search of paradise (Bran equates to Brendan). Still, its primitive pagan core, with all its marvelous episodes, will reappear in a later narrative, *The Voyage of Maelduin*.

Ṭhe Ṭwo Swịṇeheṛs

This narrative[12] is presented as a prelude to the immense epic of *The Cattle Raid of Cualngé*. It certainly postdates the *Raid*, but it includes undeniable archaisms. Thanks to it, we are plunged into the mythological depths of Ireland and the Celtic countries, specifically, into the "system" of metamorphoses, that is, the transformations of humans into animals and vice versa. Like *The Courtship of Etaine, The Story of Tuan Mac Carill*, and *The Story of Taliesin*, this text is used to support attempts to establish the existence of a belief in metempsychosis among the Celts. But this is a romantic idea that must be categorically rejected. This is not a matter of the transmigration of souls, but of changes in form, of which there are extremely numerous examples in all Celtic literature of the islands, and even in popular Armorican tales. They all refer back to the myth of Circe, which is the proof that they are not in the least related to the Indian doctrine. As far as we can make out, the cosmic vision of the Celts offers nothing comparable to any infernal cycle of reincarnations from which the soul tries desperately to escape. But let us look at the story of the two swineherds:

Friuch is the swineherd for Bodbh, king of the sidh of Munster. Rucht is the swineherd for Ochall Ochne, king of the sidh of

Connaught. Here we are introduced into the special world of the Tuatha de Danann. Moreover, the swineherds perform a function bearing little resemblance to the position they occupy in our modern society: They guard the pigs that are the food of the Tuatha de Danann, food that provides them with prosperity and immortality.[13]

Friuch and Rucht are friends. Each time acorns are scarce in Munster, Rucht invites Friuch to bring his herd to Connaught and vice versa. Now, the men of Munster and Connaught instigate a rivalry between the two swineherds that is going to bring them face to face in a different way, obliged to prove that one is better than the other. The first contest is hardly conclusive: Both the Munster and the Connaught pigs become thin, and Friuch and Rucht are relieved of their responsibilities as swineherds. "Then, for two years, they took the form of crows." Of course, since they are equally powerful, their quarrel is not resolved. At the end of the second year the two birds appear at the Munster assembly and instantly take on their human forms again. They are welcomed, but they respond with these prophetic words: "In truth, it is not proper to welcome us, because, as a result of the battle that we have fought, there will be many beautiful corpses and great lamentations!"[14] Then each of them goes to his own side and for the next two years they become fish and pursue each other cruelly through the Irish rivers and seas.

At the end of the second year we find them once again at the assembly of Connaught: "On the water they saw two animals as big as hills who struck one another in such a way that their swords of fire glistened from their throats up to the clouds in the sky."[15] Here again is a description that demonstrates the supernatural character of this struggle, out of which the natural elements erupt in fury. Next the two swineherds transform into two champions, one (now called Rinn) serving Bodbh, the other (now called Faebar) serving Fergna, king of the sidh of Nento-under-the-Waters.

One day Bodbh, his champion Rinn, and an extraordinary retinue arrive at the Connaught assembly. Bodbh's army is so rich and powerful that a good number of Connaught people die of shock, and seven times twenty queens run away with them when they leave again. Bodbh demands that someone be pitted against his champion, but none of the heroes of Connaught accepts the challenge. At just this moment another retinue arrives from the north, a barefoot army mounted on black horses. "It was said that they straddled the sea." This is Fergna, and everyone makes fun of the miserable condition of his troops. But his champion, Faebar, accepts Rinn's challenge. "They began to fight and it lasted three days and three nights. They were so ripped apart that you could see their lungs. Then someone went to separate them."

After some other adventures, the two rivals take the form of two worms, one in the Uaran Garad spring in Connaught, the other in the Glass Gruind of Cualngé, in Ulster. The second, who decides to be called Crunniuc, engages in conversation with the future queen Medb, who comes to wash in the stream. This worm recommends that she marry Ailill de Connaught. The first, who takes the name of Tummuc, makes friends with the king Fiachna. The two worms are thus fed by Medb and Fiachna for one year. One day Tummuc says to Fiachna, "There is going to be a meeting between the animal I told you about last year and myself. . . . One of your cows will swallow me tomorrow and one of Medb's cows will also swallow my comrade. Thus, two bulls will be born and because of us, there will be a great war in Ireland."

This prediction comes true, and now the two antagonists of the *Raid* appear on the scene—the two sacred bulls, the Brown One of Cualngé and the Beautiful Horned of Ae who, at the end of the war between Ulster and the other Irish provinces, will rip each other apart and die, leaving neither victor nor vanquished.

I will pass over the theme of fertilization through the mouth, which is encountered frequently in Celtic literature,[16] to consider two problems raised by this text. Upon analysis the first, that of metamorphosis (and not metempsychosis), clearly appears to be a simple matter of magic, thus of druidism. Perhaps a few vague memories of totemism are mixed in here as well. According to all the texts, druids were both sorcerers and priests. They were capable of putting the elements into motion and transforming the aspect of things. But in the epic narrative (which, we must remember, is a later version compiled and written down by Christian monks) the deep significance of these acts is lost. The editor—who is no doubt satisfying the audience of his own period in this way—sees no more than the symbolic exterior aspect of the change. When he writes that the two swineherds are transformed into birds, he takes this transformation literally, while the text allows us to think that this was only a matter of taking on birdlike characteristics (probably a bird of prey). Couldn't this be a form of ritual comparable with the shaman rituals of northern Europe and the Asian steppe? The shaman also changes himself into an animal and takes on all its characteristics—and not only does he transform himself, but he can also transform others. When, through his spells, the shaman incarnates the spirit of a wild boar into the body of a man, this man *acts as a wild boar* while remaining a man. He begins to dig up the ground to find roots with his teeth. This is no longer a matter of simply a man, but of a man and a boar combined. There are many accounts of these kinds of spells.[17] It is enough to compare them to druidic rituals to see that, if they are not perfectly parallel, at least they have many points in common. The two swineherds belong to the Tuatha de Danann and are therefore fairy creatures, magicians, druids, since, according to the tradition, the Tuatha brought druidism from the northern islands (which brings us back to the Hyperboreans, to Europe and northern Asia, and thus to the shamans). Obliged to confront each other, these two druids use their courage and their physical and moral strength as much as their magic powers. The Christian narrator who piously recorded the story, no longer knowing what to make of it, retained only the exterior metamorphoses, which were easier to describe. It is always the concrete image that survives, and not the content. The signifier takes the place of the signified, and all the more so when there is no longer anyone who can explain the real meaning. In this way images empty of meaning are formed, but they are sometimes very beautiful, very enigmatic, and they captivate the imagination.

On the other hand, in this fundamental opposition between the two swineherds is something that resonates philosophically. As far as we can tell, Celtic thought is not based on the principle of noncontradiction. Rather, it seems to be a system more pre-Socratic in nature, much like the one Hegel used. Each being gives rise to its opposite, its nonbeing, implicitly contained within it. While these two principles exist in harmony, they merge into unity, into nothingness. Rucht and Friuch, *before*, find themselves in this nonexistent state, this nonawareness of their powers. Beginning from the moment when they become conscious of their powers, each sees the other; they are thus aware of their existence, but only in relationship to each other. Now, since conscious existence is a dynamic based upon opposing forces, these forces oppose each other with violence, which explains the struggle between the two swineherds, a struggle of equal and contradictory forces, and thus an irresolvable struggle in the world of things, which is also the world of appearances. Thus, on the cosmic level, the story of the two swineherds is nothing other than an illustration of the metamorphoses of the being into its various incarnations.

The Flood of Lough Neagh

Here we are dealing with the legend of the city of Ys in its Irish version,[18] probably older than the overly Christianized Armorican version, which suffers from the analogy between Ker-Ys and Sodom—an analogy that lends itself to very edifying conclusions. Let us recall that the town of Ys is engulfed by the sea because the daughter of the king has entrusted to her lover the key to the lock of the great seawall protecting the city. Her lover, who is the devil, then uses it to open the famous bronze doors. In the Irish version, it is a *fountain* that overflows; the Welsh version of the same legend, as it appears in a poem attributed to Gwyddno Garanhir[19] and in the *Black Book of Carmarthen*, gives the same cause for the flood. We must also note that La Villemarqué, when he wanted to write (or reassemble) the *Submersion de la ville d'Ys*, decided to mention "the wells of the town of Ys" even though he made the city drown under the waves of the sea.[20]

Here, then, is the Irish version:

A king of Munster had two sons, Rib and Ecca. Ecca was very violent in demonstrating his independence with regard to his father, and one fine day, "manipulated by his stepmother Ebliu, he gravely insulted his father and fled from Munster with all his men. His brother Rib and his stepmother Ebliu left with him."

It isn't difficult to guess what type of insult Ecca inflicted upon his father. The fact that he was "manipulated" by his stepmother and that she accompanies him in his flight allows us to think of Ebliu as a Phaedra, though more fortunate than the Greek heroine. Briefly, the fugitives head north, and the druids tell them that it isn't good for the two brothers to settle in the same place. Thus they separate. Rib and his men go to live on the Arbthenn plain, "and there the water from a fountain gushed forth before them from the earth and drowned them all." But what happens to Ecca is much more complicated, and much stranger.

Ecca and his men reach Brug-na-Boyne, the fairy land of Oengus the Mac Oc, son of Dagda. They stop there to rest. Oengus approaches them and orders them to leave without delay. Since they are exhausted, they don't listen to him and set up their tents. Furious, Oengus makes all their horses perish during the night, but the next day, swayed by Ecca's reproaches, he gives them a great horse, already harnessed, so they can transport their bags. However, he also gives them this advice: "Make sure that this great steed is kept constantly moving along; do not give him a single moment of rest, because otherwise, he will surely be the cause of death."

Ecca and his troops then reach a plain where they decide to establish themselves. But while each of them is trying to unload his things from the horse, they forget to keep him moving. "And at the moment when he stopped, a magic fountain sprang forth under his feet." Ecca is very troubled by this phenomenon;[21] remembering Oengus's warning, he has a house built around the fountain and sets up his own fortress beside it in order to be better able to keep an eye on it. "And he chose a woman to take care of the fountain, charging her with keeping the door continually locked except when the men from the fortress came to fetch water."

After that Ecca gains sovereignty over half of Ulster. A town grows up around Ecca's fortress. Ecca has two daughters, probably by Ebliu, named Ariu and Libane. Ariu marries some sort of half-mad prophet, Curna the Simple. This Curnan wanders throughout uttering lamentations[22] and predicts that one day "a lake would surge forth in the midst of them because of the fountain and that it was urgent for them to build boats." He predicts as well "the death of all living being with the exception of a certain Conang, Libane, and himself." "I see the water surging, a wide and deep torrent, I see our chief and all his host engulfed by the wave, and also Ariu, my beloved—alas! I cannot save her. . . . —But Libane, to the east and to the west, will swim for a long time along the shores of the ocean, near the mysterious shores and the small hidden islands and in the depths of the sea."

Of course, like Cassandra (and Saint Gwenolé preaching in the town of Ys), Curnan's prophecies of doom are ignored; everyone laughs in his face. "Then the woman who had been put in charge of the fountain, on one certain occasion, forgot to close the door. . . .[23] Immediately water engulfs the plain and forms a great lake. . . . Ecca, his whole family, and all his men are drowned, except for Libane and Conang and Curnan the Simple.

That should be the end of the story, but it continues, and very strangely; elements that couldn't be more pagan are going to be mixed up with an attempt at Christianization. Libane herself is also submerged, but she doesn't die. "She lived an entire year, with her little dog, *in her chamber under the lake.*" The theme of the underwater palace appears throughout Celtic texts, whether they are Irish or Welsh, and here we find reminders of the tales of the Round Table. But the transcriber adds: "Because God protected her from the water." At the end of the year Libane begins to get bored, which is very natural. Then she prays and says, "*O my Lord*, I wish to be a salmon so that I can swim with the others through the clear green sea." With these words, she takes the form of a salmon; only her face and her breasts are unchanged.

To find the original text again, all we need to do is delete the "she prayed" and the formulaic "O my Lord." Let us quickly add that she swims for three hundred years before being fished out by Saint Congall, who baptizes her and gives her the name of Muirgen (born of the sea). *Upon being baptized, she dies.*

The Christianization is so badly done that we are able to discern the real meaning of the story. If Libane-Muirgen dies at her baptism, that's because she is a magical figure, a sorceress or a druid. She is the one who possesses the power to turn herself into a salmon, that is, the power to live underwater. It is an act of magic like those performed by shamans, which isn't at all surprising since there are many likely connections between druidism and shamanism.

Moreover, this transformation from a human being into a salmon is not an isolated event in Celtic literature. The two swineherds, Rucht and Friuch, live in the form of fish for two years. Tuan Mac Carill becomes a salmon before being eaten by the wife of Carill, who then brings him back to life in his human form. In the Welsh narrative of *Kulhwch and Olwen*, when Arthur leaves in search of Mabon (the god Maponos), he finds him in the form of a salmon.

But Libane has kept her female features. This is a mermaid, a fish-woman, the most ambiguous of all beings, the Breton Mary-Morgan (all the more so as she is baptized Muirgen, the Gaelic form of Morgan). This is Melusine of Poitou (formerly inhabited by the Picts, probably the same people as in Scotland, or at least one group among those making up the Britonic race). Finally, this is—and here is the most remarkable thing—the same figure as Dahud-Ahes, the daughter of the king Gradlon of Ker-Ys.

Indeed, according to the Armorican legend, Dahud is *born on the sea*. She has a town *built under the sea*. She is a sorceress who often changes her form, and after Ys is submerged, when she is rejected by Saint Gwenolé (who pulls her off her father's horse), she becomes a mermaid. She is condemned to wander forever among the great fish, under the waves of the sea, where fishermen sometimes notice her sadly singing the song of her birth.

The same type of curse befalls both Dahud and Libane. They are born illegitimately, their magic powers make them formidable and invulnerable, but this invulnerability doesn't come without a price. Dahud is the guardian of the locks for the waterways of Ys. One day, when she's had enough of being the city's prisoner, she escapes into the waves to rejoin the race of aquatic beings with whom she belongs. In her chamber under the lake Libane, a prisoner in her human form, decides to enter the world of water. She is also marked by the element of water, and even if the text doesn't say so, we can easily assume that she is the one Ecca has put in charge of watching over the fountain, and that she is the one who—intentionally—forgot to close the door. This all takes place within a very mysterious context bearing some relation to an aquatic worship, a Mother-Waters cult of which we find many indications in the Celtic traditions.

The Courtship of Etaine

The Courtship of Etaine[24] is certainly the most poetic and one of the strangest epics in the Irish Mythological cycle. We still know it only through three fragments, each coming from a complete narrative, which are sometimes very difficult to understand. Fortunately, the legend was well known; many parts of it have been retained for us in poems or even in anecdotes from other times, and these allow us to adequately reconstruct the original legend.

It all begins with the story of Oengus. The Dagda, one of the important chiefs of the Tuatha de Danann and whose real name is Eochaid Ollathir, has illicit relations with Eithne, the wife of Elcmar of the sidh of Brug-na-Boyne. She gives birth to a son, whom the Dagda entrusts to Mider of the sidh of Bri-Leith. Mider, in whom we can recognize the *Deo Medru* of a bas-relief inscription from eastern France, raises the child who bears the name of Oengus, but who is given the nickname of the Mac Oc, that is, "the young son."

When Oengus learns one day that he is the son of the Dagda and Eithne of the Brug, he asks his adoptive father to take him to the chief. So Mider brings him to the Dagda and says to him, "He wants to make himself known to his father so that land might be given to him, because it is not right that your son be without land, since you are the king of Ireland." The Dagda receives Oengus and declares that the land which he wants to give him is not unoccupied. In fact, it is the sidh of Brug-na-Boyne, which is held by Elcmar. Then the Dagda and Mider hatch a rather Machiavellian plan for removing Elcmar from his domain without killing him. The next night of *Samhain*, a day of celebration and peace when the sidh will be open and defenseless, Oengus, without Elcmar knowing it, will provoke him and threaten him with death if he doesn't grant him sovereignty over his domain for one day and one night. Then Oengus will not give his land back to Elcmar after having heard the judgment of the Dagda.[25]

The prediction comes true. Oengus and Elcmar go to hear the opinion of the Dagda and the latter declares that the expression *one day and one night*, during the *Samhain* holiday, implies timelessness, which clarifies for us a certain aspect of this Celtic celebration during which all the barriers, including those of time, are dismantled. As a result, Elcmar has given his land to Oengus for good, but as compensation the Dagda offers the evicted one sovereignty over the sidh of Cletech.

Oengus establishes himself at Brug-na-Boyne, and the following year Mider comes to visit his adopted son. During a game Mider is wounded in the eye, and despite the aid of Diancecht, the medicine-god of the Tuatha de Danann, who cures him, he considers this wound an insult. Thus the Mac Oc must make amends to him, in full compliance with Celtic custom. As a chief, what Mider demands is very substantial, but he takes into account the fact that his wound has been healed. It is a matter, this time, of "a chariot, a beautiful cloak, and the most beautiful girl in Ireland." Oengus gives him a chariot and a cloak. Then Mider reveals the name of the girl: Etaine, the daughter of Ailill, king of northeast Ireland.

Here we come, then, to the actual courtship of Etaine—the first of them, to be precise. Oengus is going to find Ailill and ask him for his daughter. Ailill is one of the Sons of Mile, that is to say, the Gaels. Under the pretext that he would have no recourse against the fairy race in case harm comes to Etaine, Ailill at first refuses, and then lets himself be tempted by the promise of gifts. Wishing to take advantage of the magical powers of the Tuatha, he requires Oengus to clear twelve uncultivated plains in such a way that houses can be built, livestock can be rounded up, and festivals can be organized there.

Oengus tells his father, the Dagda, of the pact he has just made. The Dagda has the twelve plains cleared in a single night. The next day Oengus returns to Ailill, but the latter, having become greedy, refuses to give him Etaine unless he runs twelve rivers through the marshes to irrigate the country and bring the products of the sea to its inhabitants.

The Dagda does what is asked. But Ailill responds to the Mac Oc, "You will still not have my daughter, because once you have her, I will no longer be able to profit from her or obtain what I can obtain with her." Clearly, Ailill displays a very disinterested kind of paternal love. This time he demands the weight of Etaine in silver and in gold.[26] The Dagda provides the required riches, and Oengus brings Etaine back to Brug-na-Boyne, where Mider immediately marries her. For an entire year Mider and Etaine live with the Mac Oc, then, the year having passed, Mider decides to return home to the sidh of Bri-Leith.

But we learn that Mider was already married to a certain Fuamnach, "wise and sensible, skillful in the arts and magic." There is nothing surprising about that. In short, Etaine is only a legal concubine for one year, and this union can be renewed from one year to the next. However, Mac Oc warns his adoptive father about Fuamnach's jealousy and cunning, and reminds him that Etaine was entrusted into his, Oengus's, safekeeping and that he, above all others, is responsible for her.

Very much in love with each other, Mider and Etaine arrive at Bri Leith. Fuamnach seems to receive them warmly. She makes Etaine sit on a seat in the middle of the house, then suddenly, striking her with a branch from a red service tree, transforms her into a pool of water. Then, to escape Mider's vengeance, she goes to seek refuge with her adoptive father, Brezal. However, while drying up, the pool of water produces a larva that becomes an insect, crimson in color.

It was the most beautiful insect in all the world. More sweet than the sound of pipes, harps, and horns was the sound of its voice and the noise its wings made. Its eyes shone like precious stones in the darkness. Its radiance made all those it approached envious. The dew which it scattered with its wings healed all ills, all discomfort, all epidemics. . . . Mider knew that this was Etaine who had taken on this form and for as long as the insect was with him, he wanted no women and just the sight of her nourished him. Her humming put him gently to sleep and when someone unfriendly approached, the insect immediately awoke him.

The beauty of this description demonstrates the poetic and imagistic theme of the woman-insect or woman-butterfly so appreciated by poets and painters, the surrealists in particular. We have to admit that in Mider and the insect's strange cohabitation, there is something admirable and moving. Indeed what more beautiful song of love is there than the harmonious music of the insect who nourishes and protects the one whom he (or she) loves? And what sight more touching than that of Mider ecstatic before this beloved being, no matter what form he sees her in? Isn't this the very triumph of absolute love? If love was invented by the West, it is to the Celts and specifically to the Irish that the West owes its most beautiful visions of love.

But all this is too beautiful to last. It almost seems like a tragedy by Racine, with supernatural elements added. Fuamnach's jealousy knows no bounds. Hermione, Roxanne, Phaedra—all of them at once? She casts a spell, the famous druidic wind, which seems exactly like a kind of shamanism, and a violent storm blows Etaine the insect into her whirlwinds. For seven years (the number is symbolic of one cycle) Etaine

found neither summit, nor shelter, hill nor height in Ireland to alight upon, but only the rocks and the waves of the sea. And she wandered in the air until seven years had passed. Then she fell on the fringe of Mac Oc's cloak, as he found himself on the mound of the Brug. Oengus put her on his breast, in the fold of his cloak.[27] He brought her to his dwelling place and to his *sun chamber* which had bright windows. . . .

the Mac Oc became accustomed to sleeping in the *sun chamber* close beside her every night, and he comforted her until her joy and her colors returned to her. Then he filled the *sun chamber* with beautiful green plants, and the insect flourished on the flowers of these good and precious herbs.

Here we have that famous *sun chamber* or *crystal chamber* that is a theme peculiar to Celtic literature and that we find again in *Tristan's Folly* and *Adventures of Art*. It is a matter of regeneration by the sun, the symbol of vital power.[28] But in any case, the poetry of such a portrait escapes no one. What we find here is much more than a mythological theme being employed. On the part of the author (or authors), there is a kind a delicacy and refinement that make this epic a major literary work. After this, the Irish storytellers better not be accused of embroidering upon legends they no longer understand.

However, Fuamnach has not given up. To get the Mac Oc away from the Brug, she asks him to come and be the arbitor in her conflict with Mider, and as soon as he leaves, she causes another magic whirlwind that breaks the sun chamber and carries the insect to the roof of a house in Ulster. There Etaine falls into the goblet that Etar's wife is about to drink from "in such a way that she was swallowed with the liquid in the cup. So it was that she was conceived in her [Etar's wife's] womb and became her daughter. She was named Etaine, daughter of Etar. A thousand and twelve years had passed between the first conception of Etaine by Ailill and this one."

Cases of fertilization by means of the mouth are not uncommon in the Celtic tradition. Tuan Mac Carill, who took on many different forms, is devoured in the form of a salmon by the wife of Carill and is reborn as their son. Among the Welsh, Gwyon Bach, fleeing from Keridwen, is swallowed as a grain of wheat by the latter. Keridwen immediately becomes pregnant and then gives birth to a son, the same Gwyon who will become the bard Taliesin.[29]

And thus the second Etaine is born, a reincarnation of the first. Again, we must not come to the conclusion here that the Celts believed in metempsychosis. This rebirth of Etaine is only a sign of continuity. Let us not forget that Etaine is subject to the destiny that transforms her, that turns her, a simple daughter of humans, into a divinity associated with Mider and the other mysterious beings who inhabit the mounds. Thus Etaine is not a simple mortal, like Tuan Mac Carill or Taliesin. And what is more, the life of Etaine is incomplete, her love for Mider not being fully realized. As Tristan and Iseult find each other again in death, so Etaine and Mider must find each other, not in death—as these are fairy or divine beings—but in another life, that is, in some other form, since it is the divinities' prerogative to manifest themselves in various and changing forms.

However, the Mac Oc and Mider realize that Fuamnach has duped them once again. Oengus, Etaine's legal protector, leaves in pursuit of Fuamnach, catches up to her, and cuts off her head, thus not only bringing about justice but also restoring his honor, which obliges him to avenge Etaine's disappearance. With this episode, the first fragment of the legend of Etaine, the first "courtship," ends.

The second fragment may be more obscure but is no less beautiful. Here, Etaine is the daughter of Etar, nobleman of Ulster. During this period the most powerful king of Ireland (of the Gaels, but not of the Tuatha de Danann) is Eochaid Aireainn, overlord of Conchobar, Ailill, and Medb. The Irish nobles urge the king to get married, but he doesn't know whom he should wed. He sends out messengers, who discover Etaine, and he decides to meet the young woman himself. The storyteller then gives us a description of Etaine so sumptuous and poetic that hardly another can compare:[30]

> A girl lived by the side of a fountain. She had a magnificent silver comb ornamented with gold. She washed in a silver basin, and there were four birds of gold and precious stones on the edge of the basin. She was dressed in a beautiful cloak embroidered in bright crimson, with silver brooches and a gold pin at her breast. Enveloping her body was a long gown of green silk with a collar, a border of red gold, and clips of gold and silver. She had two braids the color of gold held with four clasps on either side of her head and a golden pearl crowning each braid. Then the girl undid her hair to wash it and took it in both hands, letting it fall over her breast. Her hands were whiter than snow at night and her cheeks redder than foxglove. She had a fine even mouth with teeth as brilliant as

pearls. Grayer than hyacinths were her eyes, red and fine her lips. Light and soft were her shoulders, tender, soft and white her arms. Her fingers were long, thin, and white. She had beautiful pale red ears. Her sides were fairylike, whiter than snow and the foam on the sea. Her thighs were tender and white, her calves narrow and alive, her feet delicate, with white skin, healthy and rich were her heels, and very white and round her knees.[31]

After such a description we might imagine that the innumerable authors of sixteenth- and seventeenth-century blazons had precursors, and that they could have taken lessons from these coarse, barbaric poets from an island lost in the mists, incapable of grasping nuances and subtle shades, incapable of any artistic work whatsoever. And we might even find this description by the Irish storyteller more restrained—despite its length—and much more powerful, vivid, and spellbinding than those attempts, however admirable and *pretty*, from stylized baroque literature. Here it is life itself that is transmitted to us. This portrait is not fixed. It moves before our eyes, and for the time we are reading it truly shimmers, like a constellation, like a sun.

Needless to say, the king Eochaid falls in love with Etaine and marries her. He takes her to Tara, and the story would end there if one of his brothers, Ailill Anglonnach, had not also fallen in love with Etaine. "Then the wife of Ailill . . . said, 'O Ailill, why are you always looking aside? It seems to me that this is the look of love.'" Ailill tries not to think about Etaine anymore, but the more he struggles with this love, the more it grows within him. We might think we were hearing Phaedra revealing to Oenone the sad struggle she has undergone trying to stifle her passion for Hippolyte. Ailill suffers from an affliction of languor that keeps him in bed for one year. Eochaid sends his doctor, Fachtna, to try to cure his brother. Fachtna can only say that Ailill is suffering from lovesickness, for which he knows no cure. As for Ailill, he feels such shame over this guilty love that he admits it to no one. He becomes more and more sick, and everyone expects him to die.

Then—and this is where the parallel with *Phaedra* becomes interesting—Eochaid, who must go away, entrusts his brother to Etaine and gives her these instructions: "Let your bed be close to Ailill's for as

long as he lives, and when he dies, let his tomb be dug in the prairie."
Etaine stays alone with Ailill. And like Phaedra who cries, "Brought
by my husband himself to Trezene . . . my too open wound immediately bled," Ailill feels his love become madness: "This is Venus completely attached to her prey." In a moving dialogue in verse,[32] which
takes place when Etaine asks him the reason for his sadness and languor, he confesses that he loves Etaine, admitting his shame with regard to his brother Eochaid and declaring that Etaine alone can heal
him. Here again we find many Racinian echoes: "Here is the reason
for my wound: I have no song on my harp . . . I am not capable of
speech, I am no longer master of my senses and my heart is in agreement with them. Sad thing, oh wife of the king . . ., my body and my
spirit are sick." And he continues with extraordinary violence, in prose:
"My love is a spike, it is a strong and violent desire, it is like the four
corners of the earth, and is it endless like the sky: it is a broken neck, or
being drowned in water, it is a battle against a shadow, a race to the sky,
it is a dangerous race under the sea, it is a love for a ghost. . . ." After
such examples we can no longer believe for an instant the peremptory
judgments of Celtic scholars (and there are some) who claim that all
psychology is absent in Irish narratives. Moreover, this is a widely held
opinion: Everyone knows that *primitive* societies are incapable of grasping the least idea of psychology, and that epics present us with only
literary or mythological stereotypes. We really have to wonder where,
in fact, this wonderful psychology is to be found.

But let us return to the story. Etaine does not reject Ailill, nor does
she remain dumbfounded (and stupid) like Hippolytus.[33] She has too
much pity for him, and not wanting him to die because of her, she
forces herself to keep coming to feed him and take care of him. And
one day she even says to Ailill, "Come to my room tomorrow, in the
house which is outside of the citadel, and there I will concede to your
appeals and your desire."

We can see that Etaine has an idea of charity that goes much farther than moralizing sermons would advocate. But this is when destiny intervenes, because a strange sleepiness comes over Ailill just as
he is going to meet Etaine. Etaine is waiting and notices a shadow that
resembles Ailill and seems tired. However, she realizes that it is not
Ailill. The next day she makes the same arrangements with Ailill, but
the same sleepiness comes over him—and so it goes each successive

night, and each time the same shade appears to Etaine. Then she says to the shade, "It is not you whom I've agreed to meet. Why do you come here? Moreover, if I have agreed to meet him, it is not out of desire or adventure, but to save him, because he is lovesick for me." The shade responds that he has done well to come. He reveals to her that he is Mider of Bri-Leith and that the two of them were once married. "If we were in that situation, what was it that separated you from me?" asks Etaine. "That's not hard to answer," says Mider, "it was the incantations of Brezal and the sorcery of Fuamnach." Mider then asks, "Will you come with me?" Etaine answers that she doesn't want to leave the king of Ireland, not for Mider nor for anyone else. Mider explains, "It was me who put it into Ailill's head to love you. Then I kept Ailill from meeting you and stripping you of your honor." And Mider insists, "But will you come to my country with me if Eochaid consents?" "Yes," says Etaine.

And Mider disappears. Etaine goes to find Ailill and tell him all that has happened. Ailill feels relieved, declares himself healed, and is very glad that Mider has saved Etaine's honor. Thus ends the second part of the story of Etaine, the second courtship.

The third fragment once again features Mider as the central character. One day while Eochaid Aireainn is out walking on the prairie, in front of the Tara fortress, he sees a strange warrior arriving. "He wore a crimson tunic, and his golden blonde hair fell to his shoulders, and his eyes sparkled. He carried a five-edged lance in one hand and a white shield with golden gems in the other."[34]

Eochaid bids him welcome. The new arrival says that his name is Mider of Bri-Leith and proposes a game of chess to the king. A great lover of this game, the king does not refuse. The game begins, and Mider stakes fifty magnificent gray horses on it, complete with all their accessories. Eochaid wins; the next day Mider returns with the promised horses.

However, he demands a rematch. They play again, and Mider loses. He must provide various herds, which he gives to the king the next day. Eochaid is delighted with these exchanges, and proposes still another game. In a sort of rage, Mider accepts. He loses again and Eochaid asks him to "remove the rocks from Meath, cut the rushes in Tethba, build a dike in the marshes of Lamraige, and clear a forest in Briefne." Mider protests that this is too much, but it makes no difference, and he begins. He only makes the king promise that no one will leave Tara the night that he performs these tasks.

But Eochaid, who seems to be familiar with Molinist casuistry, immediately has his quartermaster posted to watch what takes place. The latter will have complete impunity, since he arrived *before* the work, as witness of the incredible activities of the Tuatha de Danann who come to help Mider keep his promises. And as the quartermaster reports to him that the men of the sidh put the yoke on the oxen's shoulders while the Gaels put it on their foreheads, Eochaid will hasten to put this invention into practice, which will win him the nickname *Aireainn*, that is, "plowman."[35] The next day Mider presents himself before the king, but he has "a bent back and an evil look in his eyes." He proposes another game of chess, but this time the stakes will be whatever the winner decides.

Now Eochaid loses the game. It is probable that Mider wanted him to win the preceding ones so that he would be more likely to lose this one. And Mider claims his reward, nothing less than Etaine herself. Eochaid became uneasy. "Come back in a month from this day and your request will be fulfilled," he said.

We can now understand Mider's sought-after goal. To the question posed to Etaine, "Will you come with me?" she answered, "Yes, if Eochaid consents to it." Thus he wants to place the king under the obligation to give him Etaine legitimately.

But the king of Tara has no intention of keeping his promise. One would think that he truly was the student of brilliant casuists. He assembles all his troops around Tara's fortress, convinced that Mider will not be able to reach him there on the arranged day. Thus, he, Eochaid, taking note of Mider's absence, will be absolved of his promise. But this subtle reasoning doesn't take into account Mider's magic powers. On the said date, laughing at the warriors who don't even see him, Mider presents himself in the fortress hall, where he finds Eochaid and Etaine. Mider recalls Eochaid's promise and reveals that Etaine herself has promised to follow Mider if Eochaid gives his consent. Etaine acquiesces. "I told you that I would not go with you as long as Eochaid would not give me up. But you may take me if Eochaid relinquishes me."

Eochaid tries to resist, but cannot object to Mider giving Etaine a kiss. Then Mider "seized the woman in his arms and carried her through the roof of the house. The shamefaced warriors rushed to the king's side. They saw two swans flying away from Tara, over the plain."

That is how the story of Etaine ends.[36] Much more could be said about this final image of the two swans, the birds of the Other World, who are going to find peace and happiness in the universe of the sidh. Thus we find realized, idealized, the love of Etaine and Mider despite men and gods, an absolute love if there ever was one, which nothing could alter. But what distinguishes this legend of love from romantic passion is that there is no element of fatality to it. What could be more quietly amoral than this love? What more natural than this tumultuous affection, which binds the god to the fairy? There is nothing morbid, no blood, in this story. It stands among the most beautiful and moving of tales that the human spirit has ever devoted to the exaltation of mad love. And the final image in particular, of the two birds diving into the depths of a knoll where the marvelous black lights of the Country of Dreams await them, cannot help but make us think of the words of André Breton from a chapter in *Amour fou:* "In the side of the abyss, built out of the philosopher's stone, opens the starry castle."

The Dream of Oengus

Oengus,[37] the Mac Oc, son of the god Dagda, is one of the key figures in the Gaelic epics of Ireland. Though apparently a minor character in the events related in the narrative from various cycles, he nevertheless plays an essential role. Like the image of Horus in relation to Osiris, of Baldr in relation to Odin, he is, in fact, the *young son*—that is, the old god regenerated. His strange birth, the result of adultery (and incest, since his mother, Eithne-Boann, is supposed to be the daughter of Dagda) committed outside of time in the mythic space of the festival of Samhain, makes him an exceptional being whose "immortality" is proven by the way he survives in popular traditions. Indeed, his name is closely linked to the sidh of Brug-na-Boyne, that is, the magnificent megalithic cairn of Newgrange that dominates the Boyne River valley and where many fairy or epic adventures take place.

We have seen in *The Courtship of Etaine* how Oengus took possession of the sidh thanks to a ruse devised by Dagda, a ruse that is clearly dishonest but nonetheless "legal." It is Dagda and the Mac Oc who represent the Varuna aspect of the primordial divinity. Varuna is the supreme magician, the one who acts without restraint and who *unties*—as opposed to Mitra, who is the *binding* god—the guarantor of contracts. We will find these characteristics again in the later figure of Merlin the Enchanter, and, like the latter, Oengus is a kind of demiurge who organizes the world in his own way, which runs counter to the laws in effect.

What is more, despite the aspect of the "black" and disquieting magician that he assumes in the Christian mind (parallel to Merlin, who is called "son of a devil"), Oengus has retained a Christ-like function: He is "savior" and "regenerator," if not "resurrector," as the famous *sun chamber* he establishes in the sidh proves, which he uses to regenerate the unfortunate Etaine. Now this *sun chamber* is not a poetic invention. It actually exists in the megalithic mound of Newgrange. Indeed, it became apparent over the course of the monument's restoration that on the morning of winter solstice, the first rays of the rising sun enter through an opening over the door made for this purpose, slowly lighting the sinuous corridor and finally completely illuminating the central chamber, where deposits of human bones were found. Here we are dealing with both a ritual and symbol: The corridor is the vaginal passage and the central chamber the womb, and the sun comes to deposit its seed at the very depths of the maternal belly to give back life—another life—to the dead who have been placed there. Here archaeology and the mythological tradition are in complete agreement, which demonstrates once again how important myths and legends are in trying to understand something of the religious ideas of peoples who left no written history. In this case, it is a matter of the megalithic peoples, and not the Celts, since the Newgrange monument dates back to about 3500 B.C. But the Celts are incontestably the heirs to that very ancient civilization.

However much Oengus is a god, he nevertheless remains entirely human; moreover, this is what emphasizes his Christ-like character. He is at once god and human, and is thus subject to all human suffering and passion. *The Dream of Oengus* narrative carries us to the depths of the unconscious of this "young son" at the same time as it paints for us a surprising picture of relations between the two worlds, that of the gods and that of the mortals. Because the Irish mythological epic finds justification only in an eternal and ambivalent struggle between the natural and the supernatural, it is vital that humans, who relate the actions of the gods, be in contact with them at one time or another. The two worlds are parallel, and they come together and interpenetrate under certain circumstances. But this contact can be just as much confrontational as friendly, and in either case it can only take place according to precise rules, which were established after the mythic Battle of Tailtiu that saw the victory of the Sons of Mile, that is, the Gaels, over the ancient gods, the "people of the goddess Dana," that is, the Tuatha de Danann. The surface of Ireland having been granted to the Gaels, the distant (and mythic) isles and the underground universe of the mounds having become the domain of the Tuatha, it became necessary for the latter, just as it was for the Gaels, to divide the territory among themselves. And, according to another narrative, it is the powerful Mananann, the son of Lir, who proceeded with the division, as the head chief of the Tuatha:

> Mananann's advice to the warriors was to spread out among the sidhs and establish themselves in the hills and the beautiful plains of Ireland.... And to each of the Tuatha de Danann for whom a noble residence or seat was appropriate, Mananann assigned a particular property. And he made the *feth fiada,* the feast of Goibniu and the pigs of Mananann for the warriors. That is, because of the *feth fiada,* the princes could not be seen, because of the feast of Goibniu, the high kings were immortal and did not get old, and although the pigs of Mananann could be killed, there would always be more live ones for the warriors. Mananann taught the nobles to set up their fairy residences and to establish their fortresses in such a way that they looked like the residences of the beautiful Promised Land and the beautiful Emain Ablach.[38]

Thus, the Tuatha de Danann have the gifts of invisibility (when they desire it) and immortality, since they participate in the famous festival of Goibniu, the divine blacksmith. They each have an assigned residence, and it is always a megalithic mound. We must add that Ireland is, without a doubt, the country containing the greatest number of these. But the fact that the Tuatha live in the underground world of the mounds does not keep them from having relationships of a feudal nature with the humans who control the surface. They certainly have their own hierarchy, but they must take into consideration the human hierarchy, too. Many texts illustrate this fact, *The Dream of Oengus* in particular.

We find Oengus in his home in the Sidh-na-Brug. While he is sleeping, he perceives a young girl, the most beautiful girl he has ever seen, coming toward him. He reaches out his hand to grasp her, but she makes a leap and disappears. The next morning Oengus feels himself overcome by languor and unable to eat. The following night the same girl reappears in his sleep and plays him some music, which leaves him unconscious. An entire year passes, and Oengus remains in a state of languor that his entourage finds unsettling. They send for "Fingen, the doctor of Conchobar. . . . He knew by looking at a man's face what his illness was, and he recognized by the smoke which left a house how many were sick there."[39] Fingen understands that Oengus is suffering from the love of a woman *who is absent*, declares himself powerless to cure him, and advises that Boann, Oengus's mother, be sent for.[40]

For one year Boann searches throughout Ireland, but never manages to find the girl whom Oengus has seen in his dream. The following year it is Dagda himself who sets out on this quest. But he meets with no greater success, and Oengus continues to languish. Then Fingen advises Dagda to go and see "Bodbh, king of the sidh of Munster, because his knowledge is famous throughout Ireland." Bodbh searches for the young girl and, after a year has passed, announces that he has succeeded, asking that Dagda bring his son in a chariot to the sidh of Femen in Munster so that he can identify the one he has seen in his dream. This is done. "They left for the lake and saw one hundred and fifty young women. They saw the young woman among them. The young women only came up to his shoulder. They were bound together in twos with silver chains and each wore a gold collar around her neck with a fine gold chain."[41] Even if this text is not very clear, it means that the young girls in question are the swan-women, the female fairy creatures capable of appearing in the form of both bird and girl. And in general, as many Irish (and even Breton-Armorican) narratives illustrate, these woman-swans are always in twos, linked at the neck by a gold or silver chain.

We then learn the name of the girl: Caer Ibormaith, the daughter of Ethal Anbual, of the Uaman sidh. But the established customs must be respected, and Oengus—or, rather Dagda—must ask for the girl's hand in marriage. But Dagda has no authority over Connaught, where the Uaman sidh is located. Thus, it is necessary to ask Ailill and Mebd, the king and queen of Connaught, to summon Ethal Anbual, for whom they act as some sort of overlord. Now Ethal Anbual refuses to go to Ailill and Medb, and declares that he will never give his daughter to the son of Dagda.

This attitude leads to war. Ailill and Dagda invade the Uaman sidh, killing sixty warriors whose heads they take, and bringing Ethal Anbual back as prisoner to Cruachan, the residence of Ailill and Medb. Ordered to give his daughter to Oengus, the vanquished chief declares that he cannot do that, because his daughter's power is greater than his own; he ends up admitting that she takes the form of a bird one year, and the form of a woman the next, which doesn't come as much of a surprise. Finally, to placate Ailill and Dagda, Ethal Anbual reveals that the young girl can be found at the Loch Bel Dracon the next evening of Samhain. It is up to Oengus to go there and persuade the beautiful Caer Ibormaith. With this admission, the adversaries are reconciled.

The evening of Samhain, "the Mac Oc went to the Loch Bel Dracon and he saw one hundred and fifty white birds on the lake, with silver chains and gold rings around their heads." Oengus, who was in human form, is changed into a bird and goes off to speak to the woman-swan. It does not take the two of them long to come to an agreement, because the beautiful Caer has been in love with Oengus for a very long time. That is why she appeared to him in his dream. But since she is still enchanted, she and Oengus go around the lake three times in the form of two swans before heading off toward Sidh-na-Brug. There, "they sang music together and they plunged the people into sleep for three days and three nights. Then the young woman lived with him."[42]

It is clear that at the end of three days and three nights, a symbolic number that represents the mythic time of Samhain, the enchantment is over. And since this time Oengus has reigned over all of the Sidh-na-Brug, along the slopes of the Boyne River valley, at least if we are to believe the ancient narratives and the popular oral tradition as it is still related today.

Frâech and Finnabair

Frâech[43] (heather) is the son of Idach of Connaught and Be Finn, Boann's sister. Thus he belongs to both the human race and the fairy people of the Tuatha de Danann. For eight years he lives without a wife, no doubt preferring the company of the fifty sons of kings who frequent his residence. But his beauty and his bravery are such that his reputation spreads far and wide, and without ever having seen him—which is far from extraordinary in Celtic legends—the beautiful Finnabair,[44] the daughter of Ailill and Medb, falls desperately in love with him.

Someone tells Frâech this, and after getting his men's advice he decides to go speak to the young woman. But he knows that he will only win her from her parents if he makes a good impression on them. He goes to find Boann, his mother's sister,[45] to ask her for "some marvelous clothes and presents from the fairies." Boann provides them, and Frâech leaves for Cruachan, the residence of Ailill and Mebd, with an amazing retinue:

> They wore fifty blue cloaks each of which was like the back of a scarab and had four dark gray wings and a red gold brooch; fifty white tunics with gold and silver animals; fifty silver shields with trim; a royal candle in the hand of each of the men with fifty white brass rivets, fifty lumps of gold riveted to each of them; tipped by carbuncle at their ends; precious stones crowned their heads which shone like the rays of the sun at night. They had fifty swords with golden handles and each had a gentle gray horse, with a golden bit, and a silver bowl holding golden bells. . . . Seven horn players with gold and silver horns, robes of all colors, long golden and yellow hair, brilliant cloaks. Three druids were in front of them, with silver diadems set off in gold. Each had a shield with emblems in relief, with crested hooks, with ribs of bronze on the sides. Three harpists, each with a royal demeanor.[46]

Frâech and his retinue are very well received by the king and queen of Connaught. They are given a section of the royal house, which allows the narrator to describe some of it in detail:

Seven gilded beds from the hearth to the wall, in the house all around; a bronze pediment for each bed; compartments of nicely marked red yew, three bands of bronze around each bed; seven bands of copper, a cauldron for beef[47] reaching to the roof of the house. The house was of pine, covered on the outside with shingles. There were sixteen windows to the house and copper frames around each of them. A copper beam crossed through it from the hole in the roof. Four copper pillars stand by the beds of Ailill and Mebd. They were all made of copper bronze and the bed was at the very center. Around it, there were two pediments covered with gold. From the pediment, a strip of silver connected the crosspieces of the house and went around it from one door to the other.[48]

We can see from this that Celtic fortresses had nothing in common with the classic fortified castles of the Middle Ages. But the evident archaisms of the civilization described here do not undermine the great preoccupation with aesthetics and the unrestrained attempt at the most subtle levels of refinement.

A game of chess begins and lasts for three days and three nights—that is to say, for a symbolic period during which time is suspended, signified "by the glow of the precious stones," which clearly indicates the magical nature of the story. Food is served, and Ailill asks Frâech to have his harpists play.

An otter skin sack, trimmed with scarlet leather, gold, and silver surrounded each harp; at the center, the skin of a deer, as white as snow, but with eyes of a dark gray in the middle, and trimmings of flax on the strings, also as white as the coat of a swan. The harps were gold, silver, and white bronze, with figures of serpents, birds, and dogs in gold and silver. When someone touched the strings, these figures ran in circles around the people. Then they played, and twelve men from the house of Ailill and Mebd died from crying so hard and from sadness.[49]

However, when Ailill and Mebd ask Frâech why he has come to Cruachan, Frâech responds simply, "I wanted to pay you a visit."

It seems as though Frâech is embarrassed. More than anything else, he would like to have a conversation with Finnabair, but he has not had an opportunity. Finally, one morning when he gets up early to go wash at the fountain, he meets the young girl, who is there with her servant. He asks her if she will agree to run away with him, proof that he has no real desire to ask for her hand in marriage. But Finnabair tells him that she will not leave without the consent of the king and queen. That does not keep her from giving Frâech a gold ring as evidence of her love.

But someone sees and reports to Ailill the gift of the ring and the exchange between the two young people. To put it mildly, the king and queen of Connaught are hardly disposed toward giving their daughter to Frâech.[50] This is precisely the moment Frâech chooses to make his official request. Ailill responds by requiring an exorbitant compensation from him. Frâech answers, "I swear by my shield, my sword, and my arms that I will not give such a dowry, even for Mebd of Cruachan!" And he leaves the room, full of anger. Ailill and Mebd then imagine that they are rid of Frâech once and for all.

A little while later, when everyone is by a pond, Ailill asks Frâech to show him how well he can swim. Frâech undresses and dives into the pond. Meanwhile, Ailill searches Fraech's purse and takes out the gold ring, which he throws in the water. But Frâech has seen everything, even the salmon that swallows the ring. He catches the salmon and brings it back to shore without saying anything. Ailill then asks him to dive in again and go get him a branch from the service tree on the other side of the pond.

Frâech obeys and cuts the branch, which he brings back to Ailill. Ailill asks him for more of them, and Frâech crosses the pond again. But there is a "beast" in this pond, a sort of monster, which the king is perfectly aware of, and which Frâech doesn't know about. The beast attacks the young man, who cries for a weapon to be thrown to him. Then Finnabair quickly undresses and dives in, bringing Frâech his sword. Thanks to her help, Frâech kills the monster and returns to the shore. But he is bad shape, exhausted, and suffering from many wounds.

Curiously, Ailill and Medb seem to regret their behavior. They have the young man attended to, but resolve to seek vengeance on Finnabair, whom they consider a traitor. That is when a lamentation on the fortress of Cruachan is heard, "and three times fifty women in crimson tunics were seen, with green hoods, with bracelets of silver on their wrists." These are clearly the woman-fairies or more exactly, the woman-swans, who surround Frâech and carry him away to the sidh, bringing him back the next day perfectly healed. Ailill and Mebd then make their peace with Frâech. But they do not renounce their vengeance against Finnabair.

Over the course of the celebration that follows, Ailill has his jewels brought out and spread before him. Then he sends for Finnabair and asks her to show him the gold ring he gave her the year before. Finnabair answers that she doesn't know where it is. Ailill threatens her angrily that she will die if she doesn't find the ring. But Frâech has asked one of his servants to go find the salmon and to have it prepared so that it can be served as part of the feast. Of course, just as in many other traditional tales, the ring is found in the salmon and everything works out. Ailill no longer has anything to hold against his daughter, and he is obliged to officially "betroth" her to Frâech. The marriage is planned for when he returns to his own country with his own herds.

The end of the story seems incoherent, and it is inconsistent with the beginning in that it says Frâech had no wife though he does have one, and even has three sons. Returning to his country, he learns that this wife, his sons, and his herd have been carried off. He then sets out on an expedition to get them back, and to do this he enlists the aid of the great Ulster warrior Conall Cernach, one of Cuchulainn's comrades-in-arms. After many adventures he succeeds in rescuing his wife, sons, and cows from a castle in Scotland protected by a mysterious serpent, and returns home, all ready—and again, the same interpolation—to accompany Ailill and Mebd in the Cattle Raid of Cualngé.

It is likely that this last part belonged to another narrative involving the legend of Frâech and Finnabair. It is simply a matter of a "marriage year by year," valid temporarily, which can be terminated or renewed by the consent of the two parties. This was a practice specific to Irish Celtic societies which was maintained for a long time in that country, even after it was Christianized. And this shows us that all classification of narratives in ancient Ireland is absolutely arbitrary, since many belong to all the cycles. It is true that the Celts make no distinction between myth and history, which gives their tradition a special quality found hardly anywhere else in western Europe.

2

Cohe Ulscep Cycle

This cycle is the most significant in terms of the number of
epics that can be included in it. It testifies to the dominance
that Ulster has always exercised over the whole of Ireland. It
is the richest and most heavily populated province, which, during the
period of Christianization, witnessed the establishment of the most
beautiful monasteries and both the Catholic and the Episcopal seat at
Armagh. It is also the province nearest to the sister isle and has always
had close relations with the west coast of Scotland, originally inhabited by the Picts and then by Irish immigrants.

The Ulster Cycle is thus testimony to actual fact: The Ulate heroes
are formidable warriors; their adventures are innumerable and have
left a lasting impression on both sides of Saint George's Channel. King
Conchobar, who is at the very center of this cycle, as Arthur will be in
the Breton epic later on, is the model for Celtic kings. He certainly has
many faults, and often he pays for them, but he remains the most typical
example in Celtic myth of the sovereign governing a realm without
boundaries that expands or contracts according to the influence exerted
by the king himself as equalizer of the forces present, physical and spiritual,
as mediator for the people, responsible for the growth and prosperity of
the populations that have chosen him and given him their confidence.[1]

The Malady of the Ulates

An Ulster peasant,[2] Crunniuc is a widower, with many sons. One day a
distinguished young woman comes to his home and, without saying a
word, takes charge of the housekeeping and then goes to lie down beside

Crunniuc. The peasant's fortune increases and life becomes easier. Soon after, the woman becomes pregnant and, just at the time when she is ready to give birth, the Ulate assembly takes place. Crunniuc leaves for the assembly, and the woman advises him not to speak of her to the Ulates. While at the assembly Crunniuc watches a horse race. The king's horses are the winners, but Crunniuc cannot stop himself from saying, "My wife runs faster." The king, furious, has Crunniuc arrested and sends messengers to find the woman so she can prove that her husband's words are true.

His wife asks for the race to be postponed because she is about to give birth, but under the threat that her husband will be killed, she is obliged to come to the assembly. There she pleads with the king to grant her a postponement. Unbending, the king orders her to run. She turns to the Ulates, asking them to intervene. No one dares to go against the king's wishes. Then she says, "Let it be as you wish, but because of the harm that you do me, you will be subject to even greater harm!" And she gives her name. She is Macha, the daughter of Etrange, son of Ocean.

The race between Macha and the king's horses begins, and of course, Macha beats the horses. Then she gives birth to twins right there, who are called Emain Macha (the twins of Macha), the name of the Ulate capital. Just as she is giving birth, Macha lets out a cry that casts a spell over the Ulates. And since that time, as victims of Macha's curse, all the men of Ulster must suffer the pains of childbirth for four days and five nights. Only Cuchulainn the hero will be exempt.

This strange story, all the stranger for serving as an explanation for the Ulates being indisposed during certain enemy attacks—in particular during the *Tain Bô Cualngé*—presents us with a very mysterious character: Macha. This is a very ancient divinity who becomes a fairy, but a good fairy, since she kindly comes to take care of Crunniuc and his children. She belongs to the race of the Tuatha de Danann and has magical powers. But she must be compared to Rhiannon, the Welsh goddess who appears as a mare; to Epona, the Gallo-Roman goddess of horses; and to Dechtire, the mother of Cuchulainn,[3] because there are strange coincidences, in particular the role of the mare that Macha takes on in racing with the horses and her giving birth before these very same creatures. But a complete study on Macha would be needed here, and as this narrative is the only one of many involving this figure, it only hints at what traits the great mother-goddess of the Celts might originally have had.

The Birth of Conchobar

Conchobar,[4] the king of Ulster, is the central figure in all the epics in the Ulster cycle. He is probably historical and would have lived at the beginning of the Christian era. But as he appears to us, he is so laden with symbolism, so strangely arrayed in mythological trappings, that he must be considered primarily the crystallization of Irish thinking on the role of the king. He is indeed the perfect example of the pacifying power, "equalizer," dispenser. He is the exceptional being around whom heroes gather. He maintains the country's integrity, and if he sometimes seems cruel, vindictive, even disloyal, it is because his authority, theoretically limitless, can and must be exercised without censure, either political or moral, over all of his people.

Clearly, Conchobar's birth can only be wondrous. One day during a quarrel, the druid-warrior Cathbad kills the twelve guardians of Ness, daughter of King Eochaid of the Yellow Heel. Ness goes to complain to her father, but he says that since he doesn't know who the assassin(s) is, he can do nothing. Ness then assembles a band of warriors and directs them herself, in order to avenge her guardians.

She finds herself in a desert, and while her men prepare food she takes off her clothes and her arms and goes to bathe. That's when Cathbad and his troops appear. Cathbad keeps her from seizing her clothes and her weapons and threatens her with his sword. To save her own life, the girl agrees to Cathbad's three demands: "Safety for me, your friendship, and that you will be my wife for as long as I live." And so it happens that Cathbad establishes himself in Ulster and marries Ness. One night when Cathbad is thirsty, Ness brings him some water, but there are two worms in the water and Cathbad doesn't see them. Furious, he makes Ness drink. And that night Ness becomes pregnant. She then gives birth to Conchobar: "At his birth, he had a worm in each fist, the ones that his mother had drunk."

That is how the birth of Conchobar, son of Ness, is explained. He is the son of a druid-warrior and a woman warrior. Thus he will be formidable, and he will be destined for great things, all the more so because the theme of fertilization by mouth adds the element of the marvelous indispensable for making this king a sacred figure related to the divine world.[5]

The Kingship of Conchobar

This text[6] first gives a succinct account of the birth of Conchobar, son of
Ness and Cathbad. But the marriage between Ness and Cathbad is not
permanent. Finding herself alone, Ness marries the king of Ulster, Fergus
Mac Roig, but under one very specific condition: that her son Conchobar
be king for one year. The Ulates accept this condition and even go so far
as to grant the theoretical kingship to Conchobar and the actual kingship to Fergus. But at the end of a year's reign, the Ulates prefer to keep
Conchobar as the actual king because the kingship that was given as a
dowry to Ness is now in the possession of a woman. And thus, Fergus is
completely dispossessed of his realm. Conchobar proves himself an able
king. His judgments are fair and his champions are among the best in
the world. The Ulates do him the honor of entrusting to him their nu-
bile daughters for one night so that he will be their first husband[7] and
they will prosper, since the king is the living symbol of this prosperity.
Conchobar feeds all the Ulster nobles who find themselves in his house.[8]
Each night of Samhain he invites all the Ulates, and those who do not
respond to his invitation are dead the next morning. He has three houses:
the "Red Bough," which serves as the meeting place for the kings and
chiefs, thus organized into a sort of warrior clan; the "Many Colored
House," where the weapons of the chief heroes are found; and the "Bloody
Bough," where the spoils and the heads of his enemies are collected.

This, then, is a brief portrait of Conchobar's kingship as head of a
powerful people, a king who is able to take command of all the other
Irish realms united against him.

The Siege of Dun Etair

Athirne,[9] the poet of Ulster, is a formidable sorcerer who, thanks to his
magical powers and under the threat of his spells, obtains whatever he
desires. His nickname is the Ulster Troublemaker. One day he begins a
tour of Ireland and sets off to visit all the kings and chiefs, who can do
very well without this bothersome guest. He begins with the king of
South Connaught, Eochaid son of Luchte. Eochaid is one eyed, and
Athirne, threatening worse harm, forces him to give up his remaining
eye. Then he goes to the king of Munster, Tigerna Tetbuillech, and
asks him to let him sleep with the queen that night, or else the honor

of the Munster people will be forever tarnished. Tigerna is forced to obey Athirne, who then goes on to Leinster. There he begins by threatening the men of Leinster if they don't immediately bring him a brooch of great value. After this he visits the king Mesgegra, from whom he demands his wife, Buan. "To save your honor," said Athirne, "or you kill me and there will be shame forever on the people of Leinster, and the Ulates will never cease to seek vengeance for me." So said, so done. But Athirne is not content with the queen. He remains in Leinster for one year and takes advantage of his stay by stealing three times fifty queens or wives of chiefs to take away with him to Ulster.

The day of departure arrives. Athirne sets out at the head of his retinue, and as soon as he is gone the men of Leinster are overcome with sadness. They muster their courage and decide to go off in pursuit of the poet-sorcerer to take back their one hundred fifty wives. They catch up to him, but just as they do, the Ulates—who can't stand Athirne themselves but are obliged to help him—counterattack. The Ulates are fewer in number. They retreat and take refuge in the fortress of Dun Etair—that is, Howth, north of Dublin. It is a tragic situation because there is nothing to eat or drink in the fortress except the herd that Athirne has brought with him. Now, the poet acts with total contempt and the worst kind of boorishness toward his compatriots who have come to his aid. He keeps all the food to himself and even has what remains of the milk thrown over the ramparts.

We might ask ourselves why the Ulates would tolerate such behavior. They have to, out of fear of Athirne's evil spells, his sacred powers, especially the famous geis of destruction and dishonor that he can cast upon them at any moment. The sorcerer's inordinate power—because we are not dealing with a druid—is one bit of evidence proving that the true power in Ireland was not in the hands of the kings. In Ireland the sacred imposes its laws over all actions; nowhere, even today, is there a country more subject to belief in fairies and supernatural beings. And this statement is not meant to be pejorative in the least.

Finally, thanks to Leborcham—Conchobar's messenger, for whom we are given an astonishing description ("Her two feet and two knees were in the back, her two ankles and two thighs in the front"), and who goes to warn the other Ulates—the victory is definitive. The men of Leinster retreat and hurry to build a red wall, "because it was taboo for the Ulates to cross over a red wall."

However, Conall Cernach, who has lost two of his brothers in the fighting, wants absolute revenge for them. He goes around the wall and follows Mesgegra in quick pursuit. Mesgegra just happens to be alone with his tired driver who wants to sleep. While he sleeps, the king finds a nut, eats half of it, and saves the rest for the driver. When the driver wakes with a start because he has just had a bad dream, he fights with Mesgegra over the half nut and, with a stroke of his sword, cuts off the king's hand. "Bad move," says the king. "Open my fist, o valet, and you will find the half nut!" The valet finds the half nut and turns his sword against himself. With difficulty, Mesgegra hitches up his chariot singlehandedly, and it is at this moment that Conall appears. When he sees that Mesgrega has lost a hand, Conall has one of his arms bound to make things equal, and the fight begins. Conall succeeds in killing the king, cuts off his head, and sets the head on a stone next to a ford. "A drop of blood fell from the neck and ran down the stone until it hit the ground. Then he put Mesgegra's head on another stone and the head passed through the stone." Conall then put the king's head on his own head: "The head went on his shoulder and his eyes began to squint from this moment on."[10]

Conall encounters Buan, Mesgegra's wife, and wants to take her with him, claiming that it is the king himself who commands it. He shows Buan the head, and the head changes color; now it is red, now white. She asks Conall for a moment to grieve for her husband. "Then she let out a cry of lamentation which could be heard at Tara and Allen, and then she threw herself backwards and died."

Conall demands that his driver take Mesgegra's head. "I can't lift this head," said the driver. "Then remove his brain with your sword," said Conall, "carry it with you and mix it with earth to make a shot for a sling."[11] The driver obeys. And that is how Conall returns once more in triumph (cernach in Gaelic) to Emain Macha.

The Story of Deirdre

Deidre[12] is one of the best-known heroines in Ireland itself, especially since the play by J. M. Synge revived her after Mac Pherson had already opened the door of the realm of the dead halfway for her calling her instead Darthula, the desperate lover of the beautiful Nathos. But it may be that she has become the national Irish heroine less because of the tragic side of her love story than because of the significance that the Irish have sought to attach to her. Deirdre is Ireland herself, Ireland the prisoner who yearns for her lost beloved, who deplores her unhappy fate in the chains of England, here symbolized by King Conchobar. We must not forget, however, that *The Story of Deirdre* is, first of all, an epic tragedy, within the Irish pagan framework, a tragic story of love, which develops in strange and beautiful ways.

One day, the Ulates are gathered at the home of Fedelmid, King Conchobar's storyteller. The guests are drunk, as usual. It is then that Fedelmid's wife, who is pregnant, passes among them, and the child in her womb begins to cry. This is a disturbing omen. Immediately the druid Cathbad is asked what it could mean, and after thinking about it, he chants a prophetic poem: "In the hollow of your womb has cried a woman of blond ringlets, of superb blue-gray eyes. Her cheeks are crimson as the foxglove. The pearls of her teeth are the winter's snow. Her lips are as bright as scarlet." But after this description comes the warning: "For this woman, murders will take place among the Ulate warriors." Finally, Cathbad declares that this girl will be named Deirdre.

The girl is born immediately thereafter. The Ulates, frightened by the prophecy, demand that she be killed. Conchobar is opposed to this and takes her away so that she can be raised with him. His intention is clear: Someday he wants to marry this girl, who is destined for such a dramatic fate.

Deirdre grows up and becomes a beautiful young woman. Conchobar sees to it that not a single man gets a glimpse of her. Only her nurse and Leborcham, the king's messenger, are allowed to enter her house. Now, one day the girl notices a crow in the snow that is drinking the blood of a wounded animal. So she says to Leborcham, "The only man I could love would be one who had those three colors: hair like the crow, cheeks like that blood, and a body like the snow."[13]

It must be understood, of course, that this man exists. It is Noise, one of the sons of Usnech. He is a young warrior, kindhearted and magnificent. His voice is so beautiful that when he sings, any cow that hears him gives two thirds more milk. He is quick in the hunt and courageous in battle. Of course, Noise meets Deirdre. She offers herself without shame to Noise, but Noise, knowing she is promised to

Conchobar, bluntly refuses. Then Deirdre "throws herself upon him and takes him by the ears: Here are two ears of disgrace and mockery, she said, if you don't take me with you." Thus we see Noise put under obligation by the geis of shame that comes from Deirdre throwing herself upon him.[14] He asks his brothers for advice. They tell him that he must leave with Deirdre and that they themselves will accompany the pair. And so it happens. Usnech's sons go to offer their services to foreign kings.

But Conchobar, enraged, instigates plots against them. Someone is forever trying to kill them. They cross the sea and set themselves up in Scotland in a deserted place. No longer able to find food, they go into service for the king of Scotland, building houses. "It was for the girl that they made the houses, so that no one could see her, for fear that someone would kill them because of her."

In fact, it is the king's quartermaster who notices Deirdre and tells the king that he has seen a girl worthy of a king. The king of Scotland sends messengers to court Deirdre for him each evening, but she reports everything to Noise. And when she learns that the Scottish king wants to have the sons of Usnech killed, she warns them, and they all leave during the night to go settle on an island.

Conchobar, alerted to what has happened, decides to use trickery to get his vengeance. He makes it known to the sons of Usnech that he is willing to freely receive them in Ulster and that they can designate the warriors who will guarantee their safety. The sons of Usnech accept and choose for guarantors Fergus Mac Roig, Dubthach, and Cormac, the sons of Conchobar. But this is all a trap. No sooner do the sons of Usnech arrive in the prairie under the wall of Emain Macha than Conchobar arranges for the guarantors to be removed—Fergus in particular, because one of his taboos is that he must stay with a host for the duration of any feast. The sons of Usnech are alone and the Ulates attack them. Fiacha, the son of Fergus, rushes in to protect Noise, but he is run through at the same time as Deirdre's unfortunate lover. Carnage follows: All the companions of Noise are killed, and Deirdre is taken away, bound, to the king Conchobar.

But the honor of Fergus, Dubthach, and Cormac, who were solemnly declared guarantors for the safety of the sons of Usnech, is henceforth tarnished. They get immediate revenge by declaring open revolt against Conchobar and those who murdered the sons of Usnech. This leads to such a massacre that Conchobar tries to stop them. Fergus and Conchobar fight for a whole day without definitive results. Then Fergus sacks and burns Emain Macha and takes refuge, along with Dubthach and Cormac, in Connaught at the home of Ailill and Medb, who are happy to receive them. "Thirty hundred, such was the number of these exiles; until the end of sixteen years, they never stopped causing the Ulates grief and terror." And it is these exiles, Fergus Mac Roig in particular, who play an important role in the battles of the *Tain Bô Cualngé*.

As for Deirdre, she stays with Conchobar for one year, never smiling, hardly eating, not lifting her head from her lap. When minstrels are brought to her, she always sings them the same sad song, a sort of elegy for Noise and the sons of Usnech. Conchobar himself tries to dispel her sadness. She sings to him,

> Oh Conchobar, what do you want? You have caused me grief and tears. . . . The one who was for me the most beautiful under the sky, the one who was so dear to me, you have taken him away from me. . . . Two crimson cheeks more beautiful than a prairie, red lips, eyelashes black as the scarab, teeth the color of pearl, like the noble hue of the snow. . . . Don't break today, my heart. Soon I will go to my tomb, oh Conchobar, do you know, grief is stronger than the sea. . . .

From the dark beauty of these stanzas we can well imagine Deirdre, prostrate, reliving her past, always beyond the outer world, in a kind of madness. And as for Conchobar—who clearly doesn't play a good role in this adventure, since he is both traitor and tormentor—he has had enough. In a kind of sadistic rage he asks Deirdre, "Who do you hate the most of those you see?" Deirdre answers, "You and Eogan, son of Durthacht." Eogan is Noise's assassin. Then Conchobar coldly declares, "You will spend a year with Eogan."

Thus the king gives Deirdre to Eogan. The next day Eogan comes to the Emain assembly, and Deirdre finds herself behind him in the carriage. Conchobar laughs when he sees them and says, "Well, Deirdre, you look like a sheep between two rams, between me and Eogan." Seeing a huge rock in front of her then, Deirdre throws herself at it head first in such a way that she cracks her skull and dies.

This dramatic ending crowns one of the most grueling and cruelest love stories of ancient Ireland. As in the works of all great playwrights, this passionate love brings with it its share of repudiations and dead bodies. But in this *Story of Deirdre* there is something grandiose and sublime. And it is all told with a seriousness that heightens the intensity of the love, the violence, and the tragic atmosphere from which evolve characters whom Racine, if he had known of them, would certainly have found worthy of displaying beside the Pyrrhuses, the Neros, the Roxannes and the Hermiones as examples of humanity's weakness and grandeur.

The Courtship of Luaine

After Deirdre's death,[15] Conchobar remains sad and morose for a long time. The Ulate chiefs advise him to choose a wife for himself, and Conchobar sends out his messenger Leborcham to find a young woman worthy of him. Leborcham finally discovers a certain Luaine, the daughter of Domanchenn, one of the Tuatha de Danann, "the only daughter of Ireland who had Deirdre's ways." Conchobar goes to find the girl. "When he saw her, there was not a bone in his body, not even as small as an inch, that wasn't filled with a violent love for the girl." But this isn't a propitious time for the marriage. Indeed, Mananann, "son of Athgno, king of Man and the Foreign Isles,"[16] arrives with his fleet to fight the Ulates and avenge the death of the sons of Usnech, whose children he has adopted. After a few fights, peace is declared: Mananann and Conchobar exchange vows of friendship.

However, when they learn of Conchobar and Luaine's betrothal, Athirne the poet (Troublemaker of Ulster) and his two sons go to solicit the girl in order to obtain her favors. Now as soon as they see Luaine, all three of them fall in love with her and threaten her with a *glam dicin* (a powerful bardic form of satire that causes physical harm) if she won't sleep with them. The girl refuses. They each do their lampoon, and Luaine dies of shame while the poet and his sons flee into their fortress.

Meanwhile Conchobar arrives in the company of the chief Ulates to look for Luaine. Upon discovering her dead Conchobar sinks into deep despair and asks, "What can be done for vengeance?" The Ulates answer that Athirne must be killed, as well as his sons and their men. But Cathbad the druid warns them that the poet has inordinate powers and that he will send them "beasts of prey, that is, Satire, Disgrace, Shame, Curses, Fire, and Bitter Words." The heroes Cuchulainn, Conall Cernach, Celtchar, and Cuscraid the Stutterer all recommend that Athirne be destroyed. Then, after carrying out the customary mourning practices and burying Luaine, Conchobar and the Ulates lay siege to Athirne's fortress, killing him as well as his sons and daughters and burning the fortress over them, thus ridding Ireland of a scourge and at the same time triumphing over their own superstitions.

The Death of Conchobar

This narrative[17] is the logical sequel to *The Siege of Dun Etair*, even if the events that occur in it take place many years later. Briefly, it is a matter of demonstrating how the death of Conchobar is not an accident but the final step in a series of actions that follow inevitably from one another. Conchobar's fate was decided the day he declared war against the king Mesgegra, an unjust war that he was obliged to fight because of the magical powers of the poet Athirne.

So it happens that one day, the Ulates are drunk. It must be admitted that this is often the case. And the usual quarrel over who is most powerful among Cuchulainn, Loegaire, and Conall Cernach ensues. Conall challenges the other warriors to a fight since he has a formidable weapon at his disposal: the *brain of Mesgegra*, that is, a slingshot ball made from the unfortunate king's brain. No one dares to take up Conall's challenge, so great is the power of this weapon. And Conall puts the *brain of Mesgegra* back on the shelf where it is usually kept.

But the next day Cet, the son of Maga, a Connaught warrior who can never sleep without having cut off at least one Ulate head, wanders about the area, lying in wait for a victim. He enters the Emain Macha enclosure and sees the king's two fools playing ball with the *brain of Mesgegra*. Cet knows that Mesgregra prophesied that his death would be avenged in an amazing way. He seizes the *brain of Mesgegra* and looks for an opportunity to kill Conchobar.

During the course of one of those many battles between the Ulates and the men of Connaught over stolen livestock, Conchobar finds himself in a skirmish. But the women of Connaught, who much admire the Ulster king for his beauty and his courage, ask him to withdraw from the fray and present himself to them. Very flattered, Conchobar approaches the women—and this is when Cet, who has hidden himself among the women, throws the *brain of Mesgegra* at him, and two thirds of it enters Conchobar's head.

During the battle that follows, Conchobar is taken to Emain Macha. Fingen the doctor comes to his bedside, "If this rock is removed," he says, "you will die immediately. If it is not removed, I will heal you, but you will remain deformed." Then he attaches the two parts of Conchobar's head together with a gold string the same color as the king's hair, but he makes the following recommendations: "You must never get angry, never ride horseback, never eat too much, never have too passionate relations with a woman, and never run."

Conchobar lives like this for seven years. The text of the *Book of Leinster* presents us with an edifying end for the king of Ulster, which seems too much of a Christian interpolation to be authentic. One day his druid tells him the story of the Passion of Jesus Christ. Conchobar becomes so emotional and angry upon hearing it that the *brain of Mesgegra* comes out of his head and he dies.

In fact, the authentic conclusion can be found in a gloss for a poem by Cinead na Hartacain, who died in 973—a gloss sufficiently eloquent in all its dryness: "When Conchobar finds himself in the forest of Lamraige cutting wood, the *brain of Mesgegra* springs from his head and his own brain spills out."[18] Thus perishes the great king of Ulster, after seven years of forced cohabitation with the brain of an enemy unjustly destroyed.

The Death of Cet, Son of Maga[1]

According to the commendable habit that he has had since childhood, Cet,[19] son of Maga, Conchobar's murderer, works his way into Ulster to kill his daily Ulate. But Conall Cernach, who has decided to put an end to this scourge, sets out to follow him, which is that much easier because it has just snowed. He catches up with him while Cet is settling down in a house and his driver is cooking their food.

But Conall is afraid and tells himself that, after all, it would be stupid to fight with so fierce a man. He is content with leaving his mark on Cet's horse and cart. Cet understands that he is dealing with Conall and rejoices at not having to fight a man so formidable. His driver makes him feel ashamed, however, and finally the two heroes meet each other on the ford that will come to be called Cet's Ford. They have a savage battle. Cet is killed, but Conall, wounded, falls unconscious.

He is taken in by Belchu, a Connaught man, who agrees to care for him, on the condition that they fight when he is healed. But Belchu is afraid of Conall and asks his sons to go kill the Ulate in his bed during the night, telling them that he will leave the door of the house open. However, Conall, who has overheard the conversation, makes Belchu close the door and come sleep in his own bed.[20] Belchu sleeps peacefully since the door is closed. But Conall goes out to reopen it. Belchu's sons, who are waiting for the signal, rush in and kill their father. And Conall Cernach, who earns his nickname once more, appears as the dispenser of justice, kills the three murderers, and returns home with four cut off heads.

The Death of the Sons of Conchobar

Following is the translation of this short narrative,[21] which mixes the fantastic with a tragic event:

> A man went out hunting at Emain Macha. He killed three hares. He went to cook them in the hollow of a rock. Now, while he was there, he heard a voice which said these verses to him, and this voice came from the rock: "They were noble, they were worthy, they were not seeds at the bottom of a sack, they were sweet to Emain Macha, the three princes. They were charming, they were proud, they were noble and agile, they were warriors ready for anything. Many were their guests at Emain, great was their household. These were royal heirs, without deception, true supporters of princes." The voice went on, "Pitiable is the thing you have done, because here are the three sons of Conchobar, sons of

Ness: Cormac Conlonges, son of Conchobar, Cairpre, son of Conchobar and Cuscraid the Stutterer of Macha, son of Conchobar, and they came to the sidh in the form of three hares. It is them whom you have killed, " said the voice. Then the hunter was seized with horror and fled, abandoning his game.

The Adventures of Nera

Here is a very strange story[22] coming from the earliest Celtic mythology and updated during the early Middle Ages, when it was included in the great *Tain Bô Cualngé* cycle for which it serves as a kind of introduction. Nevertheless, this narrative doesn't belong to the Ulster cycle; it centers on Conchobar and Cuchulainn. It belongs more to the tradition of the Connaught, this western realm over which the king Ailill reigns, and especially the queen Mebd—or Maeve, whom Shakespeare has named Mab, and who once adorned the banknotes of the Bank of Ireland. Mebd is the absolute model of sovereign femininity, and her name, not surprisingly, means "drunkenness." She exists on the border between the real and the imaginary, the earthly and the celestial, and when it is necessary she lavishes "the friendship of her thighs" on all the warriors she needs to ensure the success of an expedition, thus prefiguring the character of the primitive Guinevere of Arthurian legend before the introduction of Lancelot into the corpus. But around Mebd is organized a strange world; we don't know if it is on the surface or part of the underground world reserved, as we have seen, for the Tuatha de Danann. Mebd and Ailill's residence is Cruachan (now Croghan), but it is a fortress, also called a fortified enclosure, built on top of a sidh, a megalithic mound where the gods and heroes of ancient times are supposed to live. Two dimensions, two spaces, and, consequently, two times were superimposed upon each other in the most perfect harmony, and it is necessary to know this in trying to understand this narrative of the *Echtra Nerai* (The Adventures of Nera), which is certainly one of the most difficult of the texts that the Irish clerics bequeathed to us in their desire to pass on the ancient tradition of their people. Everything is mixed together here—the present, the past, the future. But since everything takes place during the festival of Samhain, time is abolished and eternity rules. Under these conditions, how can we be astonished by the apparent inconsistencies of the narrative?

Thus we find ourselves in the fortress of Cruachan one evening during Samhain. Ailill and Mebd have called their household together around them in the royal house, that is, around the central hearth where food is cooking in a cauldron. While waiting for the food, Ailill makes his guests a curious request. Two prisoners had been taken the day before, and Ailill says, "Whoever will go put a willow branch around the foot of one of the prisoners found in the torture house will have his choice of a reward." It is difficult to discern the exact significance of the ritual, but we can affirm that there was such a ritual, no matter how inexplicable. Of course, there are some volunteers, but they all return hanging their heads, because "great was the darkness of that night and its horror. It was a night when phantoms appeared."[23] Finally, it is a warrior by the name of Nera who decides to go there, and Ailill promises him his golden sword.[24]

But Nera takes certain precautions. He puts on a solid suit of armor and heads out into the night for the house of tortures. To understand these details, we must remember that a royal fortress like Cruachan is a rock outcropping surrounded by ramparts and a moat, forming a sort of entrenched camp inside of which huts, half stone and half wood and covered with thatch, are found scattered about. When Nera enters the house of tortures, his armor falls off three times in a row. One of the prisoners laughs and tells him that it won't stop falling off unless he puts a suitable nail into it. Thus Nera fixes it with a nail (but we aren't told if he nails it to his own flesh!), and the prisoner tells him that he is brave. Arrogantly, Nera answers him that there is no doubt about that. Then the prisoner eggs him on: "By your true valor, take me upon your back so that I can go drink with you. I was very thirsty when I was hung up!" Nera takes the captive on his back and carries him toward the nearest house, according to the prisoner's wishes.

We must admit that all this merits, if not an explanation, at least some commentary. Presumably (although the text doesn't mention it), Nera has just performed the ritual involving the willow branch. But the prisoner's demand is a kind of magic obligation, the druidic geis, and Nera must obey. In any case, he doesn't untie the prisoner (since he carries him on his back), and he is not unfaithful to his king's wishes. But the captive's remark, "I was very thirsty when I was hung up," has a very specific meaning. Indeed, it is a matter of a Samhain ritual represented in the engraving on the famous Gundestrup Cauldron[25] and described in the annotations to Lucan's *Pharsalia*, before being picked up again in one of the sequels to *Perceval* by Chrétien de Troyes. It is a matter of hanging upside down, which was meant to make "the old man die" and to provide a new life, briefly, a sort of rebirth or resurrection in a glorious body. Clearly, this explains nothing about Ailill and Mebd's reasons for hanging the prisoner this way in the house of tortures, but it is an indication of the sacred and ritualistic significance still attributed to this strange position during the period in which the narrative was transcribed.

This remark is all the more interesting because the captive's hanging is incomplete: Indeed, to be effective, it had to be done over a cauldron. Now, it certainly seems as though the prisoner had no cauldron underneath him, since he asks Nera to carry him elsewhere for a drink. Nera thus plays the role of the priest. He carries the prisoner on his back. But nothing happens as expected, and the literal translation is worth citing here. While going toward the neighboring house,

> They saw a lake of fire which surrounded the house. "There is nothing good for us in that house," said the prisoner, "there is no fire without sobriety. Let us go to another house, the one nearest to us." They went toward another house and saw a lake of water around it. "Let's not go into this house," said the prisoner, "there is certainly no vat here except for washing or bathing or doing the dishes, after sleeping at night. Let us go to another house." The captive said, "What I want to drink is in this house." Nera put him down onto the ground and they entered. There were vats for bathing and washing, with a beverage in each of them. Then the captive drank a mouthful from each of the tubs and blew the last drop out of his lips onto the people who were in the house, in such a way that they all died.[26]

After which Nera leads the captive back to his place in the house of tortures and prepares to go back to the royal house.

But since the prisoner has blown out the last drops of what he drank, everything has inexplicably been thrown out of balance: "The hill was burning in front of him and he noticed a heap of cut heads. They were the heads of his men. Also there were warriors on the mound." Nera no longer knows where he is. He follows the warriors, who seem to sink into the depths of the mound. Then he finds himself in the sidh, that strange Other World so close to the world of the living. The people of the sidh become aware of his presence, and the king tells him to go alone to a woman's house, where he will be able to live as he pleases on the condition that each day he brings to the king a piece of firewood.

That is what happens. The woman receives him cordially, and each day he goes to take his piece of firewood to the king. One day he notices a blind man with a lame person on his back leaving the king's house and going over to a wall. He asks the woman for an explanation. "They are going over to the crown that is in the wall," says the woman. "It is a gold diadem that the king wears on his head, and this is where it is hidden." Nera is puzzled that they set out in twos to perform this ritual. "That's easy," says the woman, "it is because the king has given them the responsibility of going to visit the crown; one is lame and the other blind." That is all we know about them, but even so, we can recall certain representations of Indo-European gods who are distinguished by physical defects: the blind one (or the one eyed) is the *seer*, like Odin-Wotan types, and the lame one is the *blacksmith*, like Hephaestus types. In any case this proves the importance of the golden crown, one of those treasures from the Other World that must be discovered in order to change the world. The quest for the Grail is constructed upon this same theme.

Nera then takes this opportunity to ask the woman what she knows of his own destiny. She reveals to him that what he has seen—that is, the pile of heads and the destruction of the Cruachan residence—is an illusion. "It is an army of shades that is coming toward you." But in fact, this illusion is a prophetic vision, because Cruachan's destruction will take place unless Nera warns his people. And after telling Nera that she is pregnant by him, the woman invites him to return to his people: "Rise and go to them. They are still around the same cauldron and what it contains has not yet been removed. Tell them to be on their guard the evening of Samhain and to destroy the sidh." But she is careful to add, "Send a message to the sidh when your people are about to come to destroy it, so you can come and find your family and your livestock."

Thus, Nera returns to the fortress and finds Ailill, Mebd, and all the others again around the hearth, as if he had only just left them. As a reward, he receives Ailill's gold sword and tells of his adventures. A year passes, a year in which Fergus Mac Roig, who is called the Ulster Exile, comes to take refuge at Cruachan after his quarrel with King Conchobar over Deirdre and Noise. In the period of the Samhain, Ailill says to Nera, "The time has come. Rise and go find your livestock and your family so that we can destroy the sidh."

So Nera goes back down into the sidh. The woman, who, during all this time has carried a piece of firewood to the king each day, presents his son to him along with a magnificent herd of cattle. She makes it clear that she has given one of these cows to his son. Then Nera sees about the herd and goes to take them to pasture. But "while he slept, Morrigan took his son's cow and had it mated with the Brown One of Cualngé, east of Cualngé. Morrigan came back west with the cow. Cuchulainn met them in the plain of Murthemne when they crossed it. Because one of Cuchulainn's powers made it so that a woman could not leave his territory with him meeting her."

This intrusion in the narrative of Morrigan—a kind of goddess of love and war whose name means "great queen" and who turns up again later as Morgan of the Arthurian legends—as well as Cuchulainn, the great Ulster hero, seems to be an interpolation. The episode serves no real purpose in the development of Nera's adventures, but it does serve as a way to link this narrative to the great Ulster epic, the famous *Cattle Raid of Cualngé*. Moreover, the transcriber takes this opportunity to present the character of Cuchulainn more fully and to flesh out some of his peculiarities: "It was another of Cuchulainn's powers that the birds could not eat on his land unless he left them something. It was another of his powers that the fish could not go into the estuaries unless he fed them. It was still another of his powers that the warriors of another people could not be on his land unless he protected them. . . . Each woman, each girl who found herself in Ulster had to be under his protection until she had a husband." Cuchulainn orders Morrigan to hand over the cow to Nera. When Cuchulainn rejoins the woman with his herd, he complains that he is missing a cow, but the woman reveals to him that she has come back alone and that she has given birth to a calf. Finally, she advises Nera to go find his people again: "Let them come the evening of Samhain, because the sidhs are always open that evening."

Nera returns to Cruachan. Ailill and Mebd ask him where he went. He answers, "I was in beautiful countries, with great treasures, precious things, rich ornaments, good foods, and marvelous treasures. The evening of Samhain, they wait for you to kill you unless you are forewarned." Ailill declares that they will certainly fight against the men of the sidh. And three days before the fateful day, Nera goes back into the mound to find his wife, his son, and his herd. But his son's cow's calf encounters a famous bull, the Beautiful Horned of Ae, who is Ailill's magical animal and who will be Brown One of Cualngé's adversary in the *Raid*. The calf is in love with the Beautiful Horned and moos. In Cruachan someone hears the mooing and asks where it is coming from, which prompts a quarrel between Fergus and the too-well-known Bricriu of the Poisoned Tongue, always ready to sow ill-feeling at any gathering in which he participates.

However, her swineherd explains to the queen Mebd the reason for the mooing. She learns that it involves a calf born of the Brown One of Cualngé, which leads to the pronouncement of this terrible oath, which is going to be one of the causes of the raid: "I swear by the gods of my people that I will not lie down, that I will not sleep, that I will not drink whey, that I will not eat, that I will not drink red beer nor white beer, that I will taste no food until I have seen these two bulls fighting each other before me!" And thus the concluding episode of *The Cattle Raid of Cualngé* is foretold.

But in the meantime the expedition against the sidh must get under way: "The men of Connaught and the black army of the Exile [Fergus] head out toward the sidh. They destroy the sidh and take possession of all that they find there. That is how they carry off the crown of Briun, which was the third marvelous find made in Ireland." In all of that, of course we find the mythological and even mystical theme of the quest for sacred objects from the Other World, but also the reminder of actual historical fact: the plundering of the great megalithic tombs that were so very numerous in Ireland and that, for the most part, contained precious objects. Once more, myth and history merge with remarkable ease.

As for Nera, he "remained in the sidh with his family. He never came out of it and he will never come out of it as far as we can tell."

Thus ends the fantastic adventures of Nera, who is an *undead*, an exceptional being who escapes the common destiny of humans and attains, by virtue of the mysterious ritual he performs, a state of semigrace. It is infinitely probable that this narrative, so hard to interpret because of alterations and interpolations to the primitive outline, is a true vestige of certain druidic beliefs held by the ancient Celts.

The Death of Fergus

Here is the translation[27] of this short narrative, devoted to the end of a hero who falls victim to a long-deceived husband's jealousy:

> How did the tragic death of Fergus Mac Roig take place? That's easy. Fergus was in exile in Connaught after his honor had been tarnished because of the sons of Usnech. Because he was one of their three guarantors, the other two being Dubthach Langue-Paresseuse, and Cormac Conlonges, sons of Conchobar. They went into exile in the west for fourteen years, and during this time there was endless lamentation and grief in Ulster because of them. . . .[28] Three thousand was the number of those in exile with them. And his companion in the house of Ailill was Lugaid Dallaces, Ailill's own brother.
>
> One day, after some valorous acts, they went to the lake at the plain of Ai where they established camp and where there were games and gatherings. At one point, the whole army went to bathe in the lake. "Come, o Fergus," said Ailill, "and drown some men!"[29] "They are no good in the water," said Fergus. Nevertheless he went. In her heart, Medb couldn't stand this, and she rushed to the lake. Now, as Fergus entered the lake, all the pebbles and gravel on the lake bottom rose to the surface. Medb kept going until she was right up against Fergus' chest and then she wrapped her legs around him. Then [Fergus] swam around the lake. Jealousy seized Ailill. Then Medb got out of the

lake and stretched. "It is delicious when the buck and the doe do that in the lake, o Lugaid!" said Ailill. "Why not kill them?" said Lugaid who never missed his mark. "Do you want me to throw a spear at them?" said Ailill. "Turn my face away," said Lugaid, "and bring me a spear."

Fergus washed himself in the lake and his chest was turned toward them. Ailill's cart was brought close to him, and Lugaid threw a spear in such a way that it passed through Fergus' back. "It was a good shot!" said Lugaid. "It's true," they both said, "it's the end of Fergus." "It's very sad," said Lugaid, "if I have killed my foster brother and companion for nothing." "It is not nothing to me," said Ailill. The army rushed over, and all the men went toward the shore, the exiles as well as the men of Connaught. Fergus pulled out the spear and threw it at Ailill in such a way that it pierced the dog who was between the cart's two shafts. Then Fergus climbed out of the lake and holding himself very straight, walked all by himself to the hill beside the lake. And his soul took flight. And his tomb is there still.

3

The Cuchulainn Cycle

Cuchulainn is certainly the most significant character in the whole Gaelic tradition, and within the Ulster cycle he occupies a dominant position, comparable to the one held by Lancelot of the Lake in the French cycle of the Round Table. His birth, his life, his feats, his loves, and his death are recounted in detail in an astonishing number of epic narratives from very diverse periods.

It has been claimed that Cuchulainn was a kind of Celtic Hercules. A priori, nothing goes against this comparison. We are certainly dealing with a character both human and divine, and thus a sort of demigod. Moreover, we are told that he is, in fact, the son of the Pan-Celtic deity Lugh, if not the very incarnation of this god. His strength is Herculean, his skill with weapons unparalleled. He possesses superhuman powers. He is capable of complete metamorphosis by means of very strange deformations when he is seized with a warrior's rage. In short, he has all the characteristics of the hero before whom all must yield, men and animals alike. He is, in fact, the embodiment of divine power. He is the agent of the abstract divinity, the mediator between creatures and their mysterious creator, like Saint Michael or Saint George, the destroyer of monsters. And when he dies, because his destiny requires it, the hero's light will shine from his brow until his soul goes to rejoin the ancient gods on some marvelous island where there is neither death, nor old age, nor disease.

The Birth of Cuchulainn

One day[1] the Ulster king Conchobar happens to be in a chariot with his sister Dechtire taking part in the Ulates' favorite pastime, pursuing a flock of birds that is ravaging the country. These birds are chained together two by two, which indicates that they are fairy beings, Tuatha de Danann, intent on avenging themselves upon the Gaels who once chased them from Ireland (or at least its surface). Night falls and snow suddenly covers the region. Conchobar orders his men to unhitch the carts and sends out Conall Cernach and Bricriu as scouts. They discover a house where they are offered hospitality, but scarcely have the Ulates settled in than their host tells them that his wife is about to give birth. Dechtire goes to help the woman, who gives birth to a boy. Because a mare has just given birth at the same time to two foals, the foals are given to the child as playthings. And Dechtire tends the child.

Now, the next day the house has disappeared. All that remains of it are the horses, the foals, and the infant. The Ulates return to Emain Macha where Dechtire raises the unknown child, but the boy soon falls sick and dies. Dechtire is overcome with grief. After the child's funeral, she asks for a drink, and from out of the cup a little animal jumps to her lips in such a way that she swallows it. That night Dechtire has a dream: A man comes to find her who declares himself to be Lugh, son of Eithne, and who informs her that she is pregnant by him. Dechtire actually is pregnant, which makes for much talk among the Ulates, who whisper that the father is surely Conchobar who slept with his sister in a moment of drunkenness. Conchobar hastily marries Dechtire off to Sualtam, but she, ashamed of her condition, secretly aborts and thus acquires a new virginity before sleeping with her husband. She immediately becomes pregnant and soon gives birth to a son who is called Setana, the true name of Cuchulainn.

This is one of the versions of Cuchulainn's birth. It seems quite archaic, but it has been truncated and some things have been added. However, some interesting elements can be found here. First, because we are dealing with a hero who will be extraordinary, his conception and birth must necessarily be extraordinary. Thus, Setana is born *three times*, the first time from the woman delivered by Dechtire, a second time by the god Lugh (or by Conchobar), and, finally, the third time by Sualtam, his legitimate father.

Next we must note the symbolic fertilization by mouth—which we also find in *The Birth of Conchobar, The Courtship of Etaine, The Two Swineherds*, and the Welsh legend of Taliesin—and especially the detail about the two foals and the mare, which sends us back to a Welsh text, the *Mabinogi of Pwyll*. Indeed, there is a parallel between the simultaneous birth of the child and the two foals in the Irish narrative, and the birth of Pryderi, son of Rhiannon. Pryderi is mysteriously carried off at the time of his birth and discovered by a certain Teyrnon at the moment when the latter's mare gives birth to a foal. If we consider that Rhiannon (Rigantona) is the same figure as Epona, goddess of horses in the Roman Empire,[2] it is quite interesting to note that Dechtire may be an incarnation of the goddess-mare so often represented in Gallo-Roman statuary, and that Cuchulainn may be the foal that accompanies this mare.

Finally, there is the possible incest between brother and sister, which is found again in the Welsh legend of Gwyddyon and Arianrhod, and which is no doubt a throwback to the period when incest of this kind, as among the pharaohs, was exclusively reserved for exceptional figures and had to result in the birth of a no less exceptional hero.

Now, the second version specifies that Dechtire flees with fifty young girls, without Conchobar's permission. They reappear one day in the form of birds, which is when the Ulates go off in pursuit of them. Night falls. Fergus, sent out to scout, comes to a house where a couple agrees to accommodate the Ulates, who soon settle in and proceed to get drunk. Then Bricriu hears music outside. He heads in its direction and discovers another house in which a young man on a crystal throne greets him and reveals to him that Dechtire and the fifty young girls are there under his power. Always greedy for riches, Bricriu thinks that Conchobar will compensate him and is very careful not to speak of Dechtire. He says only that he has seen a man and some beautiful women in this house. Now, Conchobar expresses his desire to sleep with the wife of this man. Moreover, he has the right to do so, since this man is on his land and thus is his vassal. Fergus takes it upon himself to go find the woman, but she asks for a delay because she is pregnant.

The next day a small boy is found on Conchobar's breast. It is then learned that this is Dechtire's child, and all the Ulates argue with each other for the honor of raising the one named Setana, who will later become the most famous Ulate hero.

Thus, in this second version there is an allusion to the possibility of a union between Conchobar and Dechtire, but more important is the fact that Dechtire has gone to the Other World and that there, she has been the wife of the young man on the crystal throne in whom we can recognize Lugh. In any case it is important to grant Cuchulainn a mysterious conception and far-from-ordinary birth. Now the destiny of young Setana is laid out before him: He is ready to be launched into a phenomenal career.

Cuchulainn's Childhood

The narrative[3] of Cuchulainn's first exploits is put—a bit artificially—in the mouths of the three Ulster exiles while the Irish armies are marching off to attack Ulster. Having gone into service for Ailill and Medb, Fergus Mac Roig, Cormac, son of Conchobar, and Fiacha, son of Ferfebe, present their hero, and especially his incomparable and precocious valor. But as the storyteller or rhapsodist of the *Raid* uses ancient accounts involving the character's first years, this text deserves to be set apart from the rest of the *Raid*, because it contains nearly the whole mythical explanation of Cuchulainn. And if we truly wish to understand this extraordinary figure's importance for Gaelic society in the first years of the Christian era, and beyond that, in medieval society, before becoming a hero of popular legend, it is necessary to concentrate on these *Childhoods* and draw from them as much information as possible.

The young man named Setana[4] is raised by his parents on the plain of Murthemne. He hears talk of the children's games at Emain Macha and never stops insisting on going there. Despite his mother's warnings (he is five years old!), he sets out for Emain with "his curved bronze stick, his silver ball, his javelin, and his stick which is burned on the end." Arriving at Emain, he wants to take part in the games, but one hundred fifty young boys gang up against him. They all throw their sticks, but Setana, with his one stick, turns away all of them and, in turn, takes care all their balls and javelins in the same way.

> Then he did contortions. It seemed that with a few
> blows of a hammer, each of his hairs was put back into

his head in the spot where it had grown out. It seemed that each of these hairs threw out a flaming spark. He closed one of his eyes which was no larger than the eye of a needle. He opened the other which grew bigger than a goblet of mead. He stretched his jaws so far that his mouth touched his ears. He opened his lips so wide that you could see down his gullet. From the top of his head shot forth the hero's light.

This description is very important. Since he is really named Setana, he is a predestined hero. He is in contact with the divine world, as shown by the light shooting from his head, which is the eye of divine intelligence. Moreover, we will later learn that his spiritual father is the god Lugh, which means that he himself is one of Lugh's aspects. This eye at the top of his skull, which signifies *illumination*, is familiar as well. It is the eye of Buddha (whose name means "the Awakened One, the Enlightened One"); it is the light frequently represented on the brow of Moses the prophet;[5] and it is the tongues of fire received by the apostles on the day of Pentecost, which symbolize the Holy Spirit.

And this location of the "third eye" is neither a mere convention nor the result of chance. We now know that certain areas of the cortex situated beneath the top of the skull play a specific role in the higher thought processes, and that this part of the brain would allow man to acquire enormous intelligence if it were truly put to use. But what the scientists of our era are finally able to prove has been known since the beginning of time. All that was lacking—and is lacking still—is the method of employment.

But if Setana is linked to the divine *celestial* world—that is, to Lugh, the solar god—he also belongs to the *chthonic* world, to the underground world without which the divine could not be complete. Indeed, we can notice in his contortions,[6] which are his most striking peculiarity (won't he be nicknamed the Contortionist of Emain?), a very specific feature: He closes one of his eyes and opens the other as wide as a goblet of mead, which clearly means that Cuchulainn transforms himself into a cyclops; that, more than others, he possesses a cyclopean aspect and is therefore the product of obscure underground forces.[7] On a psychological level, Setana-Cuchulainn represents the balance between the two worlds, that of the bright conscious (the hero's light) and that of the unconscious (the cyclopean aspect), where the brutal forces of the death instinct are unleashed.

Now, after using his contortions to call forth his instinctive warrior powers, Setana takes the offensive, felling fifty sons of kings and pursuing five more of them with the intention of tearing them to pieces. The five children take refuge with Conchobar, who stops Setana, asks him who he is, and finally makes peace by officially introducing the young boy to the other children and putting him under their protection. But new quarrels break out, and Setana comes out the victor. Finally, Conchobar succeeds in calming everyone down by placing the children of Emain under the sole protection of Setana—which is quite an honor, we must say, for a boy of five years old.

The year after this episode Culann the blacksmith comes to Emain Macha to invite Conchobar to a feast (which was obligatory), but as he is not rich, he asks the king not to bring many guests with him. Conchobar accepts, and on the fixed day, sets out alone when he notices the young Setana in the middle of a game, taking command of 150 boys. He asks him to come with him. Setana refuses because his comrades haven't had their fill of games yet, but finally accepts on the condition that he will come a bit later.

Thus, Conchobar arrives alone at Culann's house, where he is received with great courtesy. Culann asks the king if he has asked anyone else to join him. Conchobar, who has forgotten Setana, answers no, and the blacksmith unties his "war dog"—who "has the strength of a hundred people"—to guard the fortress and surrounding area. "He was all that is most savage, untamable, angry, ferocious, aggressive." That is when Setana appears, who, not knowing the way, has followed Conchobar's tracks. The dog sees him and begins to howl, ready to swallow him in one bite. "The boy had no means of defense, but he threw his ball at him with all his strength in such a way that it went down the war dog's throat and pushed all the guts inside him out the back door [sic]; he took it by two legs and stuck it against a block of stone, so that its limbs fell in pieces on the ground."[8]

When Conchobar hears the dog's cry, he is seized with terror at the thought of the young boy who is going to be eaten. Everyone hurries outside, Fergus Mac Roig in the lead, and they are quite dumbfounded by the results they find of the struggle. But Culann is not happy:

Because the boy has killed his dog and since he has no other, his property will no longer be protected. Then Setana says to him, "If a little dog of this kind exists in Ireland, I will raise it until it is just as brave as its father. Until then, I will be the *dog protector* of goods, livestock, and land." Everyone is delighted with this wise solution, and the druid Cathbad suggests, "Why not be called Cuchulainn[9] after this?" Setana refuses because he wants to keep his real name. But nevertheless, it is from this point on that it becomes customary to call him Cuchulainn.

We must note that embedded in this anecdote, with literary value in and of themselves, are a few invaluable points regarding the ethnological portrait of the ancient Celts. Because this episode is, in fact, Cuchulainn's first initiation, he passes the test that allows him to go from a childish state to adulthood. Thus he abandons his old name— the one of his individuality, his undifferentiated *me*, his *that* (the Freudian *Das Es*)—to take on his new name, the one that suits his personality, his *me* that has evolved through contact with the outside world and that needs a shell to protect it and differentiate it. To return to Hegelian thinking, Setana did not know that he existed and, consequently, only existed in time as absolute being. But absolute being is equivalent to nothingness, since it does not know it exists. And beginning from the moment when this absolute being sets itself in opposition to nonbeing (the dog whose infernal negative value is clear), it becomes conscious of its own existence. Thus, it exists, but this existence is no longer the same, since it has been altered. Thus Setana becomes Cuchulainn, simultaneously man and dog; the being containing its own nonbeing, its own negation,[10] it becomes relative being. And by following such reasoning, which is as much Freudian as it is Hegelian (though Freud and Hegel invented nothing; they only extracted and delineated logistical structures from human thought that had always existed and expressed themselves by means of symbolic images), we come to an essential comparison: that of the name and the mask. Indeed, even today in certain so-called primitive societies initiation is accompanied by the taking on of a mask, as in Rome, where it was accompanied by the adoption of the *toga virilis*.[11] The name, the outfit, and the mask are only three aspects of the same initiation, the one that *begins* adulthood, the one by which the personality *begins*, whereby the undifferentiated *individual* becomes a *person*. We must not forget that the Latin word *persona* means, in fact, "theatrical mask." Beginning from the moment when human beings acquire their personalities, they can *play their roles* on the stage of life, but these are roles that they do not create themselves. The role itself is not imposed, as the fatalists claim, but molded by the external world according to the traits each individual possesses. And thus we have Cuchulainn provided with a name, or a mask. That he is called Setana will be forgotten. Moreover, he must never disclose his real name, because it is not for others to use, but for himself. Only the mask can be presented to either the public or the other actors.

But Cuchulainn, let us repeat, is not an ordinary human being. Thus, his initiation is also extraordinary. It takes place at the home of a black-smith, a figure from the underground world and a master of the mysterious forces that animate the earth. Culann is one of the aspects of Hades, Hephaestus, Teutas. Moreover, he is described as possessing only his *hammer*, his *anvil*, his *fists*, and his *tongs*. We are reminded of the Germanic Thor and of Sucellos, the god of the mallet so often represented in Gallic statuary. His function as master of Hell is again demonstrated by the dog, in which we can recognize the Greek Cerberus. And when Cuchulainn kills the dog, he repeats the feat of Hercules—a hero with whom he shares many traits inherited from a primitive Indo-European mythology.[12] He forces the gates of Hell and establishes himself there for a time as guardian, which is perfectly logical, given that he belongs to both worlds.[13]

But for all that, Cuchulainn's "childhoods" are not over. A year after he enters the adult world, and even though he is still only seven years old, he follows the advice of the druid Cathbad, who has just had a prophetic vision, and abandons his playthings to go ask Conchobar for weapons who, in turn, provides them. When Cuchulainn asks for a chariot next, Conchobar takes him to the warehouse where the carts are kept. In checking their sturdiness, Cuchulainn completely destroys seventeen of them and concludes that they are worthless. Conchobar then gives him his own chariot, and this one withstands the young boy's tests. After having circled Emain Macha three times, Cuchulainn, who wants to prove himself as a warrior, claims that he will protect Ulster and goes off where the brave Conall Cernach mounts guard. Cuchulainn advises Conall to return home, saying that he will take care of everything himself. Conall refuses, and Cuchulainn decides to keep going. The boy's daring makes Conall nervous and, intent upon going with him, Conall has his own cart hitched up. But Cuchulainn throws a stone and breaks the yoke, and Conall falls and dislocates his shoulder.

With his driver, Ibar, Cuchulainn heads south, and along the way asks for information about all the places he sees. From one high hill, the highest in Ulster, he looks out over the plain of Breg; seeing the fortress of the three sons of Necht, who pride themselves in "not having left alive more Ulates than they killed," he decides to go there. Ibar tries desperately to stop him, but it does no good. Arriving in front of the fortress, Cuchulainn jumps down into the meadow. "On this lawn there was a raised stone, and around this stone, an oghamic inscription appealing to heroes. This inscription read: TO EVERY ARMED MAN WHO COMES ONTO THIS LAWN, IT IS FORBIDDEN TO GO WITHOUT HAVING REQUESTED SINGLE COMBAT."

This detail is particularly reminiscent of the trials that King Arthur's knights are often subjected to in all the legends of the Round Table. We might recall the adventures of Lancelot of the Lake at the Castle of the Sorrowful Guard, among others, or the "Joy of the Court" episode in Chrétian de Troyes's *Erec et Enide* and in the Welsh *Mabinogi of Geraint*. Clearly, Cuchulainn can only rise to the challenge. The first son of Necht comes out onto the lawn and, after considering the strange circumstances, does not take him seriously, encouraged in that respect by the prudent Ibar. But "the little boy raised his face above the ground, he put his hand over his face, he turned crimson, and from head to foot, took the form of a millstone."

The fight begins. Of course, this is another David facing Goliath, and with the help of his iron ball Cuchulainn kills his adversary and cuts off his head. He does the same with the two other brothers, after which he lays waste to the fortress.

And so we witness Cuchulainn's character as guardian and protector of the race. He has already taken on the protection of the young boys of Emain. Here he claims and earns the function of protecting all the Ulate people, and this is a role he will subsequently continue to play, (particularly in the *Tain Bô*), in being the *only* Ulate to face the armies of the four Irish provinces. At that moment Cuchulainn is no longer a man, not even a superman, but the incarnation of the spirit of the clan, the embodiment of all the joined forces of all his compatriots. There are few examples as extreme as this in the epic literature of any country, except in *Gargantua* and *Pantagruel*, which, before being *Rabelaisian* works in the worst sense of the word, were the remnants of epics stored in the memory of the people of the sixteenth century, the purest and most authentic epics in the Celtic tradition.[14]

But the end of the story goes beyond the limits of the epic and even surpasses all we can imagine. Cuchulainn and his driver, Ibar, return to Emain. They meet a herd of deer, and the little boy asks his companion to speed up so they can try to take a few. Alas, Conchobar's horses are too big and can't run fast enough! Cuchalainn gets down from the vehicle, catches two deer, and ties them to the shafts of the cart with some straps.

Next they meet a flock of swans. Cuchulainn will not stop until he has caught twenty-four of them, which he also attaches to the shafts. Then he asks Ibar to take charge of them. The driver replies that he risks being run over by the wheels of the cart and gored by the deer. The little boy says to him, "You are not a true warrior, o Ibar, the glance that I will cast at the horses will be enough to keep them on the right path. I will only have to look at the deer to make them lower their heads, they will be so afraid of me." Out of the mouth of a seven-year-old boy who has just killed three formidable warriors and seized the fastest animals alive, such words can no longer surprise us. We believe them. And we are not mistaken, because this is the solemn announcement by which he takes on symbolic possession of the world of animated beings.

Now, let us imagine the image that this unlikely procession presents: a cart drawn by horses galloping with indescribable fury, swans forming a white cloud rivaling that of the road dust, and deer dragged along at the speed of Hell. On the chariot, a boy of seven and a brave driver with his heart in his boots. The most beautiful thing of all is that this procession is not just a literary phenomenon. Very frequently we find it engraved on Gallic coins, and the claim can be made that this is a matter of a very ancient myth—probably linked to the god Cernunnos, the god with deer's antlers and surrounded by birds and mythic animals, found on one of the plates of the famous Gundestrup Cauldron.

But now, back at Emain Macha, the sorceress Leborcham, Conchobar's messenger, notices this fantastic cavalcade and announces it to everyone. Conchobar exclaims that he knows what it is: "It's the little boy, my sister's son. He went to the borders of the neighboring province, his hands are all red with blood; he hasn't had enough of fighting, and if we aren't careful, all the Emain warriors will perish because of him."

Conchobar's warning is not in vain. Cuchulainn's cavalcade has done nothing to temper the warrior zeal unleashed by his anger at the first of the Necht sons, when he turned red and took the form of a millstone. These were contortion rituals that he performed, and he put himself in a state of trance. He made all the destructive instincts hidden in the depths of his unconscious rise and manifest themselves in the form of a wheel, the symbol for thunder. But once they are unleashed, it is difficult to repress these instincts, and since they have been released by druidic (or shamanic) means, it is by these same means that they must be stemmed.

That is why Conchobar makes the women and girls of Emain go out completely naked "to show their nudity to the little hero." It is not for nothing that the woman is often called "the warrior's repose." The king's orders are carried out.

> The troop of young women went out, and not one of them hesitated to show him her nakedness. But he hid his face, turning it toward the cart, and he did not see the women's nudity. Then he was forced to get out of the cart. To calm his anger, three vats of fresh water were brought to him. He was put into the first one, and he made the water so hot that it cracked the boards and the hoops of the vat as one would crack a nutshell. In the second vat, the water made bubbles as big as fists. In the third vat, it was so hot that some men could bear it, and others couldn't. Then the little boy's anger diminished.

And the narrative ends with a description of Cuchulainn putting on fresh clothes. To begin, he makes his body into a crimson wheel—that is, he celebrates his triumph complete, he literally "does a cartwheel." "He had seven toes on each of his two feet, and seven fingers on each hand, seven pupils in each of his eyes, and in each of those pupils, seven precious stones could be seen to shine."[15]

After such descriptions, all commentary seems superfluous. How could the literature of ancient Ireland have ever been called a sequence of stupid stories stuck together one after the other with no concern for poetry or beauty? This is the triumph, not only of little Cuchulainn, but of the imagination and the dream at its highest level, and in this case all we can do is salute the genius of the author, because at this point it is no longer a matter of talent, but of pure genius.

Cuchulainn's Education

Here is a strange narrative[16] straight from the earliest centuries of Celtic civilization, despite the later version that we possess only because of the legend. If the manuscript is from the eighteenth century, and thus presents many attempts at modernization or interpretations appealing to the "antiquarian" tastes of the period, the comparisons we can make between *Cuchulainn's Education* and *The Courtship of Emer*, a text preserved in earlier manuscripts that seem to have been transcribed in the eleventh century, prove to us that the most extraordinary details we discover here are also the most archaic ones. Moreover, the literary composition of the *Education* narrative provides a neat and precise account of the story, which is unfortunately not the case for *The Courtship of Emer*, probably compiled from two or three other earlier manuscripts, that, in fact, present two different stories.

Here, we are dealing with Cuchulainn's training as a warrior. Up until now his exploits have only been part of his "childhood." If the hero has taken shortcuts to reach his initiation, he is nonetheless obliged to go on improving himself. But here is where we see some curious customs showing up among the Irish of the pre-Christian era, in particular the obligation to go off to finish one's training not with an Irish master, but with a Scottish one, or at the very least one from the British isle, because throughout this period, we never really know where Britain ends and Scotland proper begins.[17] This first observation makes us think of what Caesar says about the Gallic druids who went off to educate themselves on the British isle, which leads us to suppose that for all the Celtic peoples, Britain was truly a religious, intellectual, and military center of exceptional importance.

But there is more: This military education bears little resemblance to just any war school or training camp for Roman legionnaires. As far as we can make out from our two texts, this education was, first and foremost, *magic*. It was a matter of sorcery. And when we know that druidism and sorcery were more or less interchangeable in the manuscripts recopied by Christian monks, we can ask ourselves to what extent this was inaccurate. Doesn't the *Book of Conquests* state that the Tuatha de Danann brought both druidism *and* sorcery with them from the islands of the northern world? And from this obvious link among sorcery, druidism, and the northern world, couldn't we draw one more bit of evidence in support of the hypothesis that finds in druidism a certain aspect of the shamanism belonging to the great northern Euro-Asiatic plain?

A second custom is no less surprising. The warrior education of young men was provided not by men or heroes but by sorceresses, by women often described as "women warriors." Who are they exactly? It is very difficult to say. There is a very strong temptation to call them "druidesses," if it is really true that druidesses existed, which has not yet been proven in any satisfactory way. However, we can assert that these women warriors appear quite frequently in Celtic literature and sometimes even in Celtic history, as we see in the fight led by the Breton queen Boadicée against the Romans. Moreover, it is nearly a sacred institution, since we find this theme again engraved in Gallic coins and in the character of Bodbh-Morrigan, the warrior-goddess (and not the goddess of war!) who so often hovers over the soldiers in the form of a crow to spur them on, and who sometimes joins in the battle herself.

In any case it is clear that these women warriors constituted a sort of caste, very much apart from and outside of society, a bit like the caste of the blacksmiths. Indeed, there is a basic incompatibility between the woman, the being who gives life, and war, which destroys and devours it. War is men's business. This is the case among the Celts. Nevertheless, they are initiated into war by women who are necessarily cursed beings and, consequently, sorceresses. The bad fairy of European folklore is nothing other than the degeneration of this theme.

Thus, to complete his education, Cuchulainn leaves for Scotland in the company of Loegaire the Victorious and Conall Cernach.[18] First they go to Dordmair, the daughter of Domnall Maeltemel (the Bellicose). She begins to teach them a trick. She drives a sword into the ground, point in the air, then leaps and lands horizontally, her breast on the point, without causing the least wound or tear in her clothes.

Then she asks the young men to try.[19] Loegaire and Conall attempt the trick, but fail. It is clearly Cuchulainn who triumphs. Dordmair addresses Conall and Loegaire and advises them to be careful when they go into battle, because they lack valor. She proposes helping them and teaching them some tricks, but the two warriors answer that they don't need this help and depart again for Ireland, leaving Cuchulainn in the sorceress's care.[20]

At the end of a year Cuchulainn, who has completed his education, encounters an enormous figure, black as coal, along the shore of the sea.[21] This strange character reveals to him that he will never know anything unless he goes to see Scatach, the daughter of Buanuinne, king of Scythia.[22] So we find Cuchulainn on his way to the home of Scatach. He meets some young men practicing their throws who guide him. Along the way they come to a magic bridge, the Bridge of Leaps: "When one leaped onto the bridge, it shrank until it became as narrow as a hair and as strong and slippery as a fingernail. Other times, it rose up again as high as a mast." Cuchulainn tries to leap, but slips and falls on his back.

However, Scatach, in the company of her daughter Uatach (the very terrible), is watching this scene from the top of her house. Uatach "had white fingers, black eyebrows. . . . When the girl saw the young man, she loved him with all her soul." Scatach tells her daughter to watch the young man closely, because she has been forewarned that someone still very young would come from Ireland and that he would succeed at the test of the Bridge of Leaps in less than an hour.

Cuchulainn thrashes about. The young men make fun of him for his repeated failures. "Then Cuchulainn became angry: he jumped in the air and swung there, as if he were in the wind, in such a way that, with one furious leap, he managed to reach the middle of the bridge. And the bridge did not shrink, did not become hard and slippery under him." Scatach sends her daughter to welcome the young hero who has passed the test, and sends him to spend the night in the guards' house. There Cuchulainn quarrels with the guards, kills them, and hangs their heads on the door of Scatach's fortress. The next day he goes to speak with Scatach and challenge her to combat. The two sons of Scatach intervene, and one of them, the giant Cuar (fate), is felled by Cuchulainn's blows. Cuchulainn, somewhat wounded and worn out, carries Cuar's head to his mother.

Scatach invites Cuchulainn into her house so that he can be cared for and healed, and during the night, Uatach comes to Cuchulainn's chamber. Because her intentions are very clear, Cuchulainn puts her off by saying, "Don't you know, o daughter, that it is a violation of a taboo to sleep with a woman when one is sick?" But Uatach comes back a little later, completely naked, and slides into Cuchulainn's bed. "Cuchulainn was greatly annoyed: he extended his good hand toward the girl and ran into her finger in such a way that, in pushing her away, he pulled her skin and flesh which he hurt and roughly scratched." The girl protests, threatens Cuchulainn with a geis of destruction, and will only agree to pardon him if she can sleep next to him for the night. Cuchulainn remains firm in his refusal. Uatach promises him that he will obtain three tricks from her mother that will make him the most formidable of warriors.[23]

Cuchulainn then agrees to spend the night with the girl, and in the morning she reveals to him what he must do to obtain Scatach's secrets. Cuchulainn takes Scatach by surprise when she is unarmed and holds his sword to her, threatening her with "death and destruction." In order to save her life, Scatach accepts Cuchulainn's conditions: "The three Tricks that you have never taught to anyone before me, your daughter, and also *the friendship of your thighs.*"

Thus, the character of this initiation with women warriors becomes clear. It is as much as matter of sexual initiation as it is of war. War and sexuality are linked, which is not a new discovery, but here, more than ever, we see the link. As a result of his stay with Dordmair, the daughter of Domnall, Cuchulainn has gone through the first steps of this initiation, but it can only be completed if there are sexual relations between the "mistress" and the student. Now, the relationship established between Cuchulainn and Uatach can, in no way, exclude the relationship between himself and Scatach. Moreover, the names of the sorceress and her daughter are significant: Cuchulainn submits here to a "terrible" (Uatach) initiation, "which causes fear" (Scatach). Finally, the relationship with the daughter is an "annual" marriage, that is, a legal and temporary arrangement, while the relationship with the mother is described by the delightful euphemism, "friendship of the thighs,"[24] which indicates a different type of relationship, an amorous one with the daughter, a strictly sexual one with the mother.

This particular aspect of warrior and sexual initiation is explained by the role that the woman plays in Celtic myth. As in other Irish texts, *Diarmaid and Grainne*, in particular, or Welsh texts (*Story of Taliesin*), or even French texts with Celtic inspiration (*Tristan and Iseult*), the woman is the transformer of energy, the one who absorbs male strength and then returns it by giving birth to the child. But if the phenomenon of parturition can thus be justified on the physiological level, there is another meaning related to a subject we hardly ever come upon in the Greco-Roman world and never at all in the Christian world: *coitus reservatus*. In other words, this is not a matter of the procreative act, of the birth of a third being who is a continuation of the other two, but of the transformation of the lover in the fullness of *affective* love, that is to say, emotional and carnal at the same time.[25] The woman who "gives herself" doesn't give her whole being but the orgasmic component aroused by the man, and that she shares with him. Thus she transforms the man in returning to him a part of his energy *transformed*—and she is transformed herself, since she benefits from this experience to which she has contributed her female energy. This is the perspective from which we must view the erotic-warrior initiation of Cuchulainn. To use psychoanalytic jargon, it is in the conjunction of Eros and Thanatos that the being is able to resolve this primordial antinomy and put to use the forces thus unleashed by the potential disruption of the surface equilibrium.[26]

Thus, Cuchulainn remains with Scatach and Uatach for an entire year. After this time he heads off toward the home of another woman warrior, Aife, the daughter of the king of Greater Greece who receives him quite amicably and *amorously*.[27] For one year, he lives with her. She teaches him three secret tricks, among them the mysterious *gai bolga*. This *gai bolga* has lent itself to many interpretations, and it is generally translated as the "javelin in the bag," which certainly doesn't mean very much. The most likely interpretation comes from recognizing in *bolga* the same root as in the name of *Fir Bolg*, "thunderbolt." Thus, the *gai bolga* would be a "javelin of lightning," which is in keeping with the formidable effectiveness of this trick of war—and magic. That said, at the end of the year, as Cuchulainn is preparing to leave, Aife tells him that she is pregnant. Cuchulainn answers her that if she has a son, she must educate him, teach him all the tricks but the *gai bolga*, and send him to Cuchulainn in Ireland.[28]

Cuchulainn takes to the road again and returns to Scatach's home. But in front of the Bridge of Leaps he meets a sorceress, Ess Enchenn, who throws a geis on him. Cuchulainn does not let this affect him and, thanks to his tricks, succeeds in cutting off her head.[29] Finally he again meets up with the young men of Ireland who have come to be instructed by Scatach, among them Noise, the son of Usnech, and Ferdead, the son of Daman. He remains in their company for one year, during which all these young men learn all Cuchulainn's tricks except the famous *gai bolga*.[30] When the year comes to an end, Scatach calls the young men together and makes a long speech in which she advises them never to fight with each other. They all swear their faithful friendship, saying good-bye to Scatach and returning to Ireland.

Over the course of the voyage, Cuchulainn wants to earn the hospitality of the inhabitants of a fortress by catching seabirds alive in such a way that the women and young men will be amazed. But he sees only one girl on the shore. This is Aife, the daughter of Aed the Red, who must be delivered as a tribute to the Fomor, a more or less mythic maritime people, predecessors to the Tuatha de Danann. Cuchulainn manages to triumph over the Fomor giant who comes to collect his tribute.[31] Cuchulainn and his companions are received by Aed the Red, and Cuchulainn divides up the Fomor spoils in the following way: one third to his hosts, one third to his companions, and the final third as the king's daughter's dowry. And of course it is understood that Cuchulainn "that night had the girl to enjoy in his bed."[32]

Thus, after his extraordinary childhood and his no less curious warrior education, Cuchulainn has earned the right to be admitted among the heroes of Ireland. He is now mature enough for his adventures as an adult.

Tain Bô Cualngé — The Cattle Raid of Cualngé

The Cattle Raid of Cualngé [33] is the most famous epic not only in the Ulster cycle, but in all Irish epic literature. It is also one of the most ancient. Indeed, the events that are related in this work, and that the Tigernach annals place in the year 19 B.C., are the reverently preserved remnants of the history of pagan Ireland, marked by the rivalry between Ulster and Connaught, and of all the beliefs and customs of a perfectly archaic Celtic society. Clearly, myth and history merge here and inter-penetrate, as in all Celtic literature or literature of Celtic inspiration. This is not a matter of taking everything literally, and even less of proposing that the *Raid* be the basis of all study on pagan Ireland. It is only a matter of a truly imposing work, one of the most unusual testi-monies to a civilization that has nothing in common with classical Mediterranean civilization. This is not the *Iliad;* in fact, it is the anti-*Iliad,* so opposite are the customs, the preoccupations, and the beliefs of the people, so different the literary technique employed by the au-thor or authors.

It all begins with a domestic scene in Cruachan, the capital of Connaught. Because of an unfortunate remark, Ailill, the king of Connaught, and his wife, Medb, are quarreling over their respective wealth—whether their riches are equal or one is richer than the other. This dispute is far from petty. It is terribly important because accord-ing to Celtic law, whichever spouse, husband or wife, possesses more goods has the option of directing the household affairs and disposing freely of not only his or her own goods, but also those of the spouse.[34] The characters of these two figures become clear through this dispute: Ailill is arrogant but weak, without mettle; on the contrary, Medb is a strong woman, willful, ambitious, unscrupulous, completely capable of ensuring her own success and seeing to her triumph.

Thus Ailill and Medb are counting up their goods, furniture, tools, dishes, jewels, but especially herds, since in ancient Ireland, as in all primitive Celtic societies, true wealth was made up of livestock. Now, they discover that Ailill owns one more bull than Medb, and here we are dealing with the Beautiful Horned of Ae.[35] Furious, Medb decides to acquire a bull that is just as good or better, and she sends the mes-senger Mac Roth to Dare, son of Fachan, an Ulster nobleman, who has the magnificent bull, the Brown One of Cualngé.[36] Mac Roth says to Dare, "You yourself come with your bull, and you will have a piece of property equal to your own, in the fields of the Ae plain, and a chariot worth as much as seven captives, and the *friendship of the thighs* of Medb thrown into the bargain."

Tempted by this fine offer, Dare accepts. But following a drunken quarrel, he backs out of the agreement and refuses to deliver the bull.

So Medb decides to seize the Brown One of Cualngé by force and summons every last one of her vassals from the four provinces of Ireland: Connaught, Leinster, Munster, and Meath. Medb and Ailill assemble their army, to which are added the exiles of Ulster—Cormac, son of Conchobar, and Fergus Mac Roig who, after the murder of the sons of Usnech for whom they were guarantors, revolted against Conchobar and took refuge in Connaught. Despite all of Fedelm the Prophetess's predictions of disastrous events, the army begins to march, intent on invading Ulster. Moreover, this is a good time to act, because the Ulates are in the throes of their annual indisposition, one hundred eight hours long.[37] Fergus is sent to scout but, "swayed by his affection for the Ulates," gives false directions. Then he predicts to Medb the exploits that the terrible Cuchulainn will carry out. We understand by the queen's responses that she has also provided the friendship of her thighs to Fergus, to secure his faithfulness to her cause.

It is Cuchulainn himself, the only Ulate not subject to the effects of Macha's curse, who witnesses the arrival of the enemy. Maintaining his calm, he puts a druidic circle on the road and goes off for a rendezvous with a woman. The Irish army reaches the druidic circle, which they cannot cross because doing so is a sacred prohibition and is obliged to camp there under difficult conditions caused by snow that falls during the night.

However, in the morning Cuchulainn has his chariot hitched up and goes with his driver Loeg to survey the Irish army, which has made a detour in order to enter Ulster. In the ford he places a forked branch with four points and covered with oghamic inscriptions, and he kills four warriors who had ventured that far. The horses and decapitated bodies are discovered by Medb and her men. They believe that a large army is preparing to attack them and are astonished by the forked branch planted in the ground. Fergus tries to pull up the fork but manages only to ruin the Irish chariots that he is using. Medb says to him, "We know why you are acting like this. It is to stop the army, to slow it down, it is to make us wait while the Ulates, recovered from their malady, get up and prepare to fight us." Cut to the quick, Fergus then takes his own chariot and rips up the fork. He declares, in a poem, that this magic fork was made by one man alone. All the Irish are astonished and Fergus answers them, "This can only be my student, and Conchobar's student as well, that little boy called Cuchulainn."

And then we are given the story of *Cuchulainn's Childhood.*

But a country cannot be defended by magic obstacles alone. The Irish warriors attack Cuchulainn, and the latter defends himself tenaciously. In particular, he kills Frâech, the hero of *Frâech and Finnabair*, and Orlam, one of the sons of Medb. Then the goddess-warrior Morrigan appears—in the form of a bird—to the Brown One of Cualngé and addresses a long speech to the bull, recommending that he be cautious.[38] The author uses this occasion to extol this animal's virtues, and they are not insignificant. We can understand why one part of Ireland makes war on the other part to gain possession of this creature:

> One of the feats of the Brown One of Cualngé consisted of mating with fifty heifers which, the next day, gave birth to calves. The ones who could not deliver were ripped apart in an explosion. . . . Another of his feats consisted of his being able to provide a hundred warriors shelter from the cold, or from the heat with his shadow. Another of his feats was that no pale-faced genie or goat-faced genie or lowland fairy dared to approach the district where he lived. Another one of his feats was the melodious mooing that could be heard every day in the evening when approaching his enclosure.[39]

But the war continues. Medb and her army try to advance on Ulster and make a huge detour around to the north. Cuchulainn hunts them down and carries out a true massacre. Medb then decides to divide her army into two parts. The first will be commanded by Ailill, and the second by Fergus and herself. Ailill, who decidedly gets the worse deal, obeys but orders his driver to spy on Fergus and the queen. Of course, the driver catches them flagrantly committing adultery. As Fergus has placed his sword near at hand, the driver steals it,[40] leaving Fergus only the sheath, and returns to report everything to Ailill, who comments philosophically, "She had to do that; it was necessary for her to act in that way to assure the success of the expedition." Clearly, Ailill is the perfect model of the complacent husband. In the meantime, Fergus notices that someone has stolen his sword. He makes a new one out of wood and when he accepts Ailill's invitation to play chess, the king gets his revenge and won't give him back his sword.

Uneasy at seeing her men fighting with each other, Medb then resolves to negotiate with Cuchulainn. She sends a messenger with several proposals. Cuchulainn consents only to meet with Medb and Fergus, but the interview produces no results. Always by messenger, the queen makes exorbitant promises to Cuchulainn, all refused by him. The only thing he finally agrees to is single combat each day. That is what takes place: each day an Irish hero goes to confront Cuchulainn, but none returns.

At this juncture Morrigan appears to Cuchulainn in the form of a young girl and offers her love to the hero, who rejects it. Furious, the goddess threatens him, "I will be a nuisance to you . . . during your combat against the men. I will come in the form of an eel under your feet in the ford and I will make you fall. . . . I will take the form of a gray she-wolf and will turn the four-legged beasts against you. . . . I will attack you in the form of a red cow without horns, I will incite the horned beasts who will rush at you." Cuchulainn answers her that no matter what form she takes, he will wound her and she will only be able to be healed by him. And Cuchulainn returns to his combat.

But Morrigan makes good on her threats and appears first in the form of a cow, then an eel, and then a she-wolf. Each time Cuchulainn wounds her, but each time he is also wounded himself by his adversary Loch. Cuchulainn is overcome with despair and sadness. He chants a poem deploring his fate and asking Loeg, his driver, to go find reinforcements. It becomes very clear that this warrior, as powerful as he is, has had enough of fighting singlehandedly against the armies of all Ireland. And because he is very thirsty, a sickly old woman appears who offers him milk from her cow. He takes three drinks and promises three times to heal the old woman who, we soon guess, is no other than Morrigan—and if the goddess is healed, Cuchulainn is more and more exhausted.

At this time, the god Lugh, Cuchulainn's real father (if we are to believe the ancient tradition) appears in the form of a young warrior. He casts a magic spell over Cuchulainn that puts the younger to sleep, and then takes his place for three days and three nights. Cuchulainn awakes cured of his lethargy, regains all his warrior energy, and begins to do his fearsome contortions:

> He twisted his body in the middle of his skin; his
> feet went behind him; his heels, calves, and buttocks

went around to the front. . . . Taking the nerves at
the top of his head, he brought them behind to the
nape of his neck in such a way that each of them
made a round lump, very large, indescribable, enormous, incredible. . . . Then he deformed his features,
his face. He drew one of his eyes into his head in
such a way that a crane would not have been able to
pull this eye out of the base of his skull and onto his
cheek again. The other eye jumped out of his eyelid
and settled onto the surface of his cheek. His mouth
was transformed in a monstrous fashion. He stretched
his cheeks as wide as the arc formed by his jaws and
thus made visible the inside of his throat. His lungs
and his liver came to float in his mouth. . . . You
could hear the noise his heart made beating against
his chest; this noise was equal to the noise produced
by the cries of a barking dog of war or the cry of a
lion about to attack bears. The heat caused by his
violent and vigorous anger made . . . rain clouds appear from the sky, and in these clouds, red sparks of
fire. . . . All over his head, his hair became prickly
and like a bundle of sharp needles in the hollow of a
hedge. . . . On his forehead rose up the hero's fire, a
fire as big and long as a warrior's sharpening stone.[41]

After this display Cuchulainn (accompanied by the god Lugh, according to the primitive account) jumps into his chariot, which he has
had supplied with scythes,[42] and rushes at the enemy assembled on the
plain of Murthemne. There's a terrific massacre, needless to say: one
hundred thirty kings, without counting warriors, women, children, and
men of low rank, perish that day. "Only one third of the Irish people
remained safe and sound." In any case Cuchulainn has satisfied his
hunger for blood, and that is why, the next day, completely calm and
reasonable again, he "went to survey the army, and show his friendly
and attractive being to the ladies . . . the girls, the poets, and the men
of learning; because these marvelous forms of the magic arts in which
he showed himself the night before, his contortions, gave him no honor
and contained nothing of beauty. Thus he went to show himself in his

amicable and attractive form." Let us note the concern for elegance of this angelic young man, seventeen years old, who, the night before, was a veritable demon, preoccupied only with carnage. It is one more proof of the hypothesis that views the druidic practices of the rituals of possession as analogous to those of shamanism.

Nevertheless, dressed in magnificent garments, Cuchulainn completes his tour and finds ways to win hearts—this time the hearts of the ladies—which doesn't deter him in the least from flouting his enemies by waving cut heads before them. Single combat begins again. Medb wants to send Fergus, but Fergus refuses to fight his old student. Medb then gets him drunk and Fergus finds himself before Cuchulainn. The exile proposes a deal: Cuchulainn will flee from Fergus, but on the condition of a rematch, because the next time, it is Fergus who will flee from Cuchulainn. Cuchulainn accepts and runs off, which clearly brings Fergus great honor. It is then that Calatin and twenty-seven of his sons go to attack Cuchulainn. They have a terrible reputation because they fight with poisoned weapons and never miss their mark. Despite the fears of Fergus, who would like to protect his old student, and thanks to the presence of Fiacha, another Ulster exile, Cuchulainn finds the strength to massacre the whole Catalin family, which will be of major importance in our hero's destiny.[43]

Medb then decides to send in Ferdead, son of Daman, Cuchulainn's old comrade when they were with the sorceress Scatach,[44] who is the only one who can compete with the hero. But because Ferdead is bound by friendship to Cuchulainn, he hesitates. It is necessary to promise him a considerable fortune—and Finnabair, the daughter of Medb and Ailill, as well—before he agrees.

The combat between the two brothers-at-arms lasts three days. Each night Ferdead provides Cuchulainn with supplies, and Cuchulainn sends Ferdead medicinal plants. The two adversaries are equally matched, and their struggle could last months. Finally, Cuchulainn remembers one terrible warrior trick, the *gai bolga*, or "javelin of lightning," which the sorceress Aife taught to him and which no one else knows.[45] That is how Ferdead is killed. Immediately, Cuchulainn is overcome with sadness and laments over the body of his unfortunate brother-at-arms. He sings the praises of the deceased and his tragic destiny in a *song of death* that is entirely beautiful and in which the pathetic becomes poignant: "O Ferdead! sad is our meeting: I see you both red and very pale at the same time, I cannot use my weapon until it is washed, you, you are lying in a bloody bed. . . ." And this reminds us that even an exceptional hero, a monster of war and death, possesses a human heart and feelings, and that there are moments when tears are inherent to human nature.

However, the Ulates recover from their annual malady. A few of them come to the aid of Cuchulainn, and soon, in answer to the call of Sualtam (Cuchulainn's official father), Conchobar himself, Cuscraid the Stutterer, Sencha the Peacemaker, Loegaire the Victorious, Amergin the Poet, Celtchair son of Uthechar, Conall Cernach, and many others come. Mebd sees the Ulates arriving and it is Mac Roth who tells her the names of the chief warriors, along with interminable descriptions and comments on the valor of each of them.

Medb then asks Fergus to take command of the Irish army and defeat Conchobar. Fergus accepts on the condition that he is given back his sword. Ailill has it brought to him, and this is when we learn the name of Fergus's sword, *Caladbolg*—which is no small surprise, because it is nearly the same as the name of the sword of King Arthur.[46]

Having recovered his sword—his own strength, self-confidence, *virility*—Fergus launches an attack and comes up against Conchobar himself. The battle begins between the two old friends, and Cuchulainn comes out of his torpor and rushes to help his king. He reminds Fergus of the bargain they've made: since he has fled from Fergus one time, it is now Fergus's turn to flee from him. Fergus doesn't have to be asked twice. He turns around and races off toward Connaught, with the whole Irish army following him. It is complete pandemonium. Thus the Ulates are victorious, but Queen Mebd flees and takes the Brown One of Cualngé with her.

At this point a very curious episode takes place. Medb has a strong desire to urinate, and asks Fergus to hold the shield that shelters the Irish warriors. Fergus answers that this is very bad timing. "Be that as it may," replies Medb, "I can't do anything else; I will die if I don't let my urine flow." So Fergus holds the shield and "Medb let out her urine which filled three great channels; there was enough to turn a millstone in each of these three channels." We would have to call this a Rabelaisian element, that's undeniable, but it is not only that. The text makes it clear that Medb's urine is bloody. This is the colorful and vaguely realistic rendering of the end of the war for Medb. In fact, the flight of her army doesn't matter to very much to her; she has the coveted bull. She has no more need of war, and here she performs a ritual of dispossession. In this way she symbolically rejects her warrior rage.

Moreover, Cuchulainn, who appears at this precise moment, commits no wrong. "He did not wound her; he would not have wounded her from behind." And at Medb's request, he promises to protect her and her army until they get to the ford that divides Ulster from Connaught. Thus it all ends, order returns, and everyone finds their way back home.

But at Cruachan, the Brown One of Cualngé is in rapture at discovering a beautiful unknown country, and lets out his three loud moos. The Beautiful Horned of Ae hears him, and in a fury, rushes at the intruder. Then follows a spectacular fight between the bulls—spectacular for Medb, Ailill, Fergus, and the Irish who watch through a gap in the fence, passive witnesses of the mysterious forces that they have unleashed and that, having escaped them, play by their own rules, not affected in the least by human will. "Each of the bulls looked at the other one. In a rage, they dug up the ground and threw dirt all around them. . . . Their eyes turned as red as fireballs in their heads; their nostrils and jowls blew out like a blacksmith's bellows. . . . Each of them began to pierce the other, stab him, gore him, massacre him."[47] The fighting lasts a long time. "And the night fell and the men of Ireland were forced to listen to only snorting and mooing. That night, the bulls covered all of Ireland."[48] The Brown One of Cualngé succeeds in tearing the Beautiful Horned of Ae to pieces and dispersing his body over the four corners of Ireland, before dying himself by breaking his back against a hill.

It seems as though a terrible war with the worst possible massacres was neither useful nor necessary just to arrive at this point. But is war ever useful or necessary, no matter what the cause? The possession of the sacred bull is no less worthy a cause than the possession of Helen over whom Troy was annihilated. One could respond that Helen is a symbol. Like the moon (*Selene*) to which she is related phonetically, Helen represents riches and abundance. The Brown One of Cualngé, in this case, plainly represents the same thing. And then, do we really understand the role of this bull? Also, do we know what kind of worship was rendered, not to the bull, but to the divinity incarnated through him?

The fact remains that the *Tain Bô Cualngé* is one of the most remarkable epics of western Europe, both for the scope of the actions and events and for the literary qualities of the work. We sense a style here, a very specific epic style, intentionally rough, always poetic. The few commentators who have studied the *Tain Bô* have expressed their admiration for it, all the while regretting a certain clumsiness, a certain awkwardness—because it is good form among archaeologists and linguists, those serious scholars, to never admire what has just been exhumed from the earth or from dusty manuscripts. And when, despite themselves, they do so, reservations must be carefully added. If ever it came to be believed that these people, despite their barbarism, were capable of valuable and beautiful works, what would become of the sacrosanct culture our universities so brilliantly expound?[49] Nevertheless, it seems that in the twenty-first century, after so many new scientific discoveries have taught us humility, we are entitled to admire *without reservation* this heritage saved *in extremis* from our past, a past whose richness astounds us.

The Story of Derbforgaille

This story[50] reveals Cuchulainn's role as guardian, and also his semidivine aspect. He is not a king or a legislator, but a sort of equalizing force in the world, the ancestor of the knights-errant whom we encounter in the tales of the Round Table, who are ready to raise their swords over the least injustice committed against those whom they protect. What's more, the dramatic intensity of this story is such that a straightforward translation of it is worth more than any commentary.

> Derbforgaille, daughter of the king of Lochlann,[51] fell in love with Cuchulainn because of the beautiful stories that were told about him. She and her servant girl left for the east, in the form of two swans, and arrived at Lough Cuan, bound together by a golden chain. That day, Cuchulainn and his foster brother, Lugaid, went to the shores of the lake and saw the birds. "Let's get those birds!" said Lugaid. Cuchulainn threw a stone which passed through their sides and lodged in the

breast of one of them. Immediately, two human forms appeared on the shore. "You have been cruel to me," said the girl, "because it is for you that I've come." "That's true," said Cuchulainn. At which point, he sucked the girl's side until the stone came out and went into his mouth with the pebble of blood which was around it. "It was for you that I came," she said. "That's impossible, o girl, " he said, "I cannot be joined to a side that I have sucked." "Then you will give me whatever you wish."[52] "I would like you to go, " he said, "to the most noble of men in all of Ireland, Lugaid of the Red Stripes." "Let it thus be so," she said, "provided that I can always see you."

Then she went with Lugaid and carried his child. One day, at the end of winter, the snow was thick and the men made great pillars of snow. The women went up onto the pillars and this was their game: "Let us each pee on a pillar to see which of us can pee into it the deepest. The woman whose pee goes the deepest will be declared the best among us." But they were not able to make their urine penetrate the pillars. Then they called Derbforgaille. She didn't like all this, because she wasn't foolish. However, she went up onto the pillar and discharged her urine all the way to the ground.

"If the men knew about this," said the women, "not a single woman would be loved in comparison with her. Let us take her eyes out of her head, as well as her nose, her two ears, and her hair. Then she will no longer be desirable." She was tortured and taken into her house. The men were assembled on a mound near Emain. "I think it is strange, oh Lugaid," said Cuchulainn, "that there is snow on Derbforgaille's house." "It is a sign of death," said Lugaid.

They ran, each as fast as the other, to the house. When she heard them, Derbforgaille closed herself inside. "Open!" said Cuchulainn. "Charming is the flower in which we are parted from each other," she said (and she sang a song).

It was said that her soul was not within her for much longer after they entered the house. It was also said that Lugaid died the moment he saw her. Then Cuchulainn went to the house of the women and made it collapse on top of them, in such a way that no one was able to leave the house alive. There were three times fifty queens, but he killed them all. . . . Then he erected gravestones for Lugaid and Derbforgaille, daughter of Forgall, king of Lochlann.[53]

The Feast of Bricriu

We cannot truly appreciate *The Feast of Brucriu*[54] narrative unless we know the account given by Posidonios, the Greek stoic philosopher from the second and first centuries B.C., as it comes down to us in the work of the Alexandrian compiler Athenaeus. This account concerns certain social customs of the Celts, and shows that this Irish narrative, probably composed in its current form in about the ninth century, goes back to the most ancient times. Here is the account from *Athenaeus* IV, 9:

Posidonios says . . . that the Celts, after throwing hay on the ground, set up low wooden tables. . . . Their food consists of small quantities of bread and much meat boiled in water or grilled on the coals or roasted on a spit. These dishes are placed on the tables, but, like lions, they seize them with their bare hands, tear them apart, and devour them. They allow fish to be served at their feasts as well. . . . They season it with salt, vinegar, and cumin, these fish which they grill, and they also put cumin in their drinks. . . . If there are many guests, they all sit in a circle, the seat in the middle being reserved for the most honored among them, be it an army chief or a hero whose skill is regarded as the best, be it a noble of high birth or a man who is noteworthy because of his great wealth. The host is seated near him, and then, from one side to the other, each according to his rank. . . . Behind them remain standing those who hold the shields and weapons. . . . Those who serve drinks carry earthenware or silver cups, in the form of chalices. The plates and bowls which hold meat are of the same material, but there are also copper ones, and sometimes, there are even reed baskets.

In this description, it is not difficult to see the archetype of the Round Table that King Arthur did not invent, although he helped reinstate it. This is almost exactly how the scene for the Feast of Bricriu is presented. As for the event of the narrative itself—or more, the quarrel that serves as the basis for the narrative—it is presented in this way (*Athenaeus* IV, 154):

> The Celts, says Posidonios, sometimes engage in single combat over the course of their feasts. . . . Sometimes, they go as far as wounding each other, and sometimes, overexcited by these wounds, they even go so far as to kill each other if others don't hold them back. He also tells how, formerly, when the roasted meat was presented, the strongest one raised up the haunch. But if someone opposed him, they got up together to fight each other in single combat, to the death.

We should note that, in the first century B.C., Posidonios insisted upon the fact that this custom was very ancient, since it seemed to have disappeared by his time, at least on the Continent. This much said, let us examine the Irish narrative.

Bricriu, nicknamed Bricriu of the Poisoned Tongue, one of the chief Ulates, prepares a feast for King Conchobar and the Ulster nobles, as he is obliged to do. He is willing to go to any expense. He has a house built to hold the banquet hall and has it decorated with the most valuable ornaments. Once these preparations are complete, Bricriu goes to the Emain Macha assembly and makes his invitations. Now, the Ulates refuse to go to Bricriu's because he has the well-earned reputation of starting the worst quarrels between people. Furious, Bricriu threatens them with a geis, and the Ulates decide to go to the feast but choose among themselves some armed men in charge of keeping an eye on Bricriu to keep him from doing harm.

Very annoyed at not being free to indulge in his favorite pastime, Bricriu goes to find the hero Loegaire and suggests that he demand "the hero's portion" during the feast, since it is clear that he deserves it: "Thus when the last day's feast is ready, let your driver rise and claim the hero's portion for you." Loegaire says, "Men will be killed on this day when what you wish of me takes place." Bricriu proposes the same thing to Conall Cernach and to Cuchulainn, who both promise to claim the famous hero's portion.

At feast time Bricriu assigns seats and retires with the armed men in charge of watching him. Naturally, Loegaire's, Conall's, and Cuchulainn's drivers all rise at the same time to claim the hero's portion for their masters, which sets off a great ruckus. Conchobar and the druid peacemaker Sencha intervene. Sencha serves as judge: The hero's portion will be shared among all the guests and then Ailill, the king of Connaught, will be asked who of the three heroes deserves to be judged the best.

However, Bricriu encounters Fedelm, Loegaire's wife, who has left with her servants to "clear her head which the beer and brandy had made heavy." With malicious good cheer, Bricriu suggests that she enter the banquet hall first, since she is married to the greatest hero of Ulster, and all the other women must walk behind her. And of course, when he meets Lendabair, Conall's wife, and Emer, Cuchulainn's wife, Bricriu suggests the same thing.

There is no need to describe the pandemonium that follows, which leads to a new brawl. Sencha proposes that the women prove their superiority through poems. Each of them delivers a poem to the glory of her husband. Then Conall and Cuchulainn try to force open a passageway for their wives, and Cuchulainn finds it faster to raise up an entire part of the house. Thus Emer makes a triumphant entry with her fifty servants.

But now the house is all in shambles, and Bricriu, who was watching this show from an upstairs room, finds himself on a pile of dung. He protests that his house has been ruined, and Cuchulainn finally puts everything back in place. Then the feast resumes, and after another quarrel between the women, Cuchulainn, Conall, and Loegaire are subject to a trial. They each have their carts hitched up and go to fight a mysterious giant in the midst of the fog. Loegaire and Conall are defeated and return sheepishly to Emain Macha. Cuchulainn comes back with the giant's chariot and weapons. Then Bricriu proclaims that the hero's portion rightly returns to Cuchulainn, and all the Ulates applaud. But Conall and Loegaire refuse to accept this judgment and declare that they want Ailill to arbitrate.

The Ulates then head for Cruachan, where Ailill and Medb live. Leaving last, Cuchulainn arrives first. For each Ulate hero's arrival, we are given sumptuous and detailed descriptions of the characters as they approach, provided by Finnabair, the daughter of Ailill and Medb, who sees them from the ramparts high above the Cruachan fortress. Conchobar reveals the reason for their visit, and then the Ulates depart, leaving the three claimants at Cruachan. These three are set upon by three "druid cats" during the night. Loegaire and Conall flee, but Cuchulainn resists them.

The next day Medb makes the three heroes come to her separately. To Loegaire, she gives "a bronze cup with a brass bird on the foot," to Conall, "a brass cup with a bird of gold," and to Cuchulainn, "a cup of red gold with a bird of precious stone," which clearly constitutes a judgment of their valor. But she recommends that they not show their cups before returning to the assembly of Emain Macha. Cuchulainn is once again the victor of a completely remarkable trial. It is a matter of throwing a wheel from inside the house through an opening in the roof (that is, the central chimney) in such a way that it plunges into the courtyard of an underground "bend." This is a reference to the mysterious posture of a divinity often represented in Gallic statuary, the famous god of the wheel, who has been considered the equivalent of Jupiter. Could this be a represention of the god of thunder? Of the solar wheel? We are rather badly informed about this god of the wheel, and this passage from *The Feast of Bricriu* is the only text we have on the subject. Thus, we can only make a few hypotheses based on it. The throwing of the wheel constitutes a game, perhaps a ritual game, and given the solar nature of the wheel in the earliest periods (comparable with the solar discs of the Bronze Age), it is probable that Cuchulainn, in succeeding at the test, demonstrates his solar power, the strength of the diurnal hero, which he is in any case because of his relationship with the god Lugh.

Cuchulainn then succeeds at the Trick of the Needles. "Cuchulainn goes to find the assembly of one hundred and fifty women, and is given a needle by each of them, and throws these needles on the ground one after the other, so skillfully that the point of each needle enters the hole of the one in front of it, and the hundred and fifty needles form but one single line." And Mebd sends the three competitors to the home of a certain Ercoil, who sends them to Samera. Samera tells them they must find "the fairies of the valley," who destroy the weapons of Loegaire and Conall. Cuchulainn enters into combat against the fairies and gets beaten. Loeg, his driver, hurls insults at him: "You coward, you unlucky one, you one-eyed savage! What has become of your valor and your courage for the fairies to put you into such a pitiful state?" Then the warrior's fury seizes Cuchulainn and he emerges from the trial victorious. Samera proclaims him worthy of the hero's portion. The three comrades return to Ercoil, who proposes single combat to them. Loegaire and Conall flee. Cuchulainn disarms Ercoil and brings her, chained to his cart, to Emain Macha, while Buan—Samera's daughter, who is in love with Cuchulainn—tries to catch up with the hero. "She recognized the tracks of Cuchulainn's cart because everywhere the path got too narrow, this cart had broken through the walls, enlarged the holes, or jumped over the spot. With a terrible leap, she threw herself at the back of this chariot, but her head hit a rock and she was killed."

Arriving at Emain Macha, the three warriors go to the assembly and take out their cups. Of course, it is Cuchulainn who is declared the winner, but once more Loegaire and Conall refuse to accept this. Sencha sends them to submit to the judgment of Uath Mac Immonainn (terrible, son of great fear), a giant gifted with magic powers. Uath declares, "Here is what we will do, and the one who accepts will have the hero's portion. Here is my battle-ax; one of you must take it and cut off my head. But tomorrow, I will have to cut off his."

Loegaire and Conall refuse this disquieting proposition, but Cuchulainn takes the ax and cuts off the giant's head. "Uath got back up to his feet, held his head against his chest, picked up his battle-ax with one hand, and rushed into the lake." The next day, Cuchulainn returns and lays his head down on a rock before Uath. Then the giant twirls his ax around in the air three times without striking, and declares Cuchulainn worthy of the hero's portion.

This strange story, which has been called the "Decapitation Game," is found in almost the same form in a French Arthurian legend, *Gauvain et le Chevalier Vert*, as well as a medieval English romance, the *Green*

Knight. The hero is Gaiwan, King Arthur's nephew. It is quite clearly a matter of the enactment of a sacrifice,[55] as well as a trial meant to bring out the hero's courage.

However, neither Conall nor Loegaire wants to admit he is defeated. The Ulates are obliged to send them to Curoi Mac Daire, one of the Tuatha de Danann and a kind of god of death. When they arrive at Curoi's fortress, he is not home, and his wife Blathnait bids them welcome. She provides a good feast for them and asks them to mount guard for the night. The first night Loegaire fights with a shade, who ends up throwing him into a dung heap outside of the fortress. The second night a similar misadventure befalls Conall Cernach. Then, the third night, "united together to take and lay waste to the fortress were the three Pale Ones of the Cold Moon Swamp, the three Pale Ones of the Breg plain, and the three sons of Music at Great-Fist. That evening also, the Monster of the Lake, near the fortress, promised to swallow the fortress." Cuchulainn, who is on guard, gets rid of all his adversaries, one after the other, and turns to face the monster of the lake.

This monster of the lake who wants to devour the fortress is nothing other than the floods personified, a tidal wave.[56] Cuchulainn succeeds in beating the monster and (a characteristic detail) cuts it into pieces, which signifies that he has dispersed the energy of the natural phenomenon he has just fought against. Here we witness the Herculean aspect of Cuchulainn, righter of wrongs, destroyer of monsters, the one who maintains the balance of natural forces. Without his intervention, the fortress would have been engulfed by water and Blathnait would have been a new Dahud in another city of Ys.

But Cuchulainn has not reached the end of his trials. Now the shade who caused so much trouble for Loegaire and Conall appears. Cuchulainn carries out his warrior tricks and enters into a full-blown warrior rage, at which point the shade asks for mercy and promises the hero's portion to the Ulate champion and to Emer supremacy over all the women of Ireland. After this the shade disappears, and we understand that it was Curoi. In fact, Curoi soon makes his entrance into the fortress and proclaims his decision: Cuchulainn will have the hero's portion.

When the Ulates at Emain Macha learn of Curoi's judgment, they are delighted, but Conall and Loegaire contest it one more time. It is then decided that the hero's portion will no longer be awarded to anyone. This decision, which corroborates Posidonios's observation, is clear proof that because of the endless quarrels it set off, this custom was abolished very early, not only on the Continent but in Ireland as well.

However, the sequel to the narrative, which is incomplete in the manuscript and is most certainly a later addition, specifies that "the hero's portion was not awarded to anyone until acquisition by the first warrior at Emain Macha had taken place." Indeed, during a meeting of all the Ulates, a "Rustic" appears, the sort of woodsman so often found in Celtic literature. This rustic, who may be the shade vanquished by Cuchulainn, Curoi himself, proposes that Cuchulainn be given preeminence over all the Ulate warriors. And as the manuscript is interrupted at this point, we may imagine that finally Conall and Loegaire resign themselves to accepting the superiority of their rival, who is nevertheless their comrade-at-arms.

The Drunkenness of the Ulates

Along with *The Feast of Bricriu*, *The Drunkenness of the Ulates* [57] is the most Rabelasian of all Irish narratives, but there is nothing pejorative about that epithet—in fact, to the contrary because, despite its average length, *The Drunkenness of the Ulates* is monumental, first as an account of the habits, customs, and beliefs of the ancient Irish, and then because of its very special literary composition, very shocking to minds used to schmaltz, but nevertheless very captivating because of its originality and roughness. With *The Drunkenness of the Ulates*, we open the book on our ancestors and witness them as they really were, pigheaded brawlers, swine, complainers, revelers, and phenomenal drinkers, which is, after all, proof of good physical and moral health. [58] These aspects are inseparable from the Celts' other side, the dreamy side, capable of the most vivid imaginings and the most audacious intellectual speculation, always looking beyond the real, toward the Marvelous Land where there is no old age, no ugliness, no death, but beauty in all its forms. We must not forget that drunkenness provides vision in the two worlds. Etymologically, the one who is drunk is *in the middle*, halfway between the real and the imaginary, between Heaven and Earth. [59]

Given these circumstances, it is not surprising to see the extraordinary figures of Irish epic manifest their feelings or their instincts with so much violence, so much passion. First, because the epic is the domain of hyperbole, exaggeration; second, because the Celts live in horror of static equilibrium and dream to excess in all areas—which is one more way, like any other, of living intensely and fully, living a life that would otherwise be only a series of griefs and sufferings.

At the beginning of *The Drunkenness of the Ulates*, and perhaps because he is appalled by the violence of the quarrels between the Ulates, the author is careful to say that the Tuatha de Danann, once exiled to their mounds by the Gaels, went out of their way to wreak havoc among them by inciting the greatest possible number of disputes. And thus we are warned.

During the Samhain meeting at Emain Macha, the year when King Conchobar was required to cede two thirds of his province to the great warriors for one year, the king sends his messenger Leborcham to find Cuchulainn, and his messenger Findchad to find Fintan, son of Niall. Cuchulainn has absolutely no desire to obey, but his wife, Emer, who willingly plays the dragon, makes him leave with his driver Loeg. At the entrance of Emain Macha, he meets Sencha, Conchobar's druid, who is famous for his talents as peacemaker. Sencha asks him for a favor that Cuchulainn cannot refuse him: that he leave his third of the province, which will be rightly returned to him, to Conchobar so that Conchobar can govern Ulster for the greatest good of all. And when Fintan arrives in his turn, he finds himself obliged by Cathbad, another of the king's druids, to grant the same favor.

Everyone is received by Conchobar. But Cuchulainn begins to quarrel with Fintan. They come to blows, and all their followers with them. Sencha has trouble reestablishing peace. Still, everyone stays at Conchobar's feast for three days and three nights (that is, during the Samhain ceremonies), and then they return home.

A little later, because it is his duty, Cuchulainn prepares a feast for the benefit of the king and the Ulates, and goes off to Conchobar's to invite them. Unfortunately, Fintan is there, too, to make the same invitation because he has prepared his own feast for the same evening. Of course, the two rivals and their supporters begin to fight with each other again, so savagely that Sencha refuses to intervene and Conchobar, completely disgusted, leaves them the royal palace to use as their battlefield. However, thanks to a trick the king plays, calm is restored and Sencha makes them accept the following compromise: The guests will attend Fintan's feast for the first part of the night.

Thus they all find themselves at Fintan's once again:

> Then they arrived, the guests with their spouses, the kings with their queens, the musicians with their companions, the chiefs with their wives. If only nine men came from a town, they were served just the same. The living quarters where they were lodged were comfortable, very beautiful, with an admirable appearance, and splendid halls, vast and high for the multitude, with houses large and long, and immense kitchens. And there was also a guest house decorated in a thousand colors, with great doors . . . where the men and women took their places among the most noble of the Ulates to eat and drink. The food and drink was served in such a way that there were one hundred portions for every nine of them. Conchobar's house was also arranged so that each could drink, according to standing and clan, family, servants and artists. . . . There was singing. . . . There was entertainment; treasures were distributed, as well as jewels and art objects.[60]

Such extravagance and magnificence, which we have already encountered in *The Feast of Bricriu*, leads us to think that the Gaelic chiefs must have ruined themselves by offering the best of what they had to their compatriots because everyone was invited, or at least all free men, noble or of common rank. But there was reciprocity since everyone had to return the invitation one day or another. Surely only those who could host them well had guests, and it is hard to imagine the Ulate chiefs all gathered at the modest home of an artisan able to offer only a few shellfish. But among those who were able, it was up to each of them to surpass all the others, to go all out in proving his wealth and generosity. Here we find not only a sacred sense of hospitality but an incommensurable sense of pride—pride perfectly in keeping with the dignity of the chief, with his very function, which is to provide abundantly for those he considers, rightly or wrongly, to be poorer or weaker than he is. But let us return to the analysis of the text.

Fintan's feast proceeds in the usual fashion. As a precaution, Cuchulainn charges Loeg to let him know when the night is half over. When Loeg does so, Cuchulainn informs Conchobar, who is presiding over the feast. But "among the Ulates, there was a taboo: no one must speak before the king; and there was another taboo which applied to the king: he could not speak before his druids."[61] Then Conchobar gets up. The Ulates fall silent. Cathbad the druid asks him what he wants. The king answers by inviting the gathering to continue the feast at Cuchulainn's house.

So the Ulates reassemble and depart, following Cuchulainn's chariot.[62] Here we fall into pure Rabelais, into that grandiose and mad aspect that gives him all his charm. We can just imagine the scene with all these Ulates completely drunk, and preparing to drink more, on their wild journey in the middle of the night! "They crossed the hills they came to so violently that they leveled them to plains; the iron wheels of their carts dug up the tree roots so badly in all the forests they entered that they left a plain behind them." What is more, the mass of warriors and their horses is so imposing that they manage to empty the rivers they ford. In short, we seem to be witnessing the clearing of the Beauce by Gargantua's twin or the passing of a horde of Huns led by Attila.

Naturally, they are traveling so quickly and in such a disorderly fashion that they lose their way and no longer know where they are. To cap it all off, it begins to snow. As is his habit, Bricriu begins to complain and curse the Ulates. Finally, they succeed in taking stock, and as there is no longer a question of going to Cuchulainn's house—which is much too far away (they also find themselves outside of Ulate territory)—they agree to head toward Temair Luachra, a Connaught fortress.

It is exactly on this night, in this fortress, that Ailill and Medb, king and queen of Connaught, are celebrating the first month of their son, Mane Mo-Epirt, in the company of all the nobles of the province and of Curoi Mac Daire, his foster father. The fortress is guarded by two druids, Crom Deroil and Crom Darail, two old students of Cathbad. The two druids are engaged in a dialogue, first in prose, and then in verse, a dialogue whose meaning remains very obscure but that consists of a series of analogies prompted in their imaginations by the Ulates' arrival. First the Ulate warriors are great oaks, then chariots, fortresses, shields, stone pillars, herds of deer and horses, and finally birds. Thus the image of the trees reappears, and we again find the theme of the walking forest, as in the famous Welsh poem *Cad Goddeu*.[63] In any case the two druids are unable to come to any agreement on an interpretation of what they see and hear in the darkness. Curoi hears the druids arguing, goes to find them, and at the moment when the sun rises recites a symbolic poem concerning the presence of many herds under the Temair ramparts. Then the Ulates let out a terrifying cry that shakes all the houses and leap onto the terreplein of the fortress, where the druids and Curoi are seated. "Then the snow began to melt and turned to water thirty feet around them, so enflamed was the ardor of these intrepid warriors."[64]

Crom Deroil goes to tell Medb what he has seen, and it is Curoi who interprets the words of the druid and who declares the arrival of the Ulates with Conchobar and Cuchulainn at their head. He also names the principal chiefs, including Conall Cernach and Loegaire. But more important, Crom Deroil adds that there are three Tuatha de Danann with the Ulates, among them Oengus, the Mac Oc, son of Dagda, which corresponds to the statements the author makes at the beginning of the narrative regarding the games the men of the sidh play to stir up quarrels among the Gaels. There is more: "A man with one huge eye, enormous thighs, broad shoulders, and of enormous size, covered with a huge gray cloak [holds] a big iron bludgeon in his hand." This figure strikes the nine men who accompany him with the *evil* end of his bludgeon, and they die with a single blow. Then he puts the *good* end of his bludgeon to their heads, and that is how he revives them in the same instant.

As Curoi says to Medb, "It is not difficult" to recognize Dagda himself in this description, the Gaelic equivalent of the Gallic Teutas, a "good god" but also an ambiguous god because he is master of life and death, possessor of the bludgeon that kills and revives and of the cauldron that gives prosperity and life.[65] Thus, this epic ties the Ulster cycle, and the Cuchulainn cycle in particular, to the Mythological cycle.

Medb and Curoi (we should note that Medb's husband, Ailill, has not had his say) decide to question a blind old man to find out if there is a prophecy regarding the coming of the Ulates. He answers,

> Their coming has been predicted for a very long time
> and some thought has been given it. Here is what must

be prepared: an iron house between two houses of wood, with an underground house below, a very strong iron plate where firewood and coal will be heaped, the sort of coal that this underground house is full of. It is predicted that the Ulster nobles will all be assembled one night in the house of iron . . .[66]

Medb then decides to follow the prophecy's recommendations. She welcomes the Ulates with open arms and keeps them entertained while the famous iron house is built—which will be the ideal trap for getting rid of her enemies. When everything is ready, the Ulate chiefs find themselves in the house of iron and are brought food and drink, but they are then closed inside, and the house is fastened to seven stone pillars by seven iron chains. Then, "three times fifty smiths were brought who stoked the fire with their bellows. They made three rings around the house and they lit the fire not only under but also over the house, in such a way that the fire's heat penetrated the house."[67]

The Ulates understand the trap they've fallen into, and Bricriu blames Cuchulainn for their predicament. Very upset, Cuchulainn answers that he is going to try to get all his companions out of there. He throws his shoulder against the wall and then realizes that the walls are iron. He jumps in the air, demolishes the roof, and shakes the whole fortress. Ailill intervenes and, not very happy to find that the laws of hospitality have been flouted by his wife, has the Ulates taken to an oak house and sends them beer and food. But even though the Ulates are drunk once again, they feel like prisoners. Dubthach Doeltenga, whose tongue is as wicked as Bricriu's, challenges Cuchulainn half-jokingly to get them out of this tight spot. Cuchulainn jumps up and does the "warrior leap of the salmon," which is one of the specialties he learned from the sorceress Scatach. This allows him to remove the upper part of the roof and to find himself on the roof of another house.[68] Then he notices the warriors of the fortress, armed and ready to attack the Ulates despite Ailill, who is always respectful of the laws of hospitality and conscious of his responsibility, although no one listens to him. Fighting breaks out and continues until the middle of the following day. The Ulates shove against the house with their heads and use it as a tank to crush three hundred of their enemies, but are temporarily made to retreat because of their small number.

During this time, Ailill watches the fighting from the fortress and, lamenting, pronounces these very important words regarding the actual authority of the king and his role in Celtic society: "For a long time the proverb has said that a battle cannot be won without the king. If this battle were led by me, it would have been over a long time ago. But you see, I have no power over them [the men of Connaught]." This clearly shows that while Ailill holds the title of king, it is Medb who directs everything, which is also evident in *The Cattle Raid of Cualngé*, and by virtue of a Celtic legislative principle: The wife who possesses more goods than her husband is not only mistress of her own affairs, but can also direct those of her husband, and without asking his advice. Despite her "dragon" ways, Medb never oversteps her rights, because, as daughter of the high king Eochaid Feidlech, she possesses goods superior to those of Ailill, whom she has married because he was "conciliatory" and not in the least jealous.[69]

Moreover, in pronouncing these words Ailill once more denies his responsibility. He does not participate in the combat, nor secure victory for his own people, because victory is possible only if the king himself takes part in the action. This is the reminder of an absolute Celtic principle: Celtic society cannot exist coherently without harmony between king and subjects, even if the king has no real power.

However, Cuchulainn intervenes, strikes his enemies violently, and renews his warrior rage. The Ulates put their enemies to flight, entirely destroying the fortress, but giving protection to Ailill and his seven sons, who haven't taken part in the battle. Thus, it is finally a victory for the men of Ulster. They can now head toward Cuchulainn's fortress, and there they remain feasting for forty nights. They return home then while Ailill, probably on bad terms with Medb, seeks refuge at Emain Macha, where he is made welcome.

Thus ends this half-comic, half-tragic epic, with Cuchulain as its main character, its kings occupying a necessary but secondary role, its feasts and drunken binges, its quarrels and combats. This is a singularly captivating testimony to the vitality of the ancient Celtic peoples, who can certainly be called drunkards, but surely not cowards or decadents because all these tribulations are nothing other than a glorification of virile energy.

Cuchulainn's Malady

This narrative[70] is interesting on several accounts. First, its poetic quality brings to light the Celts' sentimental nature and their storytellers' imagination. It also provides proof that these storytellers had a sense of psychology seldom acknowledged. And finally, it gives us information on the Other World, as the Celts envisioned it, especially in its most charming and magical aspects. Indeed, there is a world of difference between this pagan concept of a peaceful and amoral (in the best sense of the word) paradise, on a human scale, and the dark stories reported by le Braz in his masochistic *Légend de la mort*, putting the emphasis on guilt and the idea of punishment. Here, in a typically Baudelairian atmosphere, we have an invitation for a voyage to the Land of the Fairies where "there is nothing but luxury, calm, and sensual pleasure."

During the time of Samhain (November 1), which is the great Celtic holiday, the Ulates are gathering at Emain Macha. But since they are missing Conall Cernach and Fergus Mac Roig, they decide to wait before beginning the assembly and giving themselves over to games. It is then that a flock of birds swoops down on a lake not far off. Wanting some of these birds for themselves, the women of Ulster ask Cuchulainn to go after them. In a bad mood, Cuchulainn begins to insult "the prostitutes of Ulster" who offer him nothing better to do. Then, as they remind him that it is because of him that certain women are one eyed (because they are in love with him and resemble the hero when he is angry and takes on the aspect of a cyclops), he finally agrees and takes all the birds, which he divides between the women in such a way that no more remain for his wife Ethne Ingube.[71] She declares that this doesn't matter, since it is because of her that the other women have obtained the birds.

However, a little while later two birds linked by a chain of red gold come to the lake and sing a soft song that puts the Ulates to sleep, except for Cuchulainn, Ethne, and Loeg the driver. Despite Ethne's warnings, Cuchulainn picks up his slingshot and attacks the birds, but for the first time in his life, he misses his shot and despairs. Then he throws his lance, which goes through the wing of one of the birds. The birds disappear under the water.[72] But immediately, Cuchulainn feels sick. He leans against a stone pillar (probably a menhir), falls asleep, and dreams that two young women come toward him and strike him

115

with a crop. When he wakes up, he says that he is sick, and he actually stays in bed for one year.

As I have noted, this episode takes place around the Samhain, the time when the sidhs, the fairy mounds in which those ancient gods the Tuatha de Danann live, are opened to human beings. At this time there is exchange between the two worlds. In addition to its religious context—about which, admittedly, we have hardly any information—the Samhain festival has a clear psychological meaning. Since it is a holiday, the taboos are temporarily revoked. Thus, the prohibition against communicating with the underground world is lifted. The conscious and methodical man can plunge into the depths of his unconscious, but the forces of the unconscious can also surge to the conscious level. Cuchulainn wounds the magic birds. During normal time, nothing more would follow; the unconscious would absorb the memory and retain it there. But since it is Samhain, the function of self-censorship is banished and the memory flows back to the surface, becoming a guilt complex symbolized by the two young women who seek vengeance on Cuchulainn. The hero is not physically sick; he is the victim of psychological trauma.

Moreover, the story takes up again the following year at Samhain. A stranger comes to visit Cuchulainn and lets him know that his malady can be cured, but only by the daughters of Aed Abrat (that is, by the two woman-birds). He also says that Fand, daughter of Aed Abrat (which means "tear, daughter of brow fire"), who was abandoned by Mananann, is in love with Cuchulainn. Then the hero gets up and goes to lean against the stone pillar [73] where he had the vision of the two women the year before. The method employed so resembles a psychoanalytic cure that there can no longer be any doubt about the narrative's meaning.

Just at this point one of the two women, a certain Libane, comes to find him and confirms that Fand is in love with him and that he may have her if he agrees to fight against the enemies of King Labraid. Cuchulainn asks, "Where does he live?" "He lives in *Mag Mell*," she says. *Mag Mell* is the Plain of the Fairies, the land of the marvelous and unreal. The battle proposed to Cuchulainn is clearly a mythic one. Let us translate: It is a matter of putting his unconscious thoughts in order, of freeing himself from his guilt complex, of struggling against his inhibitions.

But Cuchulainn, the intrepid hero who recoils before no enemy, *Cuchulainn is afraid*, afraid of the abyss of his unconscious and everything that can be found there. "I would rather go somewhere else. Let Loeg go with you to get to know the country from which you come." So it is the faithful driver Loeg who leaves with Libane in a "little bronze boat" and visits *Mag Mell*.[74]

When Loeg returns, he gives Cuchulainn an account in verse of all that he has seen, extolling the charms of this marvelous country, "the herds of gray horses, with spotted manes," "three trees crimson in color, from which birds sing, long and sweet," "a tree at the door of the castle, a tree of silver where the sun shines—its splendor is like gold," "a fountain," "a vat of mead," three times twenty trees "which feed three hundred men with their simple and multiple fruits," and especially, "a girl in the noble house, who distinguishes herself from the women of Ireland, with blonde hair which flies free," a woman who "would make whole armies lose their heads."

Because time doesn't exist in the world of the fairies, it is likely that Loeg has taken no more than a few seconds to make his voyage. It is still Samhain. Cuchulainn then leaves with Libane, meets Fand and King Labraid, engages in battle against Labraid's enemies, and returns victorious but again in such a state of warrior rage that Loeg has three vats of water prepared to calm him. It is then that Fand sings a love song for Cuchulainn in which she expresses her admiration of the hero's beauty and power:

> He juggles with fifty golden apples, they rebound on his breath; no king is his equal. . . . On each of his cheeks there are dimples red as blood, green dimples, blue dimples, dimples light crimson in color. There are seven lights in his eye, he is not easy to blind; the border of his noble eye has lashes black as tar.[75]

Cuchulainn remains with Fand for one month, having vanquished the phantoms of his unconscious for good. Then he leaves again after having arranged a rendezvous with her at the Cend Tracha Yew Tree. But Emer, Cuchulainn's wife, learns of the affair. She comes to the meeting place as well, accompanied by fifty women armed with daggers, with the clear intention of killing the girl. Cuchulainn has Fand mount his "solid chariot, in the seat bathed in sunlight," and places himself between her and Emer. Then a dramatic discussion among the three figures follows.

Emer begins by reproaching her husband for having publicly dishonored her and warns him about her stubbornness: "Surely you will never find a way to leave me, my boy, no matter what you try." With the embarrassed manner of a husband caught red handed, Cuchulainn tries to hem and haw: It isn't a question for him of leaving Emer—but, he says, "Why don't you leave me in the company of [this] woman for a little while? Because, truly, this woman is pure, chaste,[76] very skillful, worthy of a handsome king, this daughter of the waves come from the immense seas." And he concludes a bit cynically: "Oh Emer, you will never find a hero with such beautiful scars, so victorious in battle to compare to me."

Emer, who is very familiar with human psychology, and masculine psychology in particular, replies, "She is no better than me, this woman to whom you're so attached. Anything red is pretty, anything new is beautiful . . . anything you're used to is bitter, anything missing is sweet." And Emer begins to lament. Then Cuchulainn decides: "I give you my word," he said, "it is you who make me happy, and you who will make me happy as long as you live." After this choice is made, Fand interrupts, "Leave me." But Emer has a burst of generosity: "It is more just if he leaves me," she says. Fand responds that she is the one who should be abandoned because that is her destiny. In a poem in which she expresses all her sadness and all her love for Cuchulainn, she calls to her old husband Mananann, son of Lir, the king of the fairies, high chief of the Tuatha de Danann. He arrives, but only Fand can see him. Once again Fand expresses her chagrin in a moving poem: "I see here on the sea the knight of the long-haired sea.[77] . . . Farewell to you, beautiful dog (Cuchulainn), we leave you with a warm heart, even though we haven't attained what we desire; the right to flee remains."[78]

Fand disappears with Mananann. Cuchulainn begins to wander up and down the mountains without eating or drinking. Conchobar sends his druids to cure him, and they give him a potion that rids him of all memory of Fand. They use this opportunity to give Emer the potion to make her forget her jealousy. As for Mananann, he waves his cloak between Fand and Cuchulainn so that they will no longer recognize each other.

And so everything returns to order. Each world is in its place, and we conclude from the story that it is sometimes dangerous to let oneself be taken over by the people of the sidh, that is, to let oneself be caught unawares by the harsh intrusion of dream into reality. Who hasn't dreamed of making this descent into Hell, like Cuchulainn, out of love for the magic being who rules over this unconscious world, so much more beautiful and more *charming* than the conscious world? Isn't Cuchulainn Chateaubriand, haunted by the image of the sylph, that spirit for whom he searches so avidly and whom he believes he finds again, if only for an instant, in the ephemeral look of a girl with black hair and sad eyes like Lucille? Isn't Fand Atala, Velleda, Amelie, Cymodoceus, the young girl glimpsed in the Latium or the Indian Celuta? And then again, isn't there an echo of Racine in this story in which the great invincible hero, the terrible contortionist of Emain Macha, equal to a Pyrrhus or a Theseus, succumbs to "the deceptive charms" of passion and appears as weak and disarmed as any poor mortal being?

The Death of Curoi Mac Daire

The elements of this story[79] are quite enigmatic and go back to mythological traditions that are difficult to interpret. Inserted into the saga of Cuchulainn, this "violent death" of Curoi seems to be a continuation of the Mythological cycle, symbolic of the final battles between the Gaels and the Tuatha de Danann, the island's former occupants.

Curoi is a figure from the Other World. If he only appears indistinctly in the Mythological cycle, he nevertheless belongs to the race of the mounds and lives apart from everyone in a fortress that very closely resembles those "dangerous castles" so common in the French Arthurian romances. And the huge quarrel between Curoi Mac Daire and Cuchulainn, upon which this story centers, seems to have enjoyed great success in the Celtic world, since we find echoes of it again in Wales in a poem attributed to the poet Taliesin, the *Song of the Death of Corroy*.[80]

This narrative begins with a poem sung by Cuchulainn before the Ulate assembly. In this poem he tells of his very mysterious expedition to the "Land of the Shades," and, once there, into an impregnable fortress. "Seven walls surrounded the City . . . an iron fence on each wall on which seven heads were stuck." Cuchulainn successfully overcomes one trial after another, which cannot help but remind us of Lancelot of the Lake overcoming the enchantments of the Valley without Return or the Castle of the Sorrowful Guard. He does battle with serpents, toads, and dragons, and he cuts them into tiny pieces, which means that, as a solar hero, Cuchulainn brings light into the dark regions and that he destroys the phantoms of a morbid imagination—his own. He then tells how he has brought back treasure, marvelous birds, three cows, and, especially, a cauldron, and that this cauldron was given to him by the king's daughter, whom he has also brought back with him. A prose explanation that follows the poem notes that this girl is named Blathnait, and that Curoi Mac Daire participates in the expedition alongside Cuchulainn and King Conchobar.

Here we find the very Celtic theme of the cauldron, the archetype of the Grail. It is the cauldron of plenty, of inspiration and resurrection, and it seems to be the specialty of Welsh literature as well, since we find it in the *Mabinogi of Branwen*, the *Mabinogi of Perdur*, and *The Story of Taliesin*. We discover it especially in a poem attributed to Taliesin, *The Spoils of the Abyss*, which tells of an adventure almost like the one that happens to Cuchulainn, but its hero is King Arthur.[81] It concerns an expedition to a fortress on an island where a cauldron is found, an expedition that also turns into a disaster, since only seven survivors return, which links this poem to the adventure related in the *Mabinogi of Branwen*.[82]

However, after the victory of Cuchulainn, Curoi, and Conchobar, the spoils were divided but nothing was given to Curoi, which was a great injustice. Then Curoi

> ... ran toward the cows and gathered them in front of him. He put the birds in his waistband, and tucked the girl under his arm. And that is how they went off, him with the cauldron on his back. And no one among the Ulates was able to talk with him, except Cuchulainn. Curoi turned around to face him, and held him flat against the ground with his arms. Then he cut off his hair with his sword and rubbed his head with cow dung. And finally, he took off.

Curoi's supernatural character becomes very clear here since he is able to hold the Ulates in check with impunity, especially the invincible

Cuchulainn, whom he humiliates. This humiliation the hero will not very easily forget. He is so ashamed that he doesn't show himself to the Ulates again for a year. One day, in pursuit of some birds—no doubt the famous birds carried off by Curoi—he discovers Curoi's castle and has a conversation with Blathnait, whom Curoi has married. "He loved her, well before she had come from the countries of the sea. . . . He arranged a rendezvous with her for around the night of Samhain." And at the determined time, he comes with the Ulate army.

Everything is clear: At Samhain, the mounds are open and there is communication between the fairy world and the terrestrial world. It is a good time to attack Curoi, *because his fortress will be open*. But like the other Ulates, Cuchulainn is wary of Curoi's magical powers. Thus, it is through treachery that Curoi will meet his end; furthermore, Cuchulainn, who loves Blathnait, will take advantage of the situation to win her back, at the same time satisfying his desire for revenge. Actually, Blathnait betrays her husband. "She begins by advising Curoi to have a splendid fortress built with every raised stone that existed in Ireland. The Tuatha de Danann went out to build the fortress in one day, and Curoi remained alone in his fortress." We should note in this passage the clear relationship between the raised stones (the menhirs)— thus, the megalithic monuments—and the Tuatha de Danann, which once again proves that the Tuatha de Danann represent the populations from the Megalithic epoch.[83]

After that Blathnait throws milk into the stream, which is the agreed-upon signal for Cuchulainn. Then she tells Curoi to go wash. Curoi obeys, but he notices the Ulster armies. Blathnait reassures him: "It is your people," says the girl, "with stones and oakwood to build your fortress. If those are oaks, they will go quickly. If those are stones, it is a victory." But Curoi is nervous. Then Blathnait sends him off to bathe, and while she carefully washes him, she ties his hair to the rungs of the bed, draws his sword out of the sheath, and goes to open the fortress.

The Ulates rush in. Curoi manages to free himself and kills one hundred men by kicking and punching them. Then he goes to find Conchobar and is about to attack him when he notices his fortress is on fire. He rushes out to save himself, but he falls into the sea and drowns. That is how Curoi perishes, not in combat but, as the poem inserted into the text says, "drowned by the monster of the sea." This is valuable information. Curoi turns back, he reenters the mother's womb, he accomplishes the famous *regressus ad uterum* of psychoanalysis and, like Dahud in the engulfed city of Ys, he will live another life in another world, under the surface of the seas.[84]

But everything is not over. The Tuatha de Danann rush to revenge their chief, and the battle rages. However, the Ulates succeed in getting the upper hand. Thus they win back Curoi's riches and celebrate their victory. Now Ferchertne, Curoi's poet, "rushes at Blathnait, and takes her in his arms with such force that her ribs crack in her back. Then he carries her to the cliff in front of him, he throws himself into the abyss, and both of them are crushed against the rock." Thus Curoi's death is atoned for.[85] And afterward, every year, each night of Samhain, the Tuatha de Danann come to ravage the homes of the Ulates.

The Death of Cuchulainn

We have two versions of the death of the most celebrated Ulster hero,[86] two versions differing not so much in the events they relate as in the storytellers' states of mind. The text of the *Book of Leinster* is certainly the more ancient, judging from its form. The narrative is spare, almost dry, and moving for that very spareness, clearly epic in character. The Edinburgh text is longer, more developed, more detailed, and entirely bathed in a strange atmosphere of magical rites and the appearances of fantastical beings. To tell the truth, it would be hard to choose between the two versions because they are both so laden with grandeur and emotion. That is why it is good to draw from each of them when the most interesting events are unfolding.

During the *Tain Bô Cualngé*, Cuchulainn kills Calatin, the formidable warrior-magician, and his twenty-seven sons. But Calatin's wife is pregnant at the time, and gives birth to three sons and three daughters. Then Queen Medb is put in charge of their upbringing and makes them into mute, one-eyed sorcerers and sorceresses, which proves that these beings belong to the world of the cyclops. In order to avenge herself on Cuchulainn, Medb fuels Calatin's children's hatred and sends them to be initiated into magic in Scotland with the Saxons, to Babylon, and even to Hell, where the blacksmith Bhalcan makes them weapons.

It is very obvious that the murder of a hero like Cuchulainn could not be decided without long-term preparations. Like Achilles, Siegfried, and Roland, Cuchulainn can only be vanquished through treason or magic. It is also necessary that the weapons used to kill him be specially made by a blacksmith, a god of the Other World, but a hostile, malefic Other World.

When Calatin's children return to Cruachan, Medb decides to act. She assembles a great army and secures for herself the powerful aid of two formidable warriors whose fathers were killed by Cuchulainn, Lugaid, the son of Curoi, and Erc, the son of Coirpre. Then she launches her army on Ulster.

The moment is well chosen because, as in the *Tain Bô Cualngé*, the Ulates are victims of that strange malady that makes them suffer from labor pains, the result of Macha's curse. Only Cuchulainn is exempt from this disease. What is more, Cuchulainn's comrade-at-arms Conall Cernach happens to be on the British isle.

However, warned about what is happening, Conchobar understands the danger that threatens the Ulates, and because he knows Calatin's children have returned, he is nervous for Cuchulainn. Through his messenger Leborcham he sends him warning not to fight against the Irish armies and to come immediately to Emain Macha. After conferring with his wife, Emer, Cuchulainn obeys and arrives at Emain. There Conchobar entrusts him to the women's care (they are not subject to the malady), charging them with keeping him distracted and not letting him hear the noise of the battles.

Then Medb sends Calatin's children to Emain Macha. The three sisters, sorceresses of the most vile appearance, provoke an absolutely fantastic battle of trees—which proves, incidentally, that Shakespeare knew of this narrative before writing *Macbeth,* since we find not only the theme of the warrior forest in his play but also the characters of the three sorceresses.[87]

And Cuchulainn hears the noise of the fighting. Genann, the son of the druid Cathbad, has a very hard time keeping him from taking part and only succeeds by convincing him that it is a phantom army raised by druidic powers. The next day the daughters of Calatin begin again, waging huge battles still using trees and bushes. Conchobar decides to have Cuchulainn taken into the Valley of the Deaf and puts him under the protection of Niam, the daughter of Celtchair. Although she has the help of Emer and all the women of Ulster, she has a very hard time keeping Cuchulain from rushing off into battle. And since Niam has told the hero that he cannot go into battle unless she herself gives him permission, the following night one of Calatin's daughters takes the form of a crow, and then of Niam herself, and tells Cuchulainn that Conall Cernach will kill her if she does not give him her permission (Edinburgh manuscript).

Of course, Cuchulainn runs to get his weapons, despite the wise counsel of the druid Cathbad and the lamentations of the real Niam. But when he picks up his cloak, his brooch falls from his hand, which is a bad omen. Nonetheless, he orders his driver Loeg to prepare his chariot and harness his two horses, the Gray One of Macha and the Black One of the Valley without Peer. Now the Gray One of Macha turns three times to the left, which is unusual and disturbing. What is more, the chariot has been dismantled the night before by Morrigan, "because it didn't please her that Cuchulainn should go into battle" (*L.L.*).

After repairing the chariot and harnessing the horses, Cuchulainn and Loeg depart and see that Emain is on fire. The druid Cathbad shows them that it is a matter of illusion: "In these armies, there are no men, there are no troops, there are grasses and leaves" (Edinburgh). But Cuchulainn doesn't want to hear it. He says his good-byes to his mother, to Emer, and to all the daughters of Ulster. Cathbad still follows after him for a bit. Cuchulainn tells him his last wishes and bids him farewell, too. Then, all alone with Loeg on the road that leads to Tara, he encounters the three daughters of Calatin. "With poisons and venom, they prepared a dog on sorb spits" (*L.L.*). Now, one of the hero's taboos is not to visit a home without eating there, and another is the prohibition against eating dog meat. He moves away, but the sorceresses make him stay and eat. This means that he has violated one of his taboos, and his left hand, with which he was helping himself to the meat, immediately shrivels up.[88]

From this point on Cuchulainn becomes a kind of quarry that all his enraged enemies are going to track down, a kind of victim whom everyone fights for the honor of sacrificing. There is tragic grandeur here: a man alone, who was the most formidable and the most powerful of warriors, in slow agony, hunted down by one adversary after another, but never flinching before his destiny.

All the same, that doesn't stop Cuchulainn from seeking revenge and killing the daughters of Calatin (Edinburgh). But this is when the

Irish warriors, grouped around Erc, son of Coirpre, appear. Then Cuchulainn takes on his full warrior's rage: "His hair stood out from his head like the branches of red hawthorn from a bush. . . . The hero's light beamed from his head and his brow, as big and wide as a warrior's fist. This light, as dark as blood, issuing straight from his head, was great and as thick as the mast of a ship" (Edinburgh).[89] Then he advanced against the armies:

> He did the three tricks of thunder on his chariot, the thunder of a hundred, the thunder of three hundred, and the thunder of three nines. The armies were swept away. . . . As numerous as the grains of sand in the sea, the stars in the sky, the drops of dew in May, the flakes of snow, the hailstones, the leaves of the trees, the buttercups on the Breg plain, the blades of grass under the horses' feet on a summer day, so numerous were half the heads, half the skulls, half the hands, half the feet scattered across the plain.[90] (*L.L.*).

We can only ask ourselves what would have happened if Cuchulainn had had his full strength. The carnage is appalling. But Erc prepares a trap for him. He notices two men fighting each other whom no one can separate, and at this moment a jokester says to him, "Shame on you, Cuchulainn, if you can't manage to separate them!" (*L.L.*). Cuchulainn jumps upon the two men and kills them. He then picks up the javelin over which the two men were fighting, which is one of the weapons especially prepared to kill him. The jokester then threatens him with a geis if he doesn't give him the javelin. Cuchulainn throws the javelin, which goes through the jokester's head, at the same time killing nine men who happen to be behind him.

Then Lugaid, son of Curoi, seizes the javelin and wounds the driver Loeg. Once again Cuchulainn encounters two men fighting each other and a jokester. The same thing happens again, and this time it is Erc who takes the javelin and wounds the Gray One of Macha. A third time Cuchulainn undergoes the same trial. Lugaid picks up the javelin and throws it at Cuchulainn. "It happened that it went through what had been in his stomach, in such a way as to spatter it on the curtain of the chariot" (*L.L.*).

> Cuchulainn leaped from his chariot, bounded toward
> the men of Ireland and dispersed them. . . . They did
> not dare to come within the range of his voice or his
> look. His entrails hung over his legs and the crows of
> the Bodbh perched on them in such a way that the
> entrails were on the feet of the crows. Cuchulainn be-
> gan to laugh and this was the last time that Cuchulainn
> laughed. The shadows of pale death surrounded him.
> He headed for a little lake not far away from him and
> there he bathed[91] (Edinburgh).

This type of description escapes all commentary. Cuchulainn comes out of the lake and goes to lean against a stone pillar, to which he fastens himself so as not to fall down in front of his enemies and to die on his feet. The men of Ireland hang around him like vultures, but they are afraid and don't dare go close. "Then the Gray One of Macha went to Cuchulainn to protect him as his soul was there and the hero's light continued to shine from his brow. Then the Gray One of Macha charged three times around him. With its teeth, it felled fifty men and each of its hoofs killed thirty men of the army"[92](*L.L.*).

But Cuchulainn is dead. Birds perch on his shoulders. Lugaid, son of Curoi, "pushed back his hair and cut off his head. Immediately Cuchulainn's sword fell from his hand. It cut off Lugaid's right hand which fell on the ground. Cuchulainn's right hand was cut off to avenge him. Then the army left, carrying the head and right hand of Cuchulainn"[93] *(L.L.).*

Loeg reaches Emain with the Black One of the Valley without Peer and announces the death of the hero to Emer. Accompanied by the women of Ulster, Emer carries out the funeral lamentations, and then she sends Leborcham to find Conall Cernach. Leborcham meets Conall just as he reaches the Irish shore and tells him the news. Conall is over-come with anger and rushes off without a moment's delay to track down Cuchulainn's murderers. He begins by killing Mane Mo-Epirt, one of the sons of Ailill and Medb. Then, arriving at Tara, he sees two warriors playing ball with Cuchulainn's head. He kills them and entrusts the hero's head to the young Ulate Cenn Berraide, charging him with delivering it to Emer. Emer, accompanied by Loeg, performs further lamentations and sings a song in praise of the glory of the lost one (Edinburgh).

As for Conall, he attacks Erc, son of Coirpre, and kills him; then, after having caught the principal murderers, he goes to Lugaid. Lugaid asks him to tie back one of his hands, since he himself is now one handed. Conall agrees, but Lugaid's first stroke cuts the cords that held Conall's hand. Then Conall no longer holds back. He uses all his powers to fight Lugaid, decapitates him, and returns to Ulster with his collection of heads on the end of a branch. On the return trip he meets the Ulates, puts Lugaid's head on a stone, and forgets it. Remembering it afterward, he goes back to find Lugaid's head and sees that the head has melted down the stone and passed through it *(L.L.)*.

That is how the tale of Cuchulainn's death ends—a narrative of quite remarkable dramatic intensity, tinged with grandeur and savagery, imbued with an atmosphere of anguish, magic, and darkness through which that strange "hero's light" nevertheless shines, and is certainly nowhere near being extinguished.

4

The Finn Cycle

The Finn cycle, or the Ossianic cycle, is devoted to the province of Leinster. But it extends far beyond the borders of this little state and is found, alive and flourishing, throughout Scotland. Handed down orally for centuries, it is the Finn cycle that Mac Pherson knew and spread through all of Europe, the tales of Fingal (nothing other than the romantic name for Finn) and Ossian (or Oisin, the fawn).

Finn is king, but unlike Conchobar, he exercises no legal authority over Ireland or over any part of Irish territory. Indeed, Finn is king of a troop of true nomads, knights-errant, who come down to us under the name of Fiana (Fenians). These Fiana probably existed historically, during the time of the high king Cormac Mac Airt, that is, at the end of the second century A.D. They constituted a kind of state within a state, and they were often on bad terms, not only with the high king but also with the various kings of the provinces or tribes in the territories where they practiced their arts.

They were a sort of warrior militia that, from the Battle of Cnucha in 174, watched their prestige continually grow. The Fiana lived among the local people during the winter, maintaining justice and guarding the ports. In the summer they hunted in the forests. Finn, who has been classed with the heroes or the hunter-gods, and the Fiana carried out police work by chasing the bandits who overran certain regions of Ireland, and they were often responsible for collecting taxes, a task that they probably performed with much zealous interest. Their influence became so great that Cormac tried every means of getting rid of them, and it is likely that he succeeded, because no historical traces of the Fiana remain after the first half of the third century. But their prestige was enough to make their memory survive in popular legends, which are still well known even today in the remote countryside of Ireland and Scotland.

The chief of the Fiana was Finn, son of Cumall. We can recognize in Cumall the name of the Gallo-Breton god Camulos, which is proof that Finn is a purely mythic figure, analogous to the Welsh hero Gwynn, son of Nudd, whose name means the same thing. First of all Finn is the chief of a clan, that of O'Baicsne. He becomes the leader of the Fiana only after having rendered powerless the members of the adversarial clan of Morna, represented by Goll the One Eyed, another divine figure going back to the earliest and purest Indo-European tradition.[1]

Considering certain episodes in the Finn cycle, we are tempted to make a comparison to the Breton Arthurian cycle because, in the end, the institution of the Round Table has much in common with the earthy chivalry of the Fiana. Finn himself presents certain analogies with Arthur, if only because of the story of his childhood or the episode where his wife, Grainne, is carried off by Diarmaid. Whatever the case, it is a series of very accomplished narratives that this cycle presents to us, with a mix of historical references, mythological symbols, and remarkable figures, worthy of being counted among the most beautiful works of world literature.

Finn's Childhood

It is probably with the help of shorter, older narratives and poems more or less attributed to Oisin that the fili were able to compile this story of *Finn's Childhood*[2] because, though there are not many archaisms in its construction, the adventures related and certain sometimes-bizarre details show that the storyteller no longer understands very well the story he is telling, which proves the relative antiquity of the legend itself. It is clear that this was an attempt to re-create the story of the childhood and first feats of the glorious warrior Finn Mac Cumail within the peculiar atmosphere that envelops all the acts of the Fiana, an atmosphere that so often plunges us back into the earliest Gaelic mythology.

The narrative begins with a short summary of the Battle of Cnuch[3] in which Cumall, son of Trenmor, perishes.

We know that Cumall is none other than the god Camulos, known through Welsh inscriptions and often compared with Mars. After the death of Cumall, his wife, Muirne, renounced by her father Tagd, gives birth to a son whom she names Demne. But because she fears the hatred of Cumall's assassins, Urgriu, Morna, and Goll, she entrusts her son to Fiacail, son of Conchem; to Bodbmall the sorceress; and to the Gray One of Luachair.[4] These are the two women who raise Demne in secret in the Sliabh Bloom forest.

Six years later Muirne—who in the meantime has married the king of Lamraige—comes back to see her son and asks the two women to take permanent responsibility for his upbringing. Once more, a hero destined for an extraordinary future can only be raised, that is, *initiated*, by women who are both warriors and sorceresses. Let us not forget Cuchulainn's training with the sorceresses of Scotland, and Lancelot (from the Round Table romances), who is educated by the Lady of the Lake, also known as the fairy Vivian. That is how Demne grows up. He accomplishes his first feats hunting and ends up becoming the companion of a famous bandit by the name of Fiacail, son of Codna. But the two foster mothers drag him away from the bandit and take him back with them.

One day Demne goes off to the Liffey plain, where there is a fortress. He joins in the games of some young men who are playing in the field in front of the fortress, and he is the winner. Annoyed, the youths go to find the master of the fortress to tell him what has happened: "Kill him, if you know how to, if you are capable of it," he says. "We would not be able to do that," they reply. "Has he told you his name?" They answer that his name is Demne. "What does he look like?" the master asks. They answer, "He is a young man, *white, beautiful, and blonde* (Finn). "Then Demne will be called Finn," the man says."

This, then, is the origin of Finn's name, or rather, his nickname. It is a little far fetched, and there is no doubt that this is not the real origin. But no matter. Demne comes back the next day. The games turn violent, and Demne ends up drowning nine young men: "Who has drowned the young men?" everyone asks. "Finn," they answer. And so henceforth the name of Finn is attached to him.

Another day when he is at Sliabh Bloom with his two foster mothers, he catches two does. Thus Finn develops the habit of bringing them their game. "Now go far away from us," the women warriors say to him, "because the sons of Morna are looking for you in order to kill you." So Finn goes off to seek adventure. Without revealing his identity, he offers the king of Bantry his services and becomes the most skillful hunter anyone has ever seen.

He goes then to the king of Carbrige.

> One day the king came to play chess. Finn challenged him and won seven games one after the other. "Who are you?" asked the king. "The son of a peasant of the Luaigni of Tara," he said. "No," said the king, "you are the son that Muirne had by Cumall. Do not stay here any longer out of fear that you may be killed, since you are under my protection."

After this remark, which says much about the tenacious hatred that follows the clan of Cumall, Finn goes to establish himself with a master blacksmith by the name of Lochan, who has a very beautiful daughter named Cruithne. He marries the daughter (but provisionally—that is, for a year, according to the custom for concubines) and asks Lochan to make him some weapons. Lochan makes him two lances.

Here, some commentary is necessary. This is the theme, well known in all mythological literature, of the blacksmith who fashions special weapons for the hero. Let us consider Aeneas, Roland, and King Arthur. The blacksmith is always a figure from the Other World, a divinity from below, in possession of subterranean powers and secrets.[5] It is likely that this is a vestige of the revolutionary change brought about by the discovery of metal in the Bronze Age among populations that used stone tools. The weapons he makes are necessarily sacred, because the blacksmith's work is ambiguous. He forges the plow, the tool of life and fertility, but he also forges the battle-ax, lance, and sword, instruments of death.[6]

So Finn receives his weapons from the infernal divinity represented by the blacksmith Lochan, thus making him destined for great things. It is, in some way, the weaponry of the knight, and much could be said about the ritual significance of the medieval dubbing ceremony, a pagan ceremony entirely taken over by Christianity, in which the king or the lord plays the role of the god-blacksmith in presenting the young novice his weapons.[7]

But there is something very curious about Finn's adventure with Lochan the blacksmith: Finn marries Cruithne, Lochan's daughter.

This is more than just an anecdote, because *Cruithne* is the generic name for the Pict populations and by extension, the populations of the British isle.[8] Along with the names *Trenmor* and *Cumall,* the very name *Finn*—which is the exact equivalent of the Welsh *Gwynn* (going back to the Celtic-Britonic *Vindu*)—and Finn's marriage to the British isle personified say much about the ties between Finn (and the Fiana in general) and the Britonic branch.[9]

But that is not all. After having received the two lances, Finn takes leave of Lochan and Cruithne. Lochan gives him some advice: "My son, do not go on the path where the sow named Beo is found." Beo is a monstrous sow that has devastated Munster. But Finn has nothing more pressing to do than meet up with this sow. She charges the young man, but he kills her with his lance and brings her head back to the blacksmith "like a wedding present for his daughter."

This places us right in the midst of Britonic myth, and what is more, the analogy to King Arthur begins to become apparent. Indeed, the earliest Welsh narrative, *Kulhwch and Olwen,* in full agreement with the Latin text of the *Historia Britonnum,* relates Arthur's hunt for the Porcum Troit—which will become the famous Twrch Trwyth, the destructive wild boar that no one before him has been able to vanquish. In the same *Kulhwch and Olwen,* as in certain trilogies, a monstrous sow also plays a part.[10]

Arthur is like Finn (and like Heracles vanquishing the Erymanthian boar, Theseus vanquishing the Minotaur, and Saint George or Saint Michael vanquishing dragons), the purifying hero who rids the earth of its monsters, who hunts them down and thus reestablishes the balance between the forces of light and darkness, a balance threatened by the savage intrusion of the monster, necessarily dark, into the daylit world. On the psychological level this translates perfectly into the role of censor taken by the king or chief, be it Finn, Arthur, Heracles, or Theseus. He hunts the animal, thus repressing it. The animal represents the destructive forces in the unconscious that escape the threshold of the conscious and that the hero, the true superego, immediately chases back into the infernal country, that is, the Land Below, from which it came.

However, Finn sets out on his journey again, like an outlaw condemned to perpetual exile. He meets an old woman who is mourning the death of her son, killed by "a great and terrible warrior." Finn, the true defender of widows and orphans, offers to avenge his death, and that is how he kills the Gray One of Luachair, the one who struck the first blow against Cumall in the Battle of Cnuch. Not only does he get vengeance, but in addition he recovers Cumall's treasure, which the Gray One had carried off with her.

Finn then goes out in search of Crimall, Cumall's brother. He discovers him in Connaught, "in a deserted forest, an old man with a group of old Fiana gathered around him." After having cheered up these men, who are outlaws like himself, he goes off to "learn poetry from Finneces who had settled on the shores of the Boyne." It was a happy time, when the chiefs and the kings of this world still thought of learning poetry. But the Finneces episode warrants a pause:

> For seven years, Finneces found himself along the Boyne, lying in wait for the salmon of Fec. It had been foretold to him that if he ate the salmon of Fec, nothing would remain unknown to him. Now he found the salmon and charged Demne (Finn) with preparing it. But the poet forbade him from eating a single bite of the salmon. After having cooked it, the young man brought him the fish: "Have you eaten some of the salmon?" asked the poet. "No," said the young man, "but I burned my thumb while I was cooking it and afterwards I put it in my mouth." "What is your name, my boy?" he asked. "Demne," answered the young man. "Finn is your name, my boy," he said, "and you are the one the salmon is destined for, and truly you are Finn."

Whereupon, the young man eats the salmon. This is what gives Finn knowledge.[11] That is, when he puts his thumb in his mouth and sings the *illumination of the song*, then no matter what subject he has questions about, all is revealed to him. That is how he learns the three things a poet must know: *teinn laida* (the illumination of the song), *imbas forosna* (the knowledge that illuminates) and *dichetul dichennaib* (the improvisation of the song).[12]

This initiation into the gift of prophecy (and of poetry, which is the same thing) by means of a burnt thumb is quite curious. It would seem to be the storyteller's invention if we didn't find it again, nearly word for word, in the Welsh narrative, *Hanes Taliesin*. In the same way that the salmon was prepared for Finneces and not for Finn, a cauldron of inspiration and knowledge was brewed by the goddess-sorceress Keridwen for her son Afang-Du. She charged Gwyon Bach (the future bard Taliesin) with watching over the cauldron. Now "three drops of magic liquid spilled out of the cauldron and fell on Gwyon Bach's finger. And because they were so hot, he put his finger in his mouth and the very moment the marvelous drops reached it, he saw all things which were to come."[13] In both cases the initiation is the result of food tasted inadvertently that confers the gift of vision. In both cases the chosen one is not the one for whom the food was intended. In both cases it is putting a finger in the mouth that transmits the gift. The similarities are so striking that this cannot be a matter of coincidence; it is exactly the same theme. Thus, the claim can be made that this theme goes back to the primitive Celtic tradition, before the division between Gaels and Britons, and that this additional evidence supports the view of the Finn legend as a Britonic import. As to the importance of the salmon in Finn's story, it is explained by the particular symbolism of this fish: It lives in the sea, in the estuaries, and in the rivers, and it *returns to the source*. Thus it represents to him the cause and the effects—perfect knowledge of the past, present, and future. It is likely that the meaning of the salmon, an animal specific to the subpolar regions or, in any case, more closely connected to the pole than to the Mediterranean, derives from an ancient Nordic tradition in which we once more find Nordic-European or Asiatic shamanism.

After having received this initiation, Finn leaves Finneces and goes to finish his poetic training with Cethern, son of Fintan. A strange adventure then befalls him. At the Bri Ele sidh, each night of Samhain (November 1) the men of Ireland come to court a very beautiful girl named Ele, "because the Irish sidh were always opened at Samhain and so nothing of what was in the sidh was hidden then." Now, each year, one of the suitors was killed, and no one ever knew who the murderer was.

Cethern goes to court Ele along with many other suitors, but one of the suitors, the poet Oircbel, is killed. Finn wants to avenge his death, and goes to ask advice from Fiacail, son of Conchem, the husband of his paternal aunt, who advises him to go sit between the *Paps of Anu*, that is, between two mounds inhabited by fairies.[14] As it is the night of Samhain, the mounds are open, and Finn is witness to the dialogues and exchanges of food between the two sidh. Then Finn throws the lance that Fiacail has given him, and it lands on the hill of Marghe where the Ele sidh is found. Fiacail then rejoins Finn and the two hear great lamentation within the sidh because Finn's lance has killed the one responsible for the murders, the one who was in love with the girl and who killed one suitor each year out of jealousy. What is more, in order to retrieve his lance, Finn seizes one of the women from the mound and frees her only in exchange for her promise to bring him back his weapon.

After that, Finn and Fiacail compete with each other by performing various feats. The text, which is very obscure, leads us to believe that we are witnessing Fiacail giving his nephew a warrior's initiation. And then one night Finn surprises three women in the midst of their lamentations over the mound of hill of Slanga. When they notice him, they disappear into the mound, but not quickly enough. Finn, who has developed a taste for this sort of exploit, catches one of them by the brooch on her garment, which he pulls off. "Then the woman went after him and begged him to return the brooch from her cloak. She said that it wasn't proper for her to return to the sidh with such a mark of shame upon her, and she promised a reward."

Because the manuscript breaks off at this point, we will never know what the woman-fairy promises. We can guess that it involves magic powers, such as being able to heal the wounded by bringing them a drink of water. In return for this, Finn must give her back her brooch.

We can, however, make up for the gap in the *Finn's Childhood* manuscript by looking at the *Battle of Cnuch* text, already cited, which is part of the *Leabhar na h'Uidre*. Having gathered together the remaining members of the O'Baicsne clan to which he belongs, Finn presents himself before his maternal grandfather, Tagd: "He offered him the choice between a battle, a single combat, and the complete payment of what was due by law for the murder of Cumall. Tagd responded that he would like a legal judgment." And as a result of this judgment, Finn comes into possession of the fortress of Almu, which Tagd is required to give him. After this the clan of Morna "paid Finn the compensation owed by Goll for having killed Cumall." That is how Finn is able to gather together the Fiana and seek adventure.

The *Finn's Childhood* narrative has the merit of plunging us directly into the atmosphere characteristic of the Leinster cycle. It is a much less realistic atmosphere than we find in the Ulster cycle, much less colored by archaisms, and clearly the testimony of a different Irish society, perhaps influenced by contact with the Britons. What is more, we can see a very clear inclination toward fairy tale on the part of this cycle's storytellers. The old gods enter into the lives of humans, but no longer in their divine aspects. They have become fairies and enchanters. And no doubt this is what explains the persistence of this type of story in the folklore, because fairies and enchanters are the best intermediaries popular wisdom can find for linking the real and the imaginary worlds.

Finn and the Phantoms

This story[15] of modest dimensions is characteristic of the care taken by the Leinster Cycle authors to mix the supernatural with the quotidian and bring the greatest possible number of colorful elements into the telling of the hero's adventures. Here we have, quite simply, the arrival of human beings into the Other World that might always be there without us noticing it. This inevitably leads us to think of the adventures of the knights of the Round Table in their quest for the Grail, spending their nights in enchanted castles where very often very unpleasant misadventures happen to them, as with Gawain in the Dangerous Castle, or even Perceval after his first visit to the castle of the Grail.

Finn, in the company of his son Oisin and Cailte—one of his most faithful warriors and also his foster son—seeks shelter for the night in a sparsely populated region. All three arrive in front of a house they have never seen before; cries and moans are coming from it. A giant stands before the door, a giant whose description strangely resembles that of the peasant encountered by Yvain, near the Barenton fountain, in Chrétien de Troyes's *Chevalier au Lion*.

The giant bids them welcome and builds them a fire out of elderwood—which, of course, puts off terrible smoke. The three Fiana then notice some monstrous figures in the house: an old woman, completely black, with three heads, "one which cried, one which laughed, and one which slept," along with "a headless man with a single eye on his chest." The giant asks the old woman to offer their guests some entertainment. From one side of the house rise nine bodies, and from the other side, nine heads; this whole lovely assembly begins to utter horrible cries. The giant then kills Finn's horse, cuts it up, and has it cooked on a skewer. Finn refuses this food, which makes the giant terribly angry. The fire goes out. "Finn was squeezed into the corner, shaken and beaten. That is how they spent the whole night crying. . . . They [Oisin and Cailte] would not leave Finn, so that they remained stretched out on the ground and they fell into lethargy." Now, in the morning, when they come out of their stupor, they find nothing other than woods around them. The house has disappeared. Finn's horse is alive and well. Finn performs the *teinn laida* (illumination of the song), puts his thumb into his mouth, and has a revelation about what has happened: "In truth," he says, "the three phantoms of the Valley of Yews assailed us. They are the ones responsible for this outrage in order to avenge their sister . . . killed by us."

The Pursuit of Gilla the Tough One

This story,[16] probably quite recent, has for its main hero Diarmaid O'Duibhne, and marks a certain evolution in the Finn cycle. The world of the fairies and supernatural beings is still the same as that of the Tuatha de Danann, but the atmosphere is more like that of a fairy tale. Additionally, this narrative has satiric intentions: We have the impression that it is a parody, as if the author wanted to delight his audience with meaningless adventures in which the famous Fiana are not always given the best role.

One day Finn and his troop see a curious figure arriving, carrying an iron club and leading an extremely ugly horse whose hoofs make enormous pieces of mud fly up from the ground. The man says his name is Gilla the Tough One and offers Finn his services. Finn accepts, and Gilla leads his horse to pasture in the middle of the Fiana's horses. Now, the horse devours the other horses and the Fiana try to bring it under control. Twenty-eight of them mount the horse but are not able to make it budge.

Gilla then threatens the Fiana with a geis. They want to get down off the horse but are not able to. They beg Finn to come to their aid, and Finn asks Liagan to grab the horse's tail. But the horse rushes into the sea, carrying on its back the twenty-eight men—and Liagan, who can no longer let go of its tail.

Finn decides to follow the horse, but the Fiana's only remaining boat is in bad shape. Here we see the author's intention of presenting the Fiana as warriors very much in decline. Luckily, two young men appear, magicians, one of whom can produce boats with a simple wave of his wand. Finn entrusts Ireland to his son Oisin and launches out to sea with a few men in pursuit of the fantastic horse.

They arrive in an unknown land and have hardly landed before Diarmaid rushes off all alone into a very dense forest. He kills a doe, which he roasts, and builds himself a hut out of branches where he can pass the night. The next day a magician challenges him to fight. They fight all day long, and that evening the magician jumps into a well and disappears. The following day the magician comes back. They fight again, but in the evening the magician jumps into the well again, and this time Diarmaid follows him.

They come to a castle. It is clear that this is a castle from the Other World, in the underground universe of the mounds, the well here serving as a passage between the world of the living and that of the dead. Diarmaid kills the fourteen castle guards, then lies down before the door and goes to sleep. He is awakened by a stranger, who invites him to follow him. Diarmaid then learns that he is in the Tir Fohin, the "country under the sea." His host explains to him that he used to be king but was driven from his throne by an ambitious brother, and that Gilla is his friends' magician. Diarmaid offers to fight the usurper, and his host joyfully accepts.

Dairmaid succeeds in defeating the usurper and making him return the throne to his host. The next day he and the king go to find Gilla again, who greets them very warmly.

Meanwhile Finn and the other Fiana have disembarked near the castle of the King of Light, where they are well received. When the great King of the World attacks the castle, he is driven back by the Fiana. But the daughter of the King of the World has fallen in love with Finn, whom she rejoins after fleeing from her home. The King of the World has her brought back by a magician. Goll and Oscar follow the magician and set the girl free.

The Fiana then find Diarmaid again at Gilla's castle. According to one version of this story, Gilla frees the Fiana whom his horse carried off and we learn that he is really Avarrach, son of d'Alchad Ioldatach (of the Multicolored Clothes). As his domain is the "Promised

Country," we might wonder if this isn't, in fact, Mananann, son of Lir, who rules over the Land of Promise.

However, Gilla returns to Ireland with the Fiana and spends some time among them. Then one day he asks to go. The Fiana accompany him to the shore, and there he disappears all at once under the sea, which once more calls up Mananann, the knight of the sea, the one who rides the green prairies of the waves.

Diarmaid and Grainne

There is general agreement that in the story of Diarmaid and Grainne,[17] the most famous narrative in the Leinster cycle, we find one of the archetypes for the legend of Tristan and Iseult. The elements seem identical: a rivalry between the old king and the young warrior; the obligatory nature of the love potion that Tristan and Iseult drink and of the geis (taboo) that Grainne casts over Diarmaid; the solar symbolism of Iseult the Blonde and Grainne, whose name means "sun"; the violent deaths of Tristan and of Diarmaid in the same fatal and tragic atmosphere.

Along with the Cuchulainn epic, this is also one of the adventures that has remained alive the longest in popular memory, as much among the Scottish Gaels as among the Irish. But although it seems paradoxical, the oldest manuscripts have retained only a few fragments of the original story, while the oral traditions of the eighteenth century have allowed compilers like Campbell to draw from them a complete version still possessing an archaic aspect.

The story begins when the old king Finn wants to marry one more time. His choice for a bride is Grainne, the daughter of the high king of Ireland, Cormac Mac Airt. Grainne needs to be persuaded. She clearly has no desire whatsoever to marry Finn. According to the custom, she asks as a dowry "a pair of each wild animal" found in Ireland. Cailte, Finn's nephew, brings all the requested animals, and Grainne can no longer refuse.

Here the versions diverge. According to the earliest text, the *Yellow Book of Lecan (Y.B.L.)*, Finn takes Grainne as his wife, "and this was not a good thing, as there was no peace for them until their separation.

The girl hated Finn and her hatred was so great that she fell sick from it." It is then that Cormac gives a great feast to which he invites his son-in-law and all the Fiana. But in the eighteenth-century versions Grainne is not yet the wife of Finn, and it is during the wedding feast that the drama is to unfold.

After having been told the names of all the Fiana, Grainne calls her servant and asks her to go find a cup made of gold and precious stones, which she fills with a magic potion.[18] She has the cup taken to Finn and to the Fiana chiefs. All fall asleep after drinking from it, except for Oisin and Diarmaid. Oisin, the Ossian of Mac Pherson, is the son of Finn. Diarmaid is the grandson of one of Finn's relations. His foster father is Oengus, the Mac Oc, son of Dagda. Following an accident, Diarmaid's foster brother died and was transformed into a magic wild boar, with this taboo on Diarmaid: He may live as long as the boar does, but not one day more, and the boar will be the cause of his death, from which it follows that Diarmaid is strictly forbidden from killing any wild boars.[19]

Thus Grainne remains alone with Oisin and Diarmaid. She proposes that Oisin run away with her. Oisin gives no reply, taking refuge behind a prohibition: He cannot take a woman who has belonged to or is promised to Finn, because Finn is his father. Grainne doesn't insist, and turns instead toward Diarmaid, proposing the same thing to him. Dairmaid refuses. Then Grainne gets angry and cries, "I place you under a geis of danger and destruction, o Diarmaid, if you don't carry me off with you out of this house, this night, before Finn and the Irish chiefs wake up from their sleep."[20]

Here, then, the terrible geis is cast, which can hardly be translated as simply "taboo" or "ban." It is not merely a matter of a formula. It is a true spell, a *charm*, with so much power that those who shrink from it are considered outlaws and are punished by the gods. The obligatory and fatal nature of this geis appears in all Irish literature without exception and goes back to complex ancient beliefs and druidic rituals handed down since the beginning of time, in which we again find analogies to shamanism. That is why Cuchulainn, whose name (or rather, nickname) means "dog of Culann" is strictly forbidden to eat dog; the king Conaire the Great must not kill birds, because the people of the sidh who are his ancestors appear in the form of birds; Diarmaid is not allowed to kill wild boars. In these beliefs we must certainly recognize the traces of totemism. Membership in a clan requires respect for the animal symbol of that clan, the mythic ancestor, and any violation of the related taboo constitutes a self-destructive act. It is only during the clan's ritual feast that the ban is lifted and violations are not only allowed, but required (compare this to the excesses of *mi-carême* in the middle of Lent, or the Roman saturnalia, or the fools' festivals of the Middle Ages). Additionally, the hero placed under the patronage of the clan's mythic ancestor identifies with it in some way when he receives his name or nickname. He is thus transformed, by an act of magic or shamanism, into the animal that serves as his emblem; he is part of that animal race, and he cannot attack any animal of that race without undermining the natural equilibrium on which his own life depends.

But the geis that Grainne casts over Diarmaid is something else again, and no doubt this is what makes this affair particularly interesting. First of all, there is the similarity between Grainne's geis and Tristan and Iseult's love potion. For a long time this love potion was seen as a simple witch's brew—that is, just one more aphrodisiac like those we find in the tales of sorcery handed down in folklore. This is a valid but insufficient explanation. The obligatory nature of this potion (unlimited in the "courtship" version, reduced to three years in the "common" version) leads us to think that it is a *charm*, which takes the form of a seasoned wine contained in a goblet. Let us remember that Iseult's servant Brengwain, who *takes the wrong bowl* (it seems), is none other than Branwen, the daughter of Llyr, a kind of Welsh goddess of love. And if we turn again to the story of Tristan, we find that from the time she first sees him, Iseult is madly in love with him, and that, in her rage and terrible disappointment at seeing herself *bought* by him for King Mark's sake, it is she who provokes Tristan by means of the love potion. Tristan, who up until this time is completely indifferent toward Iseult, is *obliged* to love her despite his vow of fidelity to Mark and his relationship with him. Let us translate this on the psychological level: Wounded by Morholt (in the thigh, like the Fisher King in the Grail legend), Tristan has lost his masculinity. Symbolically, Tristan is the moon, a dead and decaying star, while Iseult,[21]—that is, the sun— revitalizes the one she chooses, returning to him his masculine strength and place in the social hierarchy, elevating him as well to royalty, since he will share with Mark the sovereignty that she represents.[22] Thus,

Iseult's role is essential, because it is upon her that the whole framework of the myth rests,[23] as it is upon Grainne, and Grainne alone, that the Irish legend depends.

This is all to say how important the role of the woman, both sociologically and mythologically, is in Celtic thought. The Celtic woman is free to love whomever she pleases, to possess goods, to take command. She is protected if her husband abandons her, she is respected, she is even feared because here is a being necessarily ambiguous, good and evil, the mother who gives life. Parturition is always something mysterious and disquieting, and thus the woman acquires a sacred nature. And if she gives life, materially speaking, she can become the one who gives a second life, that of the spirit, as becomes evident in the Welsh legend of Keridwen absorbing Gwyon Bach ("the killing," that is, making his former aspect disappear) and giving him back a new life under the aspect of the druid Taliesin.[24] The woman is thus the instrument of regeneration, of re-creation, the creation of the second man, the real man who sleeps within the deceptive appearance of the first. Eve gives birth to man, but this man is rough, imperfect, and he doesn't know how to use his brain. The Virgin Mary, another incarnation of Eve,[25] but immaculate this time, gives birth to a second man, the highest of spiritual beings, Christ. This idea is as old as the world and does not belong only to the Celts, but it is all to their credit that they illustrated it in the astonishing images of these legends in which the woman plays her true role as *Mater prima et secunda*.[26] She is the crucible in which the personality of man is formed, but she chooses this man, and her choice is terrible, inescapable. Then she becomes initiator, the transformer of energy.[27] We would do well to consider this admirable model now when there is so much talk about women's liberation and her "reorientation" in the modern world.

Thus, Grainne has chosen Diarmaid. Moreover, she explains to him that she has been in love with him since the day she first saw him at a great gathering before the king of Ireland: "In my room with its good view, through my blue glass windows, I noticed you and I admired you. And I turned the light of my eyes toward you that day, and since then, I have never given my love to anyone but you and I will not do it for anyone else."

Thus the process is in motion. Diarmaid asks Oisin and the other Fiana for advice. They are unanimous is telling him he has no choice.

So Diarmaid flees with Grainne, followed by Finn, who is seized with jealousy and rage. The Fiana accompany Finn reluctantly, and we get the feeling that they would protect Diarmaid if they were able to. Diarmaid manages to escape and takes refuge in a cave, always in the company of Grainne. An old woman serves as their guardian. This woman encounters the king of the Fiana, who hypocritically promises to marry her if she agrees to betray Diarmaid. "The old sorceress agreed, put her cloak in the salt, and entered the cave. Diarmaid asked her what had happened to her. 'I swear to you,' she said, 'I have never seen a day so cold and with such storms.'"[28] She then begins to sing a magnificent poem about the cold ("Cold, cold, cold is this night, the plain of Lurg, the snow is higher than a mountain, the doe can no longer find her food"), which ends with this advice dictated by Finn: "To get up out of the quilt and the featherbed would be madness for you, so much ice is there at each ford."

But once the old woman leaves, "Grainne touched the cloak, put her finger to her mouth, and discovered the curious taste of salt." She understands the treachery and flees with Diarmaid. It is then that they notice a boat on the shore, and in this boat "a companion in a strange garment, a cloak with wide yellow folds which hung from his shoulders. It was Oengus of the sidh, the foster father of Diarmaid, who had come to help him out of the shameful situation he was in with Finn and the Fiana of Ireland." Oengus proposes taking them very far away under the hem of his cloak. Diarmaid refuses to leave and arranges a rendezvous with Oengus for later on. Oengus takes Grainne away under the folds of his cloak,[29] and Diarmaid goes off to find the Fiana, but doesn't want to follow them before they answer certain questions. Finn engages him in combat, but thanks to the magical protection of Oengus, Diarmaid is invulnerable. The Fiana pass by him without even seeing him. Then he rejoins Oengus and Grainne. Oengus gives his adopted son this advice: "Never climb a tree that has only one trunk when you are fleeing from Finn. Do not go into a cave if there is only one entrance. Do not go to any island in the sea with only one channel between it and land. Do not eat in the place where you have cooked your food and do not sleep in the place where you have eaten. And no matter where you sleep, do not let the sunrise find you there."[30] After which Oengus leaves them, and the two lead an unhappy existence. Diarmaid lets his anger explode in a famous poem, the "Reproach of Diarmaid":

You have put me in dire distress, o Grainne, you have behaved grievously with me. You have taken me from the palace of a king to pass my days in exile, like a night owl, mourning my lost happiness. I am like the stag or the doe, I pass my days in forgotten valleys. . . . Because of you, I have lost my lands for good and my white-sailed boat on the sea. . . . I have lost the love and esteem of the men of Ireland and all the Fiana, I have lost honor and right. Ireland and all those found there have abandoned me, because of your love.[31]

We then learn, according to what follows in the poem, that since their flight, Diarmaid and Grainne have never lived as husband and wife. Diarmaid so distrusts Grainne's ruse that he is afraid of her. This detail is developed in another fragment of the legend, which again bears a distinct resemblance to the story of Tristan. Grainne is walking next to Diarmaid. Suddenly, "a jet of clear water sprang up through the toes of her feet and struck her thigh. Then she said softly to herself, "A plague on you, luminous stain! You are more brazen than Diarmaid!"[32]

There is nearly the identical scene in Thomas's *Tristan*: Iseult of the White Hands is taking a walk with her brother Kaherdin and a spray of mud hits her thighs. She says that this muddy water has gone farther with her than any man's hand, which tells Kaherdin that the marriage between Tristan and Iseult of the White Hands has never been consummated.

However, Diarmaid asks Grainne to explain herself. She reproaches him for having never touched her. "Diarmaid responds, 'It is true, o Grainne, and even though for a long time I have kept myself from you for fear of Finn, I don't want to endure your reproaches any longer. Truly, it is difficult to trust women.' And it was thus that Diarmaid, the first,[33] made a woman of Grainne and became intimate with her."

Basically all that precedes this moment is only a slow catharsis during which Diarmaid refuses to admit anything, despite the revelation that takes the form of Grainne, the woman-sun. The metamorphosis is not without interest in understanding how Grainne finally manages to clear away the shadows from the darkest parts of Diarmaid's unconscious, over which the superego, largely constructed out of guilt, had become the tyrant, overshadowing the most instinctive impulses of the young warrior. The climactic conclusion, that release of sexual energy, represents the victory of the sun over the darkness.

That brings us to an admirable poem, *Duanaire Finn*, certainly one of the most beautiful love songs in Celtic literature, in which Grainne is watching over Diarmiad while he sleeps:

> Sleep a bit, a little bit, and fear nothing, man to whom I have given my love, Diarmaid, son of O'Duibhne.... I will stay and watch over you, a shield against battle from the west, my heart would break from grief if ever I lost sight of you. To separate us would be to separate mother from child, the body from the soul, warrior of the beautiful lake of German. The stag, in the east, doesn't sleep. He never stops bellowing there in the bushes full of black birds, he doesn't want to sleep. The doe without antlers doesn't sleep. She cries for her little spotted one, she runs in the underbrush, she doesn't sleep in her nest.... This evening, the grouse doesn't sleep in the moors beaten by the winds. On the hill, his cry is soft and clear. Near the streams, he doesn't sleep. Sleep a bit, a little bit, and fear nothing, man to whom I have given my love, Diarmaid, son of O'Duibhne.[34]

The storytellers have embellished the adventures of Diarmaid and Grainne and have tried to maximize the "suspense" and reversals in fortune. Finn has not given up his pursuit of the two lovers, and according to the *Duanaire Finn* it continues for seven years. He even makes peace with the clan of Morna, responsible for his father's death in the Battle of Cnuch, and three sons of the Morna clan try in vain to capture the fugitives. As for Oengus, he does his best to make peace between Diarmaid and the Fiana. Thus we arrive at the denouement. There was

> An underground cave where they [Diarmaid and Grainne] lived for a long time. Each night they went out to make a raid and that is how they found . . . Oisin alone. They took him prisoner and brought him to their cave. There Oisin cut some shavings from a

lance ... and threw them into the current of the spring,
so well that they reached the Feale ford where Finn
had his camp. Then Finn took the shavings in his hand
and said, "It is Oisin who did this." And Finn's men
followed the stream to its source and discovered the
cave.[35]

Then Finn, whose rage turns to genius, makes his dog Foghaid
give the cry of the hunt. Now, among Diarmaid's taboos is this one:
He cannot hear the cry of the dogs in pursuit of prey without joining
in the hunt. In this case it is Diarmaid who is the prey, and he is well
and truly flushed out. Finn makes a show of reconciling with him and
asks him to go hunt the magical wild boar of Ben Gulbain, that is, the
very wild boar with which Diarmaid is identified. Now, another of
Diarmaid's taboos is to never refuse a request made by one of his companions. Thus, here we have Diarmaid facing his destiny.

The beast woke from her sleep and looked down into
the valley, and she saw the Fiana troops in the east
and the west coming toward her. The sight of these
warriors annoyed her, the wild boar of the sidh. Longer
than a lance were her tusks. Sharper than the *gai bolga*
[the lance of the Tuatha de Danann] were her fangs.
Diarmaid, son of O'Duibhne, threw his lance at the
wild boar; the weapon broke against a tree, but after
having pierced the boar. . . . Then he drew his old
sword from its sheath, and the beast died at the hand
of Diarmaid.[36]

Furious at seeing Diarmaid safe and sound, Finn then asks him to
go measure the wild boar. "He returned. It was a dangerous act. He
measured the wild boar, but the rough and venomous bristles wounded
the foot of the warrior ferocious in battle. Then he fell on the path, the
son of O'Duibhne, who never consented to treason, on the ground,
beside the wild boar."[37]
But the drama is not over, because Finn has the power to heal the
wounded by bringing them a drink of water himself. Diarmaid pleads
with Finn to bring him water from the spring, but Finn refuses. Then
Diarmaid reminds the king of the Fiana, of all the feats that he has

performed with him, and Oscar, son of Oisin, furious at seeing Finn taking such a stubborn stand in this special case, makes his grandfather get some water. "He filled his hands with water, but he hadn't gotten halfway to Diarmaid when he let the water run through his fingers. Then he said it was impossible for him to bring water."[38]

Oscar makes him go back again, but Finn again manages to let the water escape. "I swear by my weapons," says Oscar, "if you don't bring water quickly, o Finn, one of us won't leave this hill, whether it is you or me." Then "Finn returned to the fountain a third time because of Oscar's words and brought the water to Diarmaid at that moment when his life had just left his body."[39]

All the Fiana mourn and bury the unfortunate Diarmaid.

"When the sad Grainne saw that he was under the earth, she lost consciousness and color, and she fell senseless to the ground."[40] As for Finn, satisfied with his cruel vengeance, he concludes hypocritically, "Let us leave this hill for fear that Oengus and the Tuatha de Danann will attack us. And *even though we had no part in the death of Diarmaid*, Oengus will have nothing better to do than accuse us of it."[41]

The conclusion varies according to the version. According to the eighteenth-century version, Oengus comes with Grainne to lament the fate of his adopted son. Grainne informs Diarmaid's sons and sends them to avenge their father's death upon Finn himself, whom the Fiana refuse to protect. Finn gives up the fight, makes honorable amends for the death of Diarmaid, and manages to persuade Grainne to live with him. But according to certain allusions in various poems and narratives, it's likely that in the ancient version, Grainne died of sorrow and was buried in the same tomb as Diarmaid, which inevitably brings us back to the deaths of Tristan and Iseult. No further evidence is necessary to prove that the Tristan legend is Irish in origin (Iseult the Blonde is Irish); that it crossed through Wales (Tristan is Welsh) and British Cornwall (Mark's country) to end up in Armorique (the country of Iseult of the White Hands). It is the pan-Celtic legend par excellence, and it is contained implicitly in *Diarmaid and Grainne*.

But outside of the many ways this legend can be interpreted, there is great literary beauty in the few fragments we possess of it and also a dramatic atmosphere of remarkable intensity throughout the legend. And since a comparison with *Tristan and Iseult* is suggested from one end of the text to the other, let us conclude this brief study with the hope that *Diarmaid and Grainne* will be appreciated in the same way as the tragic story of the Tintagel lovers, and as an equal to it.[42]

The Death of Finn

Finn and the Fiana[43] organize a huge hunt on the Femen plain, well known for its sidh, and have invited nearly all the clans to it. But they find no game in the woods that day, and the next day is just the same, which is unbearable for great hunters like the Fiana. The third day Finn leads his men into the neighboring marshes and over the surrounding hills, a wasted effort because the game seems to have completely disappeared. When one of his men asks him what hero lies buried here, Finn answers that it is Failbe Findmaisch, who was killed during a hunt for the giant wild boar of Formael. Finn chants a poem to the glory of Failbe, and decides that the next day they will hunt this formidable boar.

While waiting, they have to pass the night. They go to stay with one of the Fiana, who gives them a lavish reception, and over the course of the feasting Finn comes around, describing how he obtained the magic horn that he always carries with him.

One night when he found himself in a forest with Cailte and Oisin, a magic fog surrounded them, and in this fog they heard music, probably fairy music. All night long Finn, Cailte, and Oisin wandered about in order to keep themselves from succumbing to spells, and in the morning they discovered a black giant who gave them mead to drink out of a golden horn. This is the giant who made peace between Finn and Goll, of the Morna clan, and he stayed with Finn for a year, after which time he gave Finn the horn and left. And Finn added, "If you fill it with water, the water changes into a delicious mead."

But after recalling all these memories, Finn sinks into sadness. The rest of the night is spent feasting. The next day everyone prepares to go hunt the wild boar of Formael. The description of this hunt is strangely reminiscent of King Arthur's hunt for the Twrch Trwyth in the *Mabinogi* of *Kulhwch and Olwen*, and the boar's description as well: "It was very dark and inspired terror. Covered with bristles, bold, horrible, it had no ears, no tail, no testicles, but enormous and frightening tusks coming out of its huge head."

The Fiana rush upon the animal. The best hunters succumb to the furious creature's attacks. Finn begins to regret having undertaken this hunt, which is costing him so many men, when Oscar, his grandson, fights the boar with audacity and courage. He is even lucky enough to kill it, and the Fiana celebrate his victory. The animal's victims are buried, and Finn chants a funeral hymn over their graves.

Sadness seizes Finn once again. He realizes that he is old and no longer possesses his former strength. He decides to relinquish his powers and leave Ireland. Then the Fiana hold council and agree to keep Finn from going away. Each one of them will organize feasts in Finn's honor, which will prevent him from carrying out his plan.[44]

However, the one charged with preparing the first feast is a certain Fer-Tai, whose son, Fer-Li, is the grandson on his mother's side of Goll of the Morna clan—Finn's enemy, with whom he was once reconciled but has since killed. And to avenge his grandfather, Fer-Li plans a bit of treachery. With the help of his accomplices, he rushes in on Finn and his men during the feast. Constrained by the laws of hospitality, Fer-Tai defends Finn against his own son; Fer-Li's mother, Goll's daughter, intervenes, reproaching Fer-Li for his treason and ambush. Fer-Li leaves the house, threatening Finn with a battle the next day.

The enemies assemble their troops. Fer-Li rallies the Morna clan and the sons of Urgrui, wishing in some way to begin another Battle of Cnuch. An attempt to make peace fails and fighting begins, violent and relentless. Finn throws himself into the fray

> Like a cruel and furious bull who has been badly bitten, or like a lion whose cubs have been wounded, or like a tumultuous tidal wave which once rushed like a deluge down the heights of huge mountains, breaking and smashing all that it touched. He made three assaults . . . like the honeysuckle which clings to a tree, like a woman embracing her son, and the smashing of thighs and of broken shins, of skulls under the blade of his sword, was like the wind from a blacksmith's bellows, or like the roar of dry trees that crack, or like ice under the hoofs of galloping horses. And the demons of the red mouth, and the spirits of the pale

face, and the ghosts of the valley, and the demons of
the air, and the hideous phantoms of the sky let out
piercing cries.[45]

And that is how Finn eliminates most of his enemies. The only ones
remaining before him are Fer-Tai, Fer-Li, and the five sons of Urgrui.
Finn and Fer-Li engage in single combat. Finn kills his adversary, but
just as when Arthur faces Mordret, he himself is mortally wounded.
Nevertheless, he finds the courage to fight against Fer-Tai, who wants
to avenge his son. He receives another wound from Fer-Tai's sword,
but still manages to kill him.

It is then that the five sons of Urgrui, "his eternal enemies," come
before him. Finn is weak and exhausted, and since the Egerton 1782
manuscript is incomplete, we have to turn to a fragment preserved in
the Egerton 92 manuscript.[46] Finn finds himself alone on the shore of
the Boyne. He has reached the place called the "Finn's Leap." There,
trying to jump, he falls, and his forehead strikes a rock; his brains spill
out and he dies. Then "the Boyne fishermen discover him. They were
four in number: the three sons of Urgrui and Aiclech, son of Dubdriu.
They found him and Aiclech cut off his head. And the sons of Urgrui
killed Aiclech. They carried Finn's head off with them."

Thus, the two versions agree on the fact that the sons of Urgrui are
present at the time of Finn's death. We have come full circle, and the
death that befell Cumall once more strikes the clan of O'Baicsne. Finn
Mac Cumail, the formidable chief of the Fiana, a kind of hunter-god,
purger of monsters, dies in sadness and silence.

But is he really dead? Gods don't die. Neither do fairy creatures.
And Finn will remain in the hearts of the Irish and Scottish for a long
time. For many centuries they will sing of him over the course of those
evenings when they drink beer and, crossing themselves, tell the stories of fairies and phantoms. And then, one day, a certain Mac Pherson
will inherit him and make him known to the entire world under the
name of Fingal, with his son, Ossian, as they wander forever in the
Caledonian mists under the mysterious foliage of trees or in some ruined castle. And again, the circle will be complete, but this time, who
would claim that Finn is dead?

The Story of Mongan

It is difficult to assign this narrative[47] to any one of the Irish epic cycles because, in fact, it belongs to all of them. Certainly, Mongan was an authentic Ulster king in the seventh century, but we know nearly nothing about him, and he was immediately integrated into a complex series of mythological frameworks. Moreover, outside of very clear allusions to confrontations between Gaels and Vikings, which occurred continually over a long period, it would be futile to search here for the smallest reference to any historical event. Even though marked by Ulster, it doesn't belong to the Conchobar or Cuchulainn cycle. What's more, we are dealing with a very anticlerical, indeed even outright anti-Christian, narrative—astonishing to say the least, since we know that it was transcribed by monks. Thus, it may represent quite an ancient mythological tradition rendered in a more recent language; this is all the more likely since the narrator solemnly claims that Mongan's true father is Mananann, one of the Tuatha de Danann chiefs. But another narrative, contained within an earlier manuscript,[48] makes Mongan, no matter who his flesh-and-blood father is, into a sort of reincarnation of Finn Mac Cumail, the king of the Fiana and father of Oisin-Ossian. Thus, it seems most fitting to place *The Story of Mongan* in the Leinster cycle.

The story begins when Fiachna the Blonde,[49] a descendant of Niall, leaves Ireland to go to Lochlann, that is, Scandinavia. The king of Lochlann is sick, and according to his doctors and sorcerers he can only be healed by eating a cow with white skin and red ears. The only cow answering to this description belongs to a sorceress named Caillech Dubh (black sorceress). But she will agree to give up her cow only in exchange for four others, and on Fiachna the Blonde's guarantee. It is then that a messenger comes to find Fiachna and announces to him that he has been chosen to be king of Ulster. Thus Fiachna returns to Ireland to take possession of his realm.

A year passes. One day Fiachna hears cries of distress in front of the fortress and orders his men to go see what is happening. They bring him Caillech Dubh, who complains to him that she has been tricked by the king of Lochlann and demands compensation from him by virtue of the fact that Fiachna served as guarantor for her. Fiachna proposes several cows to her, but the sorceress refuses. She asks him to

151

go make war on the king of Lochlann. A bit annoyed, but bound by his oath as guarantor, Fiachna assembles his warriors and launches his expedition.

"For three days, they fought, and the fighting turned to the Lochlann king's advantage. Three hundred warriors fell under Fiachna's blows, but a monstrous ram was released from the Lochlann king's tent, and that day, three hundred warriors were killed because of that ram." Seeing his troops falling before his very eyes, Fiachna resolves to go fight the ram himself, but his men want to prevent him from doing this. And while he is discussing it with them, he sees arriving "an immense and solitary warrior. He wore a great brightly colored cloak, a brooch of white silver on his breast, a satin shirt over his white skin, a crown of gold on his hair and two gold sandals on his feet." The new arrival asks Fiachna what he will give him for getting rid of the monstrous ram. Fiachna cries, "On my word of honor, whatever you ask for, you will have, provided that I have it at my disposal!"

This type of oath is common throughout the Celtic tradition, and totally commits the one who pronounces it. This is what will become the *constraining gift* in the Arthurian legends. Of course, at this moment a promise is made to give something without knowing what it will be, which can be very dangerous. Indeed, the unknown warrior demands an extraordinary compensation from Fiachna: "Give me that gold ring that you have on your finger so I can go to Ireland and sleep with your wife." Obviously, Fiachna tries to back out, but the stranger insists and reveals himself: "This will not be a bad thing for you, because a glorious child will be conceived by me, and you will name him Mongan the Blonde, son of Fiachna the Blonde. I will go there under your aspect, in such a way that your wife will suspect nothing. I am Mananann, son of Lir, and you, you will have the Lochlann realm, as well as that of the Saxons and that of the Bretons."

Now we can understand the origin of the episode in the Arthurian romances involving the conception of the future king Arthur by the king Uther Pendragon through the use of Merlin's magic.[50] In the same way Mongan's conception somewhat echoes the troubled circumstances preceding the birth of the hero Cuchulainn, the son of the god Lugh, or possibly of his maternal uncle, Conchobar (depending on the version used). Great legendary figures always have extraordinary births. In any case Fiachna is obliged to consent. Then the one claiming to be

Mananann releases an enormous dog out from under his cloak,[51] specifying that it is this animal who will defeat the monstrous ram. Then, equipped with the gold ring, Mananann goes off to Ireland under the aspect of Fiachna. "He slept with Fiachna's wife, and that very night, she became pregnant. As for the ram and Lochlann's three hundred warriors, they were felled by the dog. Thus Fiachna took possession of the realm of Lochlann, the realm of the Saxons and the realm of the Bretons."

We must remember that the country of Lochlann, which denotes geographically all of Scandinavia, or at least the regions occupied by the Scandinavians, has mythological resonance in Irish narratives. It is the mythic "North," a frontier zone between the visible and invisible, from which the Tuatha de Danann brought back science, druidism, and magic. We can hardly be astonished, then, at the fantastic battles that go on there, in particular the respective roles of the monstrous ram and Mananann's dog. As for Mananann's desire to sleep with the wife of the Ulster king, it corresponds to the wish to secure for the family judged worthy of ruling the world a divine element allowing them to establish—or try to—an earthly society parallel to the ideal society of the Other World. These ideas are perfectly in keeping with what we know of druidic beliefs, which again demonstrates the archaic nature of the framework upon which this narrative is built.

However, after compensating the "black sorceress" by giving her seven fortresses and a hundred head of cattle, Fiachna the Blonde returns to Ireland. His wife, who is pregnant, gives birth to a son, whom he names Mongan the Blonde. On the same day the wife of his steward, whose name is An Damh (the deer), also gives birth to a son, who is given the name of Mac an Daimh (son of the deer), while the wife of a warrior named Fiachna the Black gives birth to a daughter who will be named Dubh-Lacha (black duck). And, "when Mongan was three nights old, Mananann came to him and carried him off to the Land of Promise,[52] and vowed that he would not let him leave again until he had reached the age of sixteen years." In this way we learn the source of the magic powers that Mongan has at his disposal later in his adult life.

During this period in which Mongan is "faraway," many events befall Ulster. Fiachna the Black, ambitious and disloyal, exploits the weakness of Fiachna the Blonde's troops to turn them against him, kill him, and take control of the realm. And when Mongan returns to

Ireland at the end of sixteen years, it is to learn that Fiachna the Black has usurped the throne. To avoid war, Mongan agrees to a compromise: He cedes half of Ulster to Fiachna the Black, but in return he receives the hand in marriage of Dubh-Lacha, the daughter of his presumed father's murderer. And the two spouses are united by a passionate love.

But "one day while Mongan and his wife were playing chess [*fidchell*], they saw a little cleric dressed in dark black at the door of the room. And the cleric said to Mongan, 'This idleness which you enjoy so much isn't fitting for an Ulster king. You do not even think of avenging your father on Fiachna the Black. Whatever Dubh-Lacha may think of it, it is the just thing for you to decide. Because Fiachna the Black only has a small army at his disposal just now. Come with me, let's burn Fiachna's fortress and kill him!'" It's a Cornelian situation, but it doesn't seem to prompt a crisis of conscience in either Mongan Rodrigue or Dubh-Lacha Chimène. Mongan leads an expedition, kills Fiachna the Black, and now reigns over all of Ulster. But we must be aware, as the narrator says, that "the little cleric who carried out this treason was the great and powerful Mananann."

Mongan organizes his realm and, to prove his generosity, makes a "tour of Ireland" in order to visit the other kings and present them with lavish gifts. That is how he arrives in Leinster, where he is warmly received by King Brandubh (black crow). But the following morning, "when Mongan awoke, he saw fifty cows with red ears and a white calf beside each one of them." Brandubh notices them right away and, after having involved Mongan in an apparently meaningless conversation, concludes by saying to him, "On my word of honor, this herd is worth as much as your wife, Dubh-Lacha, because she is the most beautiful woman in all of Ireland. And this herd is certainly the most beautiful in all of Ireland. I would not give it to anyone, except perhaps to the one to whom I am bound in unconditional friendship."

Mongan wants the herd so much that he immediately links himself to Brandubh through an oath of *unconditional friendship*. We can easily imagine what such an oath can lead to, but Mongan doesn't realize this. He returns to Ulster with the herd, and a little while later he sees the king of Leinster surrounded by his followers arriving at his fortress. Obviously, Brandubh demands the herd's equivalent, in this case, Dubh-Lacha.

Under the threat of being forever dishonored and losing his soul, Mongan must cede Dubh-Lacha to the king of Leinster. The latter hurries back to his fortress, very pleased with how well his trap has worked. But Dubh-Lacha has no intention of letting herself be taken so easily. She extracts a promise from Brandubh that he will not touch her before a year has passed. Trapped into this by another trick, the king of Leinster is obliged to agree to what Dubh-Lacha demands.

During this time the unfortunate Mongan finds himself prey to the darkest and gloomiest of thoughts in a state of utter prostration. Then his steward, Mac an Daimh, reproaches him violently. We must admit that Mac an Daimh has good reason to be hard on his king: his own wife is Dubh-Lacha's attendant, and the latter, in leaving for Leinster, took her with her. Mac an Daimh comes before Mongan and says to him, "Things are bad for you, o Mongan, and unfortunate was your stay in the Land of Promise, since you learned nothing there but how to eat and amuse yourself with stupid things. As for me, it is hard for me to have my wife held prisoner in Leinster, because I am not bound by unconditional friendship to the king's steward as you have bound yourself to the Leinster king, in such a way that you are incapable of taking back your wife!"

These justified reproaches wake up Mongan a bit. He says to his steward, "Let us go to the cellar where we have left a great basket in which there's a clod of Irish earth and another one from Scotland. You will put the basket on your back and I will climb into it. That way, when the king of Leinster asks for news of me, they can tell him that I have one foot in Ireland and one foot in Scotland, and he will say to himself that as long as that's so, he has nothing to fear from me!" Here is one of the finest examples of Jesuit casuistry. . . . But that is what happens. Mongan and Mac an Daimh set out for Leinster.

They arrive in the Liffey valley just as a great festival is taking place. A great crowd is in the process of breaking up, and the king of Leinster is returning to his residence. Then they notice a cleric by the name of Tibraide, the priest of the Camain church, carrying four gospels on his head, while another cleric walks beside him with a great missal on his back. The two of them are chanting their prayers, to the great wonderment of Mongan and Mac an Daimh, who have never seen anything like this before—showing that the two men are not Christians, which shouldn't come as much of a surprise. Mongan asks his steward if he understands what the others are mumbling with so much conviction. Mac an Daimh answers, "Not in the least, except that the man carrying the missal on his back keeps repeating *amen, amen!*"

Then Mongan makes a river appear with a bridge over it. Very surprised at finding water running there where they didn't know there was any, Tibraide and his cleric climb onto the bridge. But the bridge breaks and the two men are carried off by the current, while Mongan seizes the gospels. "As long as they go on down the river, we will have some peace," says Mongan. And taking the form of Tibraide, and giving Mac an Daimh the aspect of the cleric, they head toward Brandubh's fortress.

The king of Leinster, who knows Tibraide very well, has them enter and uses this occasion to ask them to hear Dubh-Lacha's confession. The two cronies need no persuading. They go to Dubh-Lacha and drive away all the annoying bystanders. We can easily imagine what sort of confession Dubh-Lacha gives to the false Tibraide, whom she knows perfectly well to be her husband, while Mac an Daimh leads his own wife off into a discreet corner.

However, a problem arises. Along comes the true Tibraide with his cleric, knocking on the fortress door. The guards are full of admiration: "We have never seen a year in which Tibraide was more powerful than this year. There is one Tibraide inside and one Tibraide outside!" Mongan takes advantage of the situation. Still disguised as Tibraide, he says to the guards: "That's right. Mongan has come here disguised as me. Go after him and I will reward you. Kill the clerics whom you see around Tibraide, because they are Mongan's warriors who have been changed into this form!" A confused struggle follows. "The king of Leinster pursued them and Tibraide could only flee to the church of Cell Camain. No one out of the nine survivors was not wounded." The adventure seems to turn to comical, especially when the king of Leinster understands what has really happened and begins to lament, fearing that he has killed Tibraide's clerics.

Nevertheless, Mongan and his steward have returned to Ulster. And Mongan falls back into his torpor. At the end of three months Mac an Daimh comes to find him and reproach him for his incompetence. The two of them start off on another expedition of the same kind, fooling the king of Leinster and his guards, and sleeping with their respective wives. That's how it goes every three months, which is clearly not unconnected to the principal holidays of the druidic year: Imbolc at the beginning of February, Beltane at the beginning of May, Lugnasad at the beginning of August. But now the fourth festival, the Samhain, is approaching at the beginning of November, which is both the "end of the summer," and the "new year." The reprieve obtained by Dubh-Lacha cannot last any longer, and the king of Leinster proclaims that he is going to marry the one whom he has won in the game of unconditional friendship. This announcement wakes up Mongan one more time. Accompanied by Mac an Daimh, he wanders into the Liffey valley, wondering how he is going to manage to *legally* recover his wife and the wife of Mac an Diamh at the same time.

That's when they pass a mill run by an old woman named Cuimne. "This woman was as big as a weaving loom; with her she had a huge dog called Brothar, who wore a rope around its neck, and who licked the millstones. And they also saw an old mare with a large basket on her back, who carried the grain and the flour." In seeing this Mongan begins to laugh, and thinks of a plan that can't fail. He says to the old woman, "If you want to follow my advice, I will give you the aspect of a young woman, and you will appear to be my wife when I go before the king of Leinster." The mill woman, who understands none of this, agrees to try the experiment. Then Mongan calls upon all the magic he has learned in the Land of Promise.

> Thanks to a charm, he struck the dog, who then became minuscule and completely white, the most beautiful dog in the world, with a silver chain and a gold bell which could be held in a man's palm. Then he struck the old woman who became a young woman, the most beautiful ever in the world, that is, Ibhell of the glowing cheeks, the daughter of the king of Munster. He himself took the form of Aedh, son of the king of Connaught, and to Mac an Daimh, he gave the aspect of his steward. Finally he made appear a magnificent white saddle horse with an auburn mane, and the basket he turned into a golden saddle, with carved gold and precious stones. As for the mare, he turned her into a magnificent charger.

They present themselves before the Leinster king's fortress. He has no choice but to graciously receive such honorable guests. And, of course, as is required of him under these circumstances, a great feast is prepared in honor of the son of the king of Connaught and the daughter of the king of Munster. "They were brought drinks. Mongan put a charm on the cheeks of the woman and, when the king of Leinster looked at her, he was filled with love for her, so much so that there was within him not a single bone, light or heavy, which was not ablaze with desire." He then calls his steward and orders him to ask the girl what will make her happy. Mongan tells his companion to ask for as many gifts as possible and thus, a perverse game goes on under Mongan's gaze, until morning when all the guests are more or less drunk.

> Mongan said to Cuimne, "Ask the king of Leinster for his belt." Now, when anyone wore this belt, he could suffer from no malady. Thus she asked for the belt and the king of Leinster had it given to her. Mac an Daimh took it. "Now, tell the Leinster king's steward that even if the entire world was given to you, you would not want to leave your husband for him." The steward went to tell this to the Leinster king. The latter said to his guests, "Do you know this woman at my side? This is Dubh-Lacha of the White Hands, the daughter of Fiachna the Black. I took her according to the terms of an oath of eternal friendship, but if you wish, I will exchange her for your wife!" A great anger seized Mongan, but he calmed himself and said, "If I had brought steeds and ornaments with me, it would be just for you to ask me for them. However, it wouldn't be just for me to refuse anything to a lord of your rank. Even though I do this begrudgingly, it will be as you wish: take her for yourself." They made the exchange of wives. Mongan gave the girl three kisses and said, "Everyone would say that we haven't given our hearts to each other if I don't give you these kisses." Then they caressed each other and drank until they were completely drunk.

But there are those among them who pretend to be drunk:

> Mac an Daimh rose and said, "It is a great shame that no one can drink from the hand of the son of the king

of Connaught." And as no one answered him, he went to find the two best horses in the fortress, and Mongan gave them the speed of the wind. Then Mongan put Dubh-Lacha behind him while Mac an Daimh took his own wife in the same way. And they sped away from the fortress.

The awakening is more painful for the Leinster king, but the spectacle no less picturesque. "When the king of Leinster's men got up, they saw the old woman's cloak and the gray-haired old woman on the king's bed. They also saw the dog with his big collar around his neck, and the old mare with her basket." But Brandubh, the king of Leinster, can only swallow his pride. Hasn't he got what he earned? As for Mongan, son of Fiachna the Blonde, he passed his days completely content at the side of this little "black duck" whom, through his magic, he had succeeded in releasing from his rival's clutches. Apparently, morality remains intact in this story, but could we call it Christian morality?

5

The Cycle of the Kings

We know that the fili's main task was to sing of the exploits of the princes and kings for whom they served as companions. The same was true in Wales for those called "domestic bards." It's likely that most of our *chansons de geste* come from ancient poems sung by the poets who accompanied Charlemagne and his counts on their expeditions. The principle is the same throughout: It is the panegyric of the hero. But what is peculiar to Ireland is how careful the *fili* are to remain within the limits of a certain objectivity. Without considering that word's present meaning, it certainly seems as though the bard was not the least bit interested in just demonstrating the hero's courage and invincibility to his listeners, but that above all he wanted to place the hero's actions into the framework of a tradition at once historical—or so called—cultural, and mythological.

Because the Cycle of the Kings, which perhaps we should hesitate to call the "Historical cycle," evidently has as its point of departure the events that actually took place in Ireland beginning from the second century B.C. up until the period of the Plantagenets. But these events are so colored by the marvelous and demonstrate such political and metaphysical preoccupations that we can hardly believe them without first examining them with a critical eye. Moreover, it is useless to try to unearth any systematic history of Ireland here. It is much more worthwhile to focus on the marvelous gifts that the storytellers applied to their exploration of the imaginary world and to their perpetual confrontation with the tragic history of this country, devastated so many times not only by foreign invasions, Scandinavian or English, but also (which is nothing new) by incessant quarrels within.

The narratives that comprise the Cycle of the Kings are extremely diverse. First of all there are the kings' adventures, in all their grandeur and their decadence. There is the sovereign's conquest, which, because of the magic-religious rituals involved, falls more within the Mythological cycle. There are the legends involving heroes who go off to discover marvelous lands, like Maelduin, and for which, again, the mythological framework is very clear. This was primarily a matter of updating very ancient themes no longer very well understood by an already "rationalist" audience. And finally, there are the narratives attesting to the trials encountered by Christian missionaries confronting the remnants of Celtic pagan cults, as in *The Story of Mongan*, which shows us the hero, a reincarnation of Mananann, struggling against the monk Tibraide, or *Suibhne's Folly*, a true challenge to episcopal authority, or *The Death of Muirchertach*, a tragic confrontation between Christianity and druidic magic.

But what is remarkable about this Cycle of the Kings is that there is no noticeable change in tone from the cycles inspired much earlier. Moreover, certain texts in this cycle are as ancient as those others, even older in spirit. Only the formulation is modern, and again, upon analysis, we can discern in them the powerful influence of druidic traditions that are one with the expression, and psychology of the characters, and even the structures of the epic (because the Irish epic does have its own structures, different even from those of Welsh epic, despite how close the traditions are, not only geographically but also in terms of inspiration). The Cycle of the Kings is only one part of this epic, and here we find, intact, the spell cast by poets and storytellers who think of the world as a huge canvas where the imagination can play with shadows and light.

The Prophetic Ecstasy of the Phantom

By virtue of the firmly established principle that myth and history are inseparable in Celtic thinking, the authors of epic narratives are not wrong to have the ancient gods intervene in events that can be considered real, particularly when it is a matter of establishing ancestry. Any king's authority can only be strengthened by having an ancestor supported by a god. That is why the historical king Conn of the Hundred Battles, who also happens to be the hero of many narratives, finds himself "sponsored" in some way by the Tuatha de Danann. And the narrative of the *Prophetic Ecstasy of the Phantom*[1] goes back in the same way to the earliest traditions involving the sacred royalty of Ireland.

King Conn of the Hundred Battles is walking in front of the fortress of Tara in the company of his poets and druids. Suddenly, "on the mound, he felt a stone cry under his foot, and he stood on it. Now the stone cried under the weight of his body in such a way that it could be heard at Tara and over all the Breg plain." Here, then, is the stone of sovereignty, which was later supposedly stolen by the Anglo-Normans or the Scottish, and which, under the name of the "Stone of Scone" would again serve in the crowning ceremonies of British sovereigns.[2]

Of course, Conn is astonished by this wonder and asks one of his druids for an explanation. The druid fills him in on the historical background of the stone and adds, "Fal has cried under your foot today and has made a prophecy. The number of cries which she has uttered is the number of kings which will be in your lineage. But I am not the one who will name them for you." Then Conn and his companions find themselves in the midst of a thick fog that rises inexplicably. They hear a rider approach them and throw three javelins in their direction. After this, he invites them to follow him into his dwelling:

> They advanced until they came to a magnificent plain. They saw a royal fortress with a tree in front of the door, and then a splendid dwelling with a roof made of white tree trunks. It was thirty feet long. They entered the house and noticed a girl who wore a gold diadem on her head. In the house there was a silver vat with gold rings which was full of red beer. The girl held a gold vessel in her hand and lifted a gold cup to her lips.

As for the mysterious rider who led them to this place, he seats himself on a royal throne: "No one had ever seen so tall a man at Tara, a man so beautiful and with such a marvelous face."

This extraordinary being then addresses them with these words:

> I am not really a phantom, and I am going to reveal to
> you a part of the mystery which surrounds me, as well
> as my name. It was after my death that I came here. I
> am of the race of Adam. My name is Lugh, son of
> Eithne, daughter of Tigernmas.[3] Why did I go to find
> you? To reveal to you things which concern your life
> and the lives of your descendants who will be kings.
> Know that each of them will reside at Tara.[3]

Then the girl, whom we learn is the "Irish Royalty," fills a cup with red beer and asks Lugh whom she should give it to. Lugh answers, "Give it to Conn. He will win one hundred battles. He will live fifty years before dying." The girl fills another cup and repeats her question. Lugh answers, "Give it to Art, son of Conn, the man of the three cries." And the ritual continues, reviewing all the real and alleged descendants of Conn of the Hundred Battles. "Then they left the darkness of the Phantom's dwelling place and no longer saw either fortress or house. On the other hand, the vat, the vessel and the gold cup had been left to Conn." And that is how the legitimacy of the kings issuing from Conn is justified, at least in the Gaelic tradition, and how the site of Tara is named again as the omphallos of an "impossible Irish realm."[5]

The Destruction of the Inn of Da Derga

This narrative,[6] which up until now has not captured much attention from commentators, is nevertheless one of the most representative in the Irish tradition. Very dense on the surface, it is constructed with great care around religious, political, and legal themes that form a sort of breviary in which everything has significance. At the center we find the figure of the high king, but not the glorified, hallowed image of a sovereign whose merits are overexaggerated. Rather, it is much more the "splendors and miseries" of the king, such as he exists in the Celtic cosmology, representing the world and linked to it by the many ties that are so many obligations.

Men bustle about around the king. Some follow him, aware of the law that he incarnates and ready to defend him to the death because they know that the king's disappearance would leave the world orphaned. The same idea appears in the French narrative of *The Death of King Arthur*: the forces that the king, a sacred figure in a more or less mystical relationship with the divinities, brings to life are positive, coherent forces. They allow for harmony on earth, they provide fertility, abundance, the succession of the days and nights, and the seasons. The cycle completes itself in the temporal order, the world *turns* in a peaceful universe, but the balance is maintained only by the king. What a difference there is between this Celtic conception of king as provider of harmony and the Latin idea of a king's authoritarian role!

The first is a *rex*.. The first sense of the word *rex*, *rix* in Gaelic, is *rajan* in Sanskrit, which literally means, "powerful, brave, luminous." There is no idea whatsoever here of ruling. The word *rich*, which comes from the same root, originally meant "powerful, brave." So far as the radiance of the king extends, this constitutes his realm. "It is monstrous to think of realms such as they are conceived of today, with territorial limits."[7] Thus the Celtic kings' mission is to *regere*, that is to say, to cast the brilliance of his regard about him as far as he can, to play the role of the sun that gives prosperity and richness to the world. And he does this by following the example of nature, because he knows that no law can be imposed upon nature, which possesses its own rightful order. "The Indians and the Celts thought cosmically. The Roman infidels thought nationalistically. The Indians and the Celts thought mythically. The Roman infidels thought historically. The Indians and the Celts thought ritualistically, sacrificially. The Roman infidels thought legalistically."[8] The Celtic king is much more a *regulator* of the world. On the contrary, the Roman type of king is a *dux*, whose role is that of *ducere*, that is, leader, like a commander in chief of an army, imposing his order on nature in general and human nature in particular. In Rome the first kings were *reges*, regulators who, like Numa Pompilius, organized the city in harmony with the nature of the country—Latium, an agricultural plain in contrast to the hostile mountainous regions surrounding it. Then, with the republic and the policy of expansion, the king became a *consul*—that is, the civil and military head vested with power by the law but no longer by religion, *dux*—before finally becoming *imperator*, commander in chief with unlimited power.

Now, because the royal role has lost its sacred aura, since the time of Charlemagne our modern societies have adopted the Latin confusion of *rex-imperator*. We need only to reread Montesquieu to realize this because that unusually perceptive aristocrat understood that the monarchies' malaise came from this false conception of royal power. For him, any monarch who lived and ruled outside of the laws, declaring or nullifying them by his own authority (and claiming to act in the name of Heaven), was a tyrant. For Montesquieu, the true monarch is the king who obeys the laws previously established, who does not overstep them, but maintains and executes them. Isn't there a striking analogy here with the Celtic conception of the king, submitting to the laws and customs and exclusively at the service of the people? In the Welsh narrative *Branwen, Daughter of Llyr*, when Bran the hero and his army find themselves before a river they can't cross, Bran lies down over it (he is a kind of giant) so that his men can use his body as a bridge, and he pronounces these important words: "Let the one who is chief be the bridge!"

But Montesquieu is not the only perceptive one in this European society that lives by routine alone and no longer understands the meaning of functions and rituals. In the seventeenth century this spirit—particularly subversive in relationship to the established rule—was already found in the *Etats du Soleil* by Cyrano de Bergerac, who, before becoming a grotesque character in the dull play by Rostand, was a thinker of the highest order. Indeed, in the strange countries of the sun, the king is truly the servant of his subjects, who can condemn him to death if they are not satisfied with him.

And that was thought and written in the epoch when the doctrine of royal absolutism took shape, defined by Richelieu, a man of the Church, and codified by Bossut, also a Church dignitary, both of whom had clearly forgotten Saint Thomas Aquinas's formula—which nevertheless applied to the entire Christian Church—*A deo per populum*. This Christian formula is the one that prevailed in Christian Ireland as well as in pagan Ireland: the power, or more exactly, the function, of the king comes from God or the divinities, but through the intermediary of the people who themselves choose their king and by this choice take part in their own destiny.

But organized around the king, the Celtic city—beginning from him and not *for* him—can only survive if there is perfect accord between this king who resides at the city's center, the *omphallos* (which is generally his palace, the religious, political, and, a fact too often ignored, *economic* center within the fortress), and the members of the community in which everyone has a function in a very complex hierarchy, the details of which often escape us. "As it was with the world, the order of the world, so it had to be with their society. In the same way, they had to conform within to the order of the world, which is essentially circular, essentially cyclical."[9] Thus, this city is in the image of the universe. The sun occupies the center of the system. With its rays it warms and nurtures the planets that are its subjects.[10] It regulates their course. It removes the errant stars that could upset the workings of the system. It intervenes to *correct* (again, from the word *regere*) the faults in the course. But under no circumstances is it free to do as it pleases. It obeys a superior, inescapable law. If it lapses in its vigilance, the whole system collapses and it itself is destroyed, since it is an integral part of the whole.

Now if the figures surrounding the king have an interest in seeing that the established (but not preestablished) harmony is maintained, there is, nevertheless, a category of antagonistic, negative, and destructive forces—*evil*, if we must speak of a moral order here. These are the figures eliminated by the king or who eliminate themselves from the system. To return to the solar image again, let us say that these figures cling to the dark sides of the planets, where the light of the sun can absolutely never go. The old Indo-Iranian Manicheanism reappears here, but philosophically transformed. This means that each being, by the very fact of its existence, gives rise to its nonbeing, which is inherent to it. In the same way that the God-Organizer cannot exist without the concept of Satan (the Hebrew *Shatam* is "the destroyer" or the Devil (*Diabolus*, or "who throws himself in the way"), the Celtic king, the harmonizer, can only exist because there is a Disorganizer hidden somewhere and ready to take advantage of the smallest weakness, the least lapse in attention. This is not a metaphysical observation; it is a reality brought into focus by psychoanalysis. We need look no farther than the unconscious for those negative powers that oppose the coherent and *conscious* function of the king. That is why a text like *The Destruction of the House of Da Derga* is such an important document, not only for learning about the Celtic legal and political system, but also for learning about human history. Thus, here are the principal episodes of this narrative constructed as an epic, with its stereotypical characters, its familiar places—though for us they have a kind of exotic charm—and also its atmosphere, imbued with surrealism over which floats the disquieting shadow of fatality.

The story comes grafted to *The Courtship of Etaine*, and is presented as its sequel. Eochaid Feidlich (in fact, this is Eochaid Aireainn) meets Etaine next to a fountain. The description of the young girl is more or less the same as in the *Courtship*. Etaine marries the king of Tara and has a daughter by him named Etaine, like herself. This second Etaine, the daughter of Eochaid, marries Cormac, king of Ulster. But as she has only been able to bear him a daughter, Cormac renounces her, and then takes her back on the condition that the daughter be killed, because she is cursed.[11] Now, since the king Eterscel discovers her, and as he is without descendants and it has been foretold to him that a woman of unknown stock will give him a son, he takes her as a concubine. Then Mess Buachalla gives birth to a son, Conaire, who will be this epic's hero.

We must note Conaire's unknown lineage and his illegitimate birth, since it was legal to have one or many concubines, but nonetheless irregular and kept a bit of a secret. We find this theme again in many ancient traditions, and, among the Celts, in the legend of King Arthur, born of the clandestine love affair of Uther Pendragon and Ygerne de Tintagel. In addition, Conaire belongs both to the race of men, of Gaels, and to the race of the Tuatha de Danann, since he is the grandson of Etaine. Thus, he is subject not only to human laws but also to the customs of the sidh, all the while benefiting from the helpful aid of the fairy people during the time when he can commit no wrong.

At his birth Conaire is placed in a foster home, as was the custom, and there he has three foster brothers: Fer Le, Fer Gal, and Fer Rogain, the grandsons of Donn Desa, the hero. Conaire possesses three gifts: "the gift of hearing, the gift of seeing, and the gift of judgment." Thanks to these gifts, he can even teach his foster brothers, and all four lead lives identical in all respects.

However, King Eterscel dies. Since Tara's high royalty is elected, it is necessary to find a successor for him. According to the narrative's author, this is how the new king is chosen:

> The men of Ireland prepared a festival of the bull,
> which is to say, that a bull was killed, and one man ate

the whole thing and drank the broth from it. Then a
charm was said over him in his bed: the one whom he
saw in his sleep had to the king; if he lied, the sleeper
would be killed [literally: his lips had to perish].

Now, on that day, having left his foster brothers to their games,
Conaire finds himself in his chariot near Ath Cliath (the future site of
the city of Dublin). He sees a flock of unusual-looking birds and follows them, hoping to shoot them down with his slingshot, but the
birds dive under the sea and soon reappear in human form. These are
clearly people of the sidh. They reveal to Conaire the vision that the
sleeping man at Tara had after having eaten the bull: an entirely nude
adolescent, alone on the road to Tara at the end of the night, carrying
in his hand a sling and a stone. Thus it is Conaire who will be the high
king.[12]

But to all this, conditions are added, the famous geisa, prohibitions
or taboos, which Conaire must promise to respect and which are, in
some ways, the guarantees that the sovereignty will be well managed:

> It was forbidden (at your birth) for you to kill birds. . . .[13]
> You will not go around the city of Tara by the south nor
> the plain of Breg by the north.[14] The wild beast of Cerna
> must not be hunted by you. Every ninth night, you will
> not leave Tara. You will not sleep in a house where the
> light from the hearth is visible after the sun has set. . . .
> Three men in red must not go in front of you toward a
> red house [or "the house of a man in red"]. No theft
> must be committed under your reign. After the sun sets,
> no male or female company must enter the house where
> you are. Finally, you must not put an end to the quarrel-
> ing between two of your servants.

We can see that everything is foretold down to smallest detail. It is
clear that these taboos cover ancient beliefs that we do not understand,
and that the epic's author certainly no longer understood, concerning
the role and function of the king—beyond the solar role, of course,
which aimed at maintaining the system's harmony—and the role of
upholder of justice, which aimed at, if not the disappearance, at least
the repression of evil forces, of the famous *Açuras* of the Indian tradition.

However, Conaire reigns during a time without history. It is a kind of golden age: Brotherly love shines through human relationships, the climate is kind, there is neither storm nor thunder, and abundance is widespread. The world has finally found its balance, and Conaire is given the nickname of Conaire Mor (Conaire the Great).

But Conaire's three foster brothers, Fer Le, Fer Gal, and Fer Rogain, who, in fact, represent the bad instincts of the king, are devoured by jealousy and pride. They call together one hundred fifty men from among the sons of the Irish chiefs, the "rich brats" of the period, with the very deliberate intention of living outside the limits of the law. As this epoch continually slips into the fantastic, it is not astonishing to see these outlaws take the form of wolves. But they are soon captured and asked to go practice their talents elsewhere, that is, in Scotland and Britain.[15] Conaire's three foster brothers and their one hundred fifty men thus take to the sea. They encounter the son of the British king, Ingcel the One Eyed,[16] with his one hundred fifty men who are themselves exiles from Britain for the same reasons. The two groups of pirates form an alliance under the following conditions: The Irish will help Ingcel lay waste to Britain, and Ingcel will help the Irish lay waste to Ireland.[17] Then they set sail for Britain.

Now, Conaire's two foster fathers begin to quarrel, and Conaire goes to make peace between them. But since they are his servants, he has just violated one of his taboos. He returns to Tara, but on the way back, he notices the country being ravaged by fire. The southern country is being attacked by the men of the north. The infernal machine has thus been put in motion: To this second violated taboo (no theft may be committed during his reign) will be added an inexorable series of transgressions. Since he cannot continue on his way straight ahead, Conaire goes around Tara by the south and the plain of Breg by the north, and passing through Cerna, he hunts wild beasts there. He then gets lost in a magic fog caused by the men of the sidh "because Conaire's taboos had been violated."

Conaire becomes frightened and asks his men where they can pass the night. Someone replies that the inn of Da Derga, the head-host,[18] is not very far away and he will be received very well there. Accompanied by the two heroes Mac Cecht and Conall Cernach, Cuchulainn's comrade-at-arms, by his son, Le Fri Flaith, and his warriors and servants, Conaire thus heads toward Da Derga's residence.

This is when Conaire notices in front of them three horsemen who are also going toward Da Derga's hotel. "They wore three red garments and three black cloaks. They carried three red shields, and in their hands they had three red swords. They rode three red chargers and their three heads had red hair." So here is another broken taboo. Conaire sends his son Le Fri Flaith to ask them to go behind them; they refuse despite the rewards they are promised. Then the king understands that these are "three red ones of the banished people," that is to say, three Tuatha de Danann sent to bring about his ruin.

And the unfortunate Conaire is not at the end of his troubles. He is joined by an unpleasant character whose poorly defined role could be compared with that of all the rustics we encounter in Celtic epics, in the tales of the Round Table, and even in the story-song of *Aucassin et Nicolette*: This is the man of the woods, the prophet heralding catastrophes. Moreover, his name is Fer Caille, which means literally "man of the woods." The description the author gives of him deserves notice:

> His hair was rough and frizzy; if someone had turned
> a bag of wild apples over on his head, not a single
> apple would have fallen to the ground, because each
> of them would have gotten caught in his hair.[19] If his
> head had been thrown against a branch, the head and
> the branch would have stuck together. Long and thick
> as a beam were each of his shins. Each of his buttocks
> was shaped like a cheese on a willow twig. In his hand
> he carried a stick, forked and black at the tip, and on
> his back, a red pig with black spots which never stopped
> crying.[20]

Nevertheless, at nightfall Conaire and his troops finally reach the hotel of Da Derga. The proprietor gives them the warmest of welcomes. Everyone is made comfortable, including the three men in red and Fer Caille, his pig, and his wife, who is just as monstrous and ugly as he is. Mac Cecht lights a great fire that is clearly visible from some distance, another violated taboo, and this is the moment that a woman by the name of Cailbe chooses to come ask for refuge in the inn. Conaire is obliged to let her in even though he is forbidden from receiving the company of man or woman into whatever house he happens to be in after the sun sets. Now that all the taboos have been broken, the machine of destruction is going to begin to work.

This machine takes the form of the pirates. Conaire's three foster brothers, Fer Rogain, Fer Gal, and Fer Le, accompanied by Ingcel and a large troop of all the adventurers from both sides of the Irish sea, arrive in their boats in view of the coast where the house of Da Derga is located. They are attracted by the fire that Mac Cecht has lit and decide to undertake the systematic destruction of the inn, which they guess to be occupied by the king of Ireland. But first, Fer Rogain, who seems to have taken charge of the operation, sends Ingcel as scout to find out what is going on within.

Here the narrative takes a curious twist. Ingcel is one eyed, but his only eye, "which stands out from his forehead," is able to stretch way out and penetrate the interior of the house. Clearly, this figure is comparable with the cyclops of Greek legend. And each time that he observes someone or something, he returns to report it to Fer Rogain, who, very up to date on what's going on in Ireland, explains to him what he has seen. Thus we overhear, among other things, a detailed description of the chamber of the Picts, of Mac Cecht ("Good is the hero Mac Cecht. He was lying in bed when you saw him. The two naked hills that you saw near the hairy man, those are his two knees near his head. The two lakes near the mountain . . . , those are his two eyes next to his nose. The two caves near a tree . . . , those are his two ears beside his head. . . . The stream of rushing water that you saw, on which the sun shone, that is the glimmer of his sword"), of the Fomor's room, and of Conall Cernach ("He carried a crimson cloak. White as snow was one of his cheeks, the other was red and spotted as the foxglove. Blue as the hyacinth was one of his eyes, dark as the back of a capricorn was the other. His head was covered with beautiful golden hair, bushy and as wide as a basket, which touched his bulging thighs. It was also curly, like the head of a sheep. If someone had thrown a sack full of nuts at the red scallop on the crown of his head, not a single nut would have fallen to the ground, but they would all remain in the curls and the tresses and the spikes of his hair."). As for Conaire, this is how Ingcel saw him: "He had the ardor and the energy of a king, the determined and wise air. The cloak that I saw around him was like the mist on a May day. . . . In front of him, on the cloak, I saw a gold wheel, which went from his chin to his navel. The color of his hair had the brilliance of dark gold."[21]

We must note the extraordinary artistry of the storyteller. This epic is not only *epic* poetry, with all the various threads that this genre requires; it is also *lyric* poetry. And this lyricism is singularly audacious. Compared with what was being written in the same period on the continent, riddled as it was with dogmatism and Latinism, this lyricism—which sacrifices everything to analogy, which uses bold metaphor and plunges into the depths of dream and imagination—is clear evidence that there was something peculiarly and singularly modern about Celtic society, something that, in any case, no longer existed in classical Roman-Christian society.

And each time Ingcel describes a figure and Fer Rogain gives his explanation, a great cry of lamentation goes up among the pirates. They know their enemies' strength, and they know the future in store for them. Few of them will return from the destruction. But they are all committed to the business and can no longer retreat, not Ingcel nor Fer Rogain nor any of the others. They are the executors of fate: The world is completely out of balance now, only a single blow is needed to demolish the whole system, and it is the pirates, symbolic of man's destructive instincts, who must carry out this mission. Then "the pirates walked toward the inn and made a murmuring all around."

Combat begins, violent and deadly. Conaire and his men kill six hundred pirates, but the pirates set the hotel on fire. The fire is extinguished with all the available water, and the pirates are obliged to beat a retreat. "I told you," Fer Rogain, son of Donn Desa, says, "that if the champions of Ireland and Britain attacked Conaire in the house, destruction would only be complete if Conaire's ardor and fury were brought to an end." Then the sorcerers who find themselves among the pirates throw a spell over Conaire, an unquenchable thirst. The king asks Mac Cecht, who is nearby, for a drink. Mac Cecht replies insolently, "There are servants and cupbearers to bring you a drink. The order I received from you is to protect you!"

Conaire asks his servants for a drink, but all the fluids have been thrown on the fire. Conaire begs Mac Cecht to bring him water. Mac Cecht, furious, argues with Conall Cernach, who ends up saying to him, "Leave us to defend the king and go find him water, since that is what he asks of you!" Mac Cecht begrudgingly agrees and rushes out of the inn, bearing "Conaire's gold cup in which both a beef cow and a pig can be boiled." The pirates want to keep him from passing. "He gave nine blows with the iron stem (of the cauldron) and with each blow, nine men fell. Then he spun his shield around at an angle, and sliced with his sword overhead: six hundred fell from the first attack, and after having cut off a hundred heads, he passed through the troops."

The king's defenders launch violent assaults against the pirates. They kill them (more than there are of them!) and succeed in escaping. But Conaire is the victim of a spell: "His great thirst oppressed him and he perished of a consuming fever, because he had nothing to drink." We should take note that the king's death is not due directly to the pirates. Like Siegfried, like Achilles, like Cuchulainn, the hero is invincible; he cannot be killed by honest enemies. He is a victim of either treason or enchantment.

But Mac Cecht runs into trouble. He cannot find water anywhere, which proves that the druidic spell cast over Conaire was absolute in nature. He is obliged to make a tour of all the principal lakes in Ireland, but all in vain, until he comes to Uaran Garad, in the plain of Ai. Then he fills the cup and returns to the hotel of Da Derga just as a pirate is in the process of carrying off Conaire's head. "Mac Cecht felt a block of stone under his feet, on the floor of the inn. He threw it at the man who was carrying off Conaire's head, and the block passed through his spine in such a way that it broke his back. After this, Mac Cecht decapitated him, and then he threw the cup of water onto the mouth and nose of Conaire."

Mac Cecht wants to show that he has accomplished his mission, that he has freed himself from responsibility for the king's death. And the head of Conaire begins to speak. It recites a poem of praise and thanks to Mac Cecht: "Brave man, Mac Cecht, excellent man, Mac Cecht! Good warrior without, good warrior within. He gives a drink, he saves a king, he accomplishes a feat. . . . Good would I be for the famous Mac Cecht if I were alive, brave man!"

But Mac Cecht is wounded. Exhausted, he is cared for by a woman who is passing by and who extracts from the champion's wound an enormous wolf that Mac Cecht took to be a simple ant. After having rested, at the end of the third day he carries Conaire's head to Tara to be buried. As for Conall Cernach, covered with wounds, he returns home, where he is respectfully received by his father, Amorgen.

As for the pirates, they are subject to heavy losses. To tell the truth, only five of them remain, among them, Ingcel the One Eyed.[22] All the others, including Conaire's foster brothers, have perished in this systematic destruction of the inn of Da Derga.[23]

Thus ends this grandiose and tragic epic. Beyond the story, beyond the clearly Gaelic context, we find developed here the eternal theme of man facing his destiny, of man facing the universe that crushes him, but who, as Pascal says, finds his grandeur in the fact that he knows himself to be miserable and he knows the universe crushes him. A Jansenist epic, we could almost call it, and that would be all the more true because the atmosphere that the drama's characters inhabit is a typically Racinian one. When the heroes appear, whether they belong to one side or the other, we know who will be saved and who will perish. And as with Racine, their destinies intersect in the vast hall of the inn of Da Derga. Finally, the style of this narrative, the astonishing descriptions, the extraordinary imagination, the violent and surreal poetry that permeates it, make it a work of the highest order, which deserves to take its place beside the human spirit's most beautiful achievements.

The Disappearance of Condle

The great Celtic specialist from the beginning of this century, Joseph Loth, often used to make the ironic observation with regard to his ancestors that it seemed as though they were haunted by the Other World in this period, but that really they just wanted to send their enemies there as quickly as possible to be rid of them. This is partially true, but we must acknowledge that this desire is not peculiar to the Celts, while recognizing that, among those peoples who inhabited western Europe from the fifth century B.C. until the end of the Middle Ages, the Celts went the farthest in their speculations about this Other World, attributing to it characteristics not found anywhere else. *The Disappearance of Condle* narrative[24] is completely in harmony with the Celtic vision of the relationships between the visible and invisible worlds.

King Conn of the Hundred Battles, a historical figure of the second century A.D. turned legendary hero in the collective unconscious, finds himself in his Usnech fortress in the company of his son, Condle the Beautiful. We must remember that Celtic fortresses have nothing in common with the fortified castles of the Middle Ages and even less with those restored by Viollet-Le-Duc. These are fortified enclosures at the top of a rocky outcrop, containing a collection of homes and storehouses scattered throughout. Thus, Conn and Condle are walking in the meadow surrounding these buildings, followed by a few druids and men-at-arms. Suddenly, Condle notices a woman of exceptional beauty, who comes toward him and tells him that she comes from the "Land of the Living where there is neither death nor sin nor error." Conn doesn't see the woman and asks his son whom he is talking to. He then hears a voice that says to him, "He is talking to a pretty young woman, of noble birth, for whom neither death nor old age await." The voice reveals to him that she loves Condle and that she would like to take him with her to her magical country. Then she addresses Condle directly: "Come with me, Condle the Beautiful of the jeweled neck, red as a light. Blonde is your hair over your crimson face, treasure of your royal beauty! If you consent, your beauty will never fade and your youth and grace will shine forever."[25]

As a good father of the family and good king concerned about preserving his lineage, Conn of the Hundred Battles immediately reacts. He asks his druids to use their spells to get rid of this dangerous woman. One of the druids promptly pronounces an incantation, and Condle no longer sees the woman. "But before withdrawing at the sound of the druid's chant, the woman threw an apple to Condle, and for one month, Condle neither ate nor drank. He refused all food except for the apple. However much he ate of it, it never diminished, but remained whole. And Condle was overcome with longing for the woman he had seen."

This is a classic formula in the mythological tradition. We find it again in an almost identical form in *The Voyage of Bran, Son of Febal*. We find it just a bit altered in *The Voyage of Maelduin*. It is clear that the woman-fairy who appears to Condle, and who declares herself to be from the world of "peace" (of the sidh, in Gaelic), literally attaches the young man to herself by giving him an enchanted apple to eat. It is equivalent to the pomegranate that Kore-Persephone eats in Hades's domain, according to the Greek tradition. As for the Marvelous Land that the woman comes from, it is the *Emain Ablach* of *The Voyage of Bran*, also called the isle of Avalon in the Arthurian legend, this "isle of apples" where fruits are ripe all year long and where Morgan reigns, the image of the goddess of beginnings, dispenser of nourishment, sensuality, and immortality. The realm of the Grail when it is finally restored isn't far from this isle of women and eternal youth.

Nevertheless, a month passes. Condle is with his father in another of the royal fortresses, and the fairy-woman reappears to Condle, while Conn only hears her voice. The woman repeats her invitation to Condle, and Conn immediately appeals to his druid and orders him to counter the temptress with all his magic powers. The druid goes into action, but this time he remains powerless in the face of this being from the Other World, who even allows herself to ridicule druidism and prophesy the advent of a new religion, that is, Christianity: "Oh Conn of the Hundred Battles, the druidic art is not well-loved, it will not last very long. Soon, for the Judgment, a righteous man[26] with a large and magnificent following will reach the great river. Soon his law will extend to you. It will break the druids' perverse spells before the black demon and magician." We must not forget that the transcribers of these clearly pagan legends were Christian monks, and that there are many interpolations from the Middle Ages in the narratives. But what is essential remains, and the original schema is fully respected. Condle is more and more bewitched. He confesses to loving his own people but having unbearable desire for this woman. And the latter lays it on: "You struggle hard against the wave of your desire which, far from your own people, sweeps you away. Let us climb into my glass boat to go to the sidh of Boadag.[27] There is no land harder to reach. I see that the bright sun is setting. We will arrive there before night. It is the land where joy fills the soul of whoever travels there. There, there are only women and girls."

Who could resist such an appeal? Bran, the son of Febal, was not able to control his desire to rejoin the woman who had given him the branch from the Emain apple tree. Neither can Condle resist this woman. Silencing all the feelings that still connect him to his father and to the world of the living, he rushes onto the glass boat, a marvelous image of what may be the crystallization of desire: "They were seen going away. It was hard for the eyes to follow them, as they were carried on the sea. Afterwards, they were never seen again and no one knew where they had gone." And that is how King Conn of the Hundred Battles watches his oldest son disappear. Fortunately for him and for Ireland, he has another son, Art, but, not surprisingly, Art too will have adventures with the fairies.

What is interesting in all of this is finding the myth, fully intact, in a hagiographical story from Armorican Brittany involving Saint Tugdual, the more or less legendary founder of Tréguier. But the atmosphere changes, the context is purely Christian, and the sexual guilt is emphasized. Here, we are dealing with an ecclesiastical school student from Tréguier who, while walking with his comrades along the sea, is abducted by a "girl of the sea," that is, a mermaid. His comrades' prayers to Saint Tugdual makes him reappear, but "his right foot was still wrapped in a silk sash." And the young student, "fooled for a moment by the devil," as the text says, confesses (we may well wonder why!), takes communion, and, one year to the day after the event, dies.[28] Beneath the Christian tones of this Latin life of Saint Tugdual, beneath a new morality that put emphasis on the concept of sin (essentially sexual sin), it is not difficult to recognize the outline of a story familiar throughout the world, which the Celts, the Gaels and Britons alike, have given a special place.

The Adventures of Art, Son of Conn

Conn of the Hundred Battles,[29] a historical figure who lived in the second century B.C., is the high king of Tara, and his reign is marked by good fortune and plenty. There are three harvests a year, which is proof of the role of harmonizer and balancer of natural forces attributed to the king of Tara. But Conn has the misfortune of losing his wife, whom he dearly loves. He is overcome with grief. One day he leaves Tara all alone and goes off to meditate sorrowfully on the banks of the Ben Etair.

Now this same day, the Tuatha de Danann have held council in their famous Land of Promise to judge one of their own, a certain Becuna Cneisgel, guilty of some unspecified crime. The king of the fairy people, Mananann, has made the decision that Becuna will be exiled from the Land of Promise and has sent messengers out to make it known that "Becuna Cneisgel must not be given asylum in any sidh." She must mingle with the men of Ireland so that the curse she bears will fall upon them, "because the Tuatha de Danann hated the Sons of Mile (the Gaels) because they had been chased from Ireland by them."

Thus is happens that Becuna, on board a coracle, a little boat covered with skin and particularly easy to maneuver, crosses the sea and reaches the shores of Ben Etair. "She wore a great, brightly colored cloak, edged with reddish gold, a red satin blouse against her white skin, and sandals of white leather. Her hair was soft and blonde, her eyes were gray in her head, her eyebrows black,[30] her knees small and round, her feet tender and light. Beautiful was the appearance of the girl." We are carefully informed that Becuna was in love with Art, son of Conn, although she has never seen him. It is Conn whom she meets, and Conn is dazzled by the stranger's beauty. Becuna must choose, and she accepts Conn's advances only so that the latter will consent to exiling Art for a year. Conn agrees, and thus Becuna becomes the concubine of the high king of Ireland for one year.

But everything doesn't turn out for the best. Becuna is guilty of some fault and carries with her a curse. This is the femme fatale who causes catastrophes. Also, Art's exile is unjust. Thus, for one year, "there was neither wheat nor milk in Ireland," which is as expected, since the king is no longer maintaining the balance. The druids who are consulted obviously accuse Becuna and declare that "relief would be possible if the son of a faultless couple was brought to Tara to be killed there so that his blood was mixed with Tara's soil."[31]

Unable to part with Becuna, Conn decides to ward off danger by going himself in search of the child born of a faultless couple. He entrusts the realm to Art, discovers a magic coracle at Ben Etair, embarks, and wanders aimlessly over the seas until he comes to a marvelous island, which is the Land of the Fairies so often described in Irish epics. "The island had beautiful apple trees, many lovely fountains from which flowed wine, a forest full of shining grapes, hazel nut trees with magnificent hazel nuts near fountains, yellow gold, with little bees who buzzed about fruits trickling sweet-smelling juices." There Conn is received by the queen, who treats him with great hospitality and to whom he reveals the purpose of his voyage. Indeed he discovers that Segda Saerlabraid, the queen's son, is the very young man who corresponds to the druids' demands. The queen and her husband refuse Conn's request to take the young man away with him, until the young man himself asks to leave with the king. The queen then consents, placing her son "under the protection of all the kings of Ireland, of Art, son of Conn, and of Finn, son of Cumall."

After three days and three nights of sailing on the coracle, the travelers reach Ben Etair and present themselves to the Tara assembly. The druids want to sacrifice the young man right away. Conn calls upon the protection of Art and Finn, who keep the fanatics from proceeding with their plan.[32] Then a woman appears, leading a cow. This is, in fact, the young man's mother. Here is a fine example of sacrifice through substitution. The men of Ireland kill the cow, and the woman demands that the guilty druids be punished for claiming the blood of an innocent victim.[33] She also orders Conn to send Becuna Cneisgel away, since she is responsible for all the misfortune that has befallen Ireland. But Conn hides behind his obligations: He cannot send his concubine away. Then the woman leaves with her son Segda, saying, "I want there to be a third less wheat, a third less milk, a third less of the Irish harvest while this woman is with you."

One day Becuna meets Art, and under the threat of a geis, she makes him play chess with her. Art wins and thinks that he has found the means of getting rid of Becuna. Now threatening her with a geis, he requires that she bring back Curoi Mac Daire's magic wand, convinced that she won't be able to do it.

But after wandering about unsuccessfully, Becuna is received by her foster sister, Aine, daughter of Eogabal, who procures Curoi's magic wand for her. She returns to Tara triumphantly and gives Art the wand. This is an act of some significance because, thanks to this initiation by a fairy, Art is now in possession of a symbolic and magic object, the symbol of command and power. In fact, he is now the true king, and no longer Conn, who plays a secondary role in the rest of the story.

However, Becuna wants her revenge. She challenges Art to another game of chess. But it seems as though Becuna has made peace with certain Tuatha de Danann, because the people of the sidh, protected by their invisibility, come to her aid and move the pieces on the chessboard:

> Art noticed it and said, "The men of the sidh are moving your pieces; it is not you who are winning, but they." "Here is a forfeit for you," said the girl. "So it is, in truth," said the young man, "tell me what you want." "What I want," she said, "is for you not to be able to eat food in Ireland before having brought back

Delbchaen, the daughter of Morgan." "Where is she?" asked Art. "On an island in the middle of the sea, that is all that you can know."[34]

Thus we find the unfortunate Art in the grip of a formidable geis. It is Becuna's vengeance that sends him into an exile she considers to be final. But Art is not discouraged. Moreover, he now has Curoi's wand. Going to the shores of Imber Colphta, he discovers a well-equipped coracle, which allows him to cross the sea and reach the Marvelous Island where his father, Conn, has already landed.

We should take note here of the theme of the boat that leads human beings toward their destinies. There is no need to row it, nor to hoist the sails. It is enough to let the skiff be carried along by the wind and waves. There is already a little of this in the *Odyssey*, but taking Mediterranean logic into account, the intervention of Aeolus, Neptune, and the divinities is needed to explain the phenomenon. For a Celt, no explanation is needed. The boat is headed toward some destination—it is a mystery, and mysteries cannot be understood. That is why we find this theme again in the story of the Lady of Shalot, who dies out of love for Lancelot of the Lake and whose boat magically arrives at the ramparts of Caerlion on Usk *(The Death of Arthur)*, and again with King Salomon's boat and the marvelous vessel that allows Lancelot to explore the islands and promontories surrounding Brittany *(The Quest for the Grail)*. But it is especially with *The Story of Tristan* and *The Lay of Guigemar*, by Marie de France, that the resemblance is striking. Tristan, wounded by Morholt, can only be healed by the woman who is destined to him. The doctors of Cornouaille are powerless to save him. Thus, he takes a boat and goes to sea, as the winds will blow him. The boat reaches Ireland, where Tristan is healed by the queen and her daughter Iseult. In *The Lay of Guigemar*, the hero has wounded a doe during a hunt, but the arrow has ricocheted and also wounded Guigemar in the thigh. The doe then begins to speak and says that Guigemar will only be healed by the one whom he loves and who will love him. Guigemar climbs aboard a mysterious vessel without a pilot, which takes him to the foot of the castle where the lady who is supposed to love him and heal him is found.

The symbolism is clear: Tristan and Guigemar are wounded in the thigh, which is a standard euphemism meaning that they have lost their virility. The geis Becuna casts over Art is nothing but that: Art will rediscover his virility only with the woman destined to him, and he can only win her after difficult trials. The question that presents itself here is whether this is a matter of an actual magic, and thus psychological prohibition—today it would be called a traumatism, a block—or whether this is, in fact, a glorification of unique and absolute love: the hero being able to love physically only the woman whom he loves psychologically.[35]

Art is then welcomed to the Marvelous Island by Queen Creide, who sets him up in a "crystal chamber. Beautiful is the appearance of this chamber, with its crystal doors and inexhaustible vats because even though they were never filled, they were always full." This crystal chamber is strangely reminiscent of the *sun chamber* where Oengus keeps Etaine when she is in the form of an insect, and also of the famous crystal chamber where Tristan, disguised as a fool, says he wants to take Queen Iseult. It is one of the aspects of the Isle of Glass, of the Glass Castle found almost everywhere in Celtic legends. In fact, this theme is quite enigmatic. Perhaps we must view it as a kind of ritual of regeneration by the sun, the Sun, which, since the Bronze Age, had become the god who gives life and who revitalizes. But isn't this also the sense of the actual, physical role the sun plays in the phenomenon of life? We now know that the solar rays were there at the beginning when life appeared on our planet, and that the energy of the solar rays is beginning to be harnessed by men.[36]

For one month, Art remains in this crystal chamber as a guest of the queen. There he acquires new strength, the energy that he will need to fulfill his destiny. And it is Queen Creide who reveals to him what he must do and who warns him about the dangers he will face. Art takes leave and sails across a sinister sea inhabited by strange monsters, which he succeeds in killing. He lands on an island and crosses through a forest where he must fight cruel stags and *Coincuillind*. The word *Coincuilland* literally means "dogs of holly." It is a name that the eighth-century Irish gave to Viking invaders, but here, it is clearly referring to animals, like the stags, who kept bold visitors out of the Promised Land, the blessed country where the sought-after treasure is found. This is not the only trial he goes through. He comes to a mountain of ice, inhabited by hideous toads and lions with long manes. After that follows a passage down an ice river. There appears a formidable warrior, Curnan Claibhsalach (the atrocious breast), who must keep him from going farther. But Art is triumphant. He then confronts Ailill Dubhdedach (of the black teeth), another formidable figure. Art succeeds in cutting off his head, entering the fortress, and making Ailill's widow reveal to him "the way to the Land of Wonders and Morgan's fortress," the final destination of his expedition.

That is how Art comes within sight of Morgan's fortress. "There was found Coinchend Cenfada (head of the long dog-head), Morgan's wife. She had the strength of a hundred men in battle. She was the daughter of Conchruth (red head), king of Coinchind (heads of dogs)."

As it was prophesied that Coinchend would perish the day her daughter was courted by a man, she has studded the long road that leads to her fortress with various dangers, and she puts to death all those incautious fools who, having succeeded in passing them, still dare to ask her for Delbchaen's hand in marriage.

We might wonder why so many names referring to the head of a dog are found grouped together in Morgan's family. It is an invaluable indication of the location where the action takes place. We are at the entrance to Hell, in the pagan sense of the word, the Hell guarded by dogs and that, even better, is called dog heads, which shows us the Celtic aspect of the Cerberus myth. Art's penetration into this infernal world can thus be explained as the deliverance of the imprisoned soul, another version of the Orpheus myth, or even—and this interpretation is more in keeping with Art's royal character—as the acquisition of sovereignty represented by Delbchaen, by nature an infernal divinity, and consequently, the dispenser of riches from the Other World (isn't Pluto *the rich*?).

Art's adventure recalls one of the most ancient Welsh narratives, *Kulhwch and Olwen*. There, as well, the hero must submit to initiation trials before being able to win Olwen, the daughter of Yspaddaden Penkawr (big head). And as it has been predicted that Yspaddaden would lose his life the day his daughter is married, he puts all incautious suitors to death. Moreover, the details are strictly identical. The suitors' heads are stuck onto the stockade around the fortress, and there is only one empty post.

At first, Art is received courteously—and deceptively—by Coinchend and Queen Creide's two sisters, Arb and Finscoth. They offer Art two cups, one full of wine, the other of poison. But remembering

Creide's warnings, Art drinks the cup on the right, which is the one containing the wine. Again, he has successfully passed the test, he has chosen the wine of life and also of love, because, as in the Romance of Tristan, there is a symbolic link between the cup and love.

Thus, the last action to be accomplished remains, the struggle against Coinchend. Art cuts off her head and just like Kulhwch with Yspaddaden's head, goes to place it on the one empty post of the stockade. Then he takes possession of the fortress, and without further ado sleeps with Delbchaen. But this is when Delbchaen's father arrives, Morgan of the Black Teeth. He challenges Art to single combat. It is a terrible fight, but of course Art comes out of it the hero. And after seizing all the riches in the Land of Marvels, he returns to Tara accompanied by Delbchaen and makes it clear to Becuna that she must leave the vicinity for good. Sad and helpless, eternally cursed, condemned to wander, Becuna Cneisgel gets back into her coracle and disappears. As for Art and his wife, they are received with joy and enthusiasm by the chiefs and the men of Ireland.

That is the epic of Art, son of Conn. It is an epic tinged with the marvelous, a fairy voyage to which is added ancient myths, ancient beliefs. Perfectly ordered, perfectly clear, this narrative can be compared with certain episodes from the Arthurian romances. It has something of the same beauty, intensity, and color. We are in the presence of an authentic literary masterpiece coming straight from the powerful imagination of Irish storytellers whose anonymity must not let us forget their astounding and surprising genius.

The Siege of Druim Damhgaire

Here is a strange epic[37] in which the most diverse traditions merge. It is based on history, but mythology comes in with the appearance of Oengus, the Mac Oc, one of the principal Tuatha de Danann. And what is more, druidic magic constitutes the very web of the work, which makes it an invaluable document for the study of druidism, the powers that the ancient Irish druids claimed to possess in particular.

It is a matter of the underhanded struggle that the two kings of Ireland indulge in beginning from the year A.D. 300. They have divided Ireland into two zones of influence, the Leth Cuind (Conn's

Half) in the north, and the Leth Moga, (Mogh's Half) in the south. Cormac Mac Airt, Conn's grandson, is king of Tara, thus high king, while Fiacha, grandson of Eogan the Great, known as Mogh Nuada, has acceded to the Munster throne. Fiacha is the student of the famous druid Mogh Ruith. As for Cormac, he has a reputation for great wisdom.

One day when someone is praising the riches of Oengus's residence in front of Cormac, Cormac expresses such skepticism that Mac Oc appears to him and uses the occasion to reveal to him his future. Cormac will have a brilliant reign, but will experience great difficulties at the end of a certain number of years. The prophecy comes true. The royal treasure depleted and Cormac desperately seeks ways to replenish it. He then realizes that Fiacha, the king of Munster, owes him taxes that he has never paid.

But Fiacha refuses to give in to Cormac's demands. Each of the two kings prepares for war. Cormac asks his druids what will be the result of this expedition he is planning, and the druids reply with few encouraging words. Cormac is furious with them and considers getting rid of them in order to avoid the bad outcome.

One day while Cormac is hunting, he falls asleep in a magic fog and is soon awakened by a young woman, Bairrfhinn Blaith (the beautiful one of the golden hair), from the Bairche sidh. She takes him back with her to the underground world and keeps him there for three days and three nights. Then Bairrfhinn provides him with three magicians, Ergi, Eang, and Engain, as well as two druids, Colphta and Lurga, all with formidable magical powers, in order to assist Cormac in his endeavors.

Thus Cormac launches an attack against Munster. But his two old druids, Cithruadh and Fis, who are threatened with being put to death and annoyed at having been supplanted, cast a magic wind over Cormac's army. His warriors fight against each other in an atmosphere of total confusion, which completely demoralizes the high king's army.

Nevertheless, Cormac lays siege to the Munster fortress of Druim Damhgaire. His new druids make the hill on which he is camped higher. Single combat follows, and taking the aspect of sheep, the magicians Ergi, Egan, and Engain harass the Munster warriors. Colphta and Lurga, the druids, manage to make the springs that supply the men of Munster disappear. Lacking water, the latter are on the verge of surrender when Fiacha thinks of asking his old master, the druid Mogh Ruith, for help because "there are no spells at all that he cannot do either outside or inside the sidh."

Mogh Ruith sets his conditions for taking part in Munster's defense. He wants a large piece of land, which Fiacha immediately agrees to. In response, Mogh Ruith pushes his demands even farther. He must have a hundred cows, a hundred steer, a hundred horses, fifty mantles, and, what is more, a beautiful girl to marry as well as the head position in parades and assemblies. Since Fiacha has no choice and the situation is becoming desperate, he gives in to the druid's exorbitant demands.

Then Mogh Ruith makes waters spring forth from Munster, because his magic is more powerful than that of the druids furnished by Bairrfhinn. He lowers the hill on which Cormac is camped. Cenmar, one of Mogh Ruith's students, even manages to kill the druid Colphta with the help of a magic eel; then it is the turn of Lorga, Cormac's second druid. And when the three magicians come to do battle, still in the form of sheep, Mogh Ruith creates three ferocious dogs that chase and devour them.

It is clear that this is a magic battle between druids who match their powers. The men aren't given anything much to do in the conflict except keep score. And having lost the magicians and druids Bairrfhinn provided him with, Cormac is reduced to negotiating with Mogh Ruith. He promises him a fortune if Mogh Ruith will switch sides. But mercenary that he is, Mogh Ruith has a certain respect for the given word and refuses to betray Fiacha. Then Cormac makes peace with his former druids. One of them, Cithruadh, lights a druidic fire with sorb wood and, thanks to his incantations, directs that fire at the enemies. But Mogh Ruith lights another fire, no less druidic and more powerful, which annihilates his adversary's. "Mogh Ruith was brought his skin from the hornless brown bull and his headgear from the speckled bird of winged flight, and his other druidic tools. He rose into the air and into the sky at the same time as the fires and began to beat them in such a way so as to turn them toward the north."[38]

The description we are given of Mogh Ruith recalls an African or Native American sorceress. It is an image we rarely have of the Celtic druid, whom we imagine—from the stories of our childhood—more often to be dressed in a white robe and wearing a gold billhook at his waist. In fact—and this is where this narrative becomes most valuable—

the druid is not only a priest, he is also a warrior, like Cathbad, the Ulate druid. He is a poet as well, because he chants his incantations. He is a jurist, because he judges and can draft the laws. He is a master teacher. And finally, and *especially*, he is a sorcerer, a magician possessing formidable powers, which explains the importance and seriousness of the geisa and lampoons, of curses and charms, which he can pronounce at any moment on anyone at all.

All this must draw our attention to the character of Mogh Ruith, the most striking of all the druids in Irish literature, rich as it is in magic and druidic figures. The description we are given of him, his powers, the rituals he performs, is particularly detailed. He possesses superhuman strength. He has limitless power over the elements, fire, water, air, and earth. He is able to create monsters and raise ghosts. With one gesture he can create and destroy. He holds the secrets of life and death. He has acquired his knowledge in the mounds, in the universe of the Tuatha de Danann. Let us translate: Even though he himself is mythical, or at least an idealization, in a historical epic, he is heir to the ancient science of the Tuatha, the divine science. He can exercise his powers as easily inside the sidh as outside. And what is more, he has all the paraphernalia of a sorcerer. Can we see in this figure the image of a druid from ancient times, that is, a *shaman*?

There again, druidism and shamanism present such similarities that it is difficult not to notice relationships that are not only possible, but also likely. How else to think of those descents into the Other World that could be interpreted as the shaman's voyage to the subterranean universe? How else to think of these practices of sorcery that constantly put the universes of the dead and the living into contact with each other?

But let us return to our story. Mogh Ruith's druidic fire causes Cormac's army to disband. The men of Munster pursue their enemies and cause great carnage among them. Mogh Ruith himself goes after Cormac's unfortunate druids and turns them to stone. Thus, he is the victor because his magic is the most powerful. Cormac and Fiacha make peace. Cormac renounces his claims as overlord of Munster and they exchange hostages. Connla, son of Tadg and cousin to Fiacha, is entrusted to Cormac, who will take responsibility for the young man's education.

There is an epilogue, however. A woman from the sidh, Locha

Gabar, falls in love with Connla and invites him into her magic dwelling. Connla does not come to the arranged meeting. This fairy then throws a curse and dishonor over Connla. Completely vexed, Connla goes to find Cormac and tell him what has happened to him. Under the pretext of cleansing him of his dishonor, the king suggest that he bathe himself in the blood of a king to whom he is related, which is a blatant invitation to kill Fiacha. And returning to Fiacha's home, Connla delivers a great blow to him with his lance. Thus Cormac is avenged for the defeat inflicted upon him by Fiacha, with the help of Mogh Ruith, the druid.

The Tragic Death of Muirchertach

If we were dealing with a popular tale out of the oral tradition, this narrative[39] could easily be entitled "The Sorceress and the King" because it is a story, pure and simple, of a terrible confrontation between a king and a young girl gifted with magical powers who wants to avenge the death of her father. But this doesn't take place without inner conflict because the sorceress's love for her victim is more than obvious, which opens interesting horizons on the ancient Gaels' psychological sophistication and immediately destroys the too widely held opinion that any analysis of characters' behavior or feelings is totally absent from epic or mythological narratives. That said, *The Tragic Death of Muirchertach* is very complex because, beginning from an apparently historical core (Muirchertach actually lived in the fifth century A.D.), the narrative encompasses numerous reminders of druidism, even reduced as it has been to sorcery, and episodes concerning very understandable power struggles between Christian clerics and adherents to the ancient religion.

Muirchertach, the king of Ireland, lives in his Cletech fortress in the Boyne River valley. He is married to Duaibsech, daughter of the king of Connaught, who has provided him with many children. He rules wisely for the greatest good of the kingdom. Now, one day when he goes off hunting, he leaves his companions and finds himself alone on a plain.

He was not alone for long before he noticed a girl of great beauty, with beautiful hair, fair skin, wrapped in

a great cloak, and it seemed to him that he had never
gazed upon a woman more beautiful or more fine. And
his body was seized with desire for her. Filled with
admiration for her, he said to himself that he would
gladly give up all of Ireland for a single night with her,
so powerful was his love. Then, he went to greet her
as if he knew her, and to ask her for news.

The girl is not at all frightened by the king's presence. Indeed, she
speaks quite frankly to him: "You are Muirchertach, son of Erc, king
of Ireland, and I have come here to meet you." Very favorably im-
pressed, the king asks her to come with him. She answers immediately: "I will go, provided that your gifts be agreeable to me." As the
king is completely overcome by desire, he doesn't think for very long.
"I will give you power over me," he says. The girl seems to jump at the
chance and asks him to confirm his promise with a solemn oath.
Muirchertach cannot resist. He pronounces the oath, and, completely
happy, suggests a program of celebrations and festivities. Then the girl
abruptly lays her cards on the table. "That is not what I want. I ask that
my name never be pronounced by you, that Duaibsech, your wife, the
mother of your children, never be present when I am with you and that
the clerics can never enter the fortress of Cletech as long as I can be
found there."

Muirchertach has no choice but to give in to the girl's demands.
He promises to do all this, but cannot keep himself from murmuring,
"It would have been easier for me to give you half of Ireland! But tell
me, what is your name so that I can refrain from saying it." Then he
chants two astonishingly beautiful lines:

Tell me your name, oh young girl
you, the most loved, woman sparkling star . . .

The girl gives a strange response. She says, "Sin!" But this name
has many different meanings, and for being so concise her response is
no less evocative because this simple word means "Sigh, rustle, tempest, rough wind, winter night, cry, lamentation, groan." That is indication enough of the ambiguousness of this woman who claims her
name is Sin, and her allegiances to the world of illusion and magic.
Muirchertach doesn't recognize the significance of this name, which,

in any case he is not allowed to pronounce, having taken an oath but meaning that inevitably, at one time or another, he will violate the prohibition and fall into the trap. Sin's demand is equivalent to a Melusinian prohibition: "Do not try to find out what I do on Saturday," and as a result, "Do not try to find out who I really am!" It is very evident that Sin is a fairy, one of those images derived from an ancient divinity from the period when the woman was still a model for the divine. And henceforth, Muirchertach, king of a realm regulated according to androcratic, if not "paternal," principles, finds himself engaged in a gynocratic process entirely opposed to his essential nature. He will be Sin's "plaything" even more than her victim.

Muirchertach takes Sin to Cletech. "What are you going to do now?" the girl asks. "Whatever you want," answers the king, thus giving up all his freedom. And Sin occupies the territory she has conquered. "I want Duaibsech and her children to leave this fortress and I want every warrior and artist in Ireland to come to the drinking hall with their wives." Sin also takes advantage of the situation to make it clear that she is excluding the members of clan of Niall of the Nine Hostages, the famous O'Neill clan—that is, those who might oppose her own wishes. And she presents herself as the rival or adversary of this illustrious family.

Duiabsech, her children, and all those belonging to the clan of Niall are thus expelled from the Cletech fortress. But we are in an Ireland that has become Christian: The scorned wife rushes off to the Tuilen monastery, whose bishop-abbot is the holy figure Cairnech, to whom she tells all that has happened. Indignant, Cairnech rushes to Cletech accompanied by his monks. "But Sin didn't let them approach the fortress." Then the bishop-abbot acts like all the druids he is, in fact, the heir to. He digs a grave in front of the fortress, designating it explicitly for the king, according to the purest magical tradition—Christian or druid, that remains to be determined! He begins by putting himself into a state of anger, and then pronounces a formidable curse on the king and his fortress:

In this mound, forever,
everyone will know lies the tomb
of the hero Mac Erca ["son of Erc"].
His actions were nothing.
A curse on this hill,
on Cletech and its hundreds of warriors!

189

Let its wheat and its milk be bad,
let it be full of hatred and evil!
Let neither king nor prince live there,
let no one come out of it victorious!
On this day, here on this mound
the tomb of the king of Ireland!

Even though this "satire" is pronounced by a bishop-abbot, it contains unmistakable pagan resonances and recalls ancient Irish pre-Christian rituals, as well as all the ceremonies performed by Roman priests along their enemies' frontiers. We are firmly entrenched here in the primitive European tradition, and it can be said that Christian Ireland has forgotten nothing of its origins, which has certainly unleashed the anger of the Roman Catholic Church in certain periods. And neither can we forget that Saint Patrick, Ireland's supposed evangelist, did his apprenticeship with a druid when he was a prisoner of the Gaels.[40]

Nevertheless, while returning to his monastery, Cairnech encounters Muirchertach's enemies, who want to make peace with the Irish king. He agrees to accompany them to sanctify the treaty. Of course, Sin forbids Cairnech from entering the fortress, and the king is obliged to leave it to take the vow of friendship in the company of these ex-enemies. "Then the treaty was sworn and after having used a vessel to mix the blood taken from two of them, Cairnech wrote out the clauses of the treaty," cursing in advance all those who would break it. Then Muirchertach goes back into the fortress, and Cairnech heads off again for his monastery.

The Irish king can finally turn his attention to Sin. And clearly, this mysterious woman deeply intrigues him. "He asked her questions, because it seemed to him that this was a very powerful goddess." Finally, he asks her these questions, in the form of a poem:

Tell me, o beautiful girl,
do you believe in the God of the clerics?
How did you come to this world?
Tell me your origin . . .

And it is also in the form of a poem that she responds:

I believe in the same true God,
my body's savior against the attacks of death.
But he can do no miracle in this world
that I cannot perform just as quickly.
I am the daughter of a man and a woman
of the race of Adam and Eve.
I am very well disposed toward you
provided that you aren't overcome with remorse.
I can create a sun, a moon,
radiant stars.
I can create cruel men,
implacable warriors.
I can, honestly, make the water
of the Boyne into wine, just as I can form
sheep out of rocks
and pigs out of ferns.
I can make silver and gold
before great crowds,
I can create famous men
for you, now, I tell you . . .

The program Sin proposes is tempting. And what is more, it is presented in accordance with the Christian spirit: "I believe in the same true God." But Sin claims to possess semi-divine powers that are weighed against those that the bishop-abbot Cairnech himself claims to have. It is true that most of the great Irish saints—at least according to the legends of their lives—are heirs to both the druids and the apostles at the same time. Thaumaturgy and "miracles" make up part of their initiation, and on many occasions Saint Patrick engaged in magical sparring matches with the druids, who refused to recognize his supremacy, exactly like the apostles confronting Simon the Magician. All this calls up the problem of magic within religion, and it is always in the name of the one God that miracles are performed, whatever name that God is given. In this narrative Sin clearly appears as a "sorceress," but what is a sorceress in the fifth century A.D.? What is a sorceress according to this story's fourteenth-century transcriber? Even if the Inquisition hardly took place in Great Britain and Ireland, something of Roman ideology remains in the way in which traditional texts are treated, especially during one period in which Ireland, long cut off from the dogmatic turbulence of Rome, began to feel the pressure of Anglo-Norman authoritarianism, in full allegiance itself with the papacy. This story of Sin and Muirchertach poses more problems than it resolves in the obvious confrontation it presents between an ancient druidic tradition and a triumphant Christianity.

Whatever the case, Muirchertach gives Sin a kind of challenge. He says to her, "Perform a few of these great miracles for us." The girl doesn't hesitate. She "came forward and lined up matching troops, each as strong and as well-armed as the other. And it seemed to them that on the earth there had never been troops more valiant or more brave, because one of them attacked the other and vanquished it in a few moments in the presence of everyone." We will recognize here the same marvels the three sorceresses, the daughters of Calatin, performed in *The Death of Cuchulainn* narrative, and we cannot help but think of the mysterious Welsh poem attributed to Taliesin, the *Cad Goddeu*, when the magician Gwyddyon changes the Bretons into trees and makes them fight victoriously against their enemies. Here we have a typical Celtic myth that we find echoes of in Gaul, Great Britain, and Ireland, a myth that in ancient times was also coupled with probable knowledge of an extraordinary organic energy we no longer have any idea of beyond the symbolic images that recall it.[41]

But that isn't all. Wanting to further assure her hold on the king and all present, Sin has three tubs filled with water from the Boyne and casts a spell over them. "It seemed to the king and his companions that they had never drunk wine of better taste or quality. Then, out of the ferns, she formed pigs, by means of enchantment." That, of course, recalls the fourth group of the Welsh *mabinogi* when Gwyddyon the magician conjures beautiful, rapid horses out of tree boughs, and then, with the help of his uncle Math, master of the magic wand, he forms a woman out of flowers and various plants; she is given the name Bloddeuwedd, which means "born of the flowers," or "aspect of the flowers."[42] It is plainly a matter of the same tradition involving powers attributed to the druids with relation to the use of organic energies. But it also reveals deep insight into the mysterious correspondences between the mineral, vegetable, and animal worlds. And it shows, in any case, the point at which the druids and their immediate successors, the Christian priests and bishops of Ireland, had arrived in their research. There is always one question we could ask ourselves in this regard: What has become of this apparently lost "magical" knowledge? Even if the question remains unanswered, it may be useful to ask it.

During an extraordinary feast, Muirchertach and his companions share the pig meat and the wine, and all night Sin keeps an eye on the king. But in the morning, the king and all those who took part in the feast feel very weak. At the least, they would be weak, since this was only an illusion; in reality they had nothing to eat or drink. There is an analogy here to the supposedly historical incidences taken up by the Council of Epernay in 1148 regarding the strange figure of Eon of the Star, a visionary monk and magician who held sway in that period in the forest of Brocéliande, and who created a veritable heretical sect. All those who came away from his table, no matter how richly furnished it was, felt as though there was nothing in their stomachs and almost fainted from hunger.[43] Maybe the very real figure of Eon of the Star was a distant descendant of the Irish druids after all.

This exhaustion doesn't in the least stop the king from asking the girl to show him more marvels.

> Then Sin took stones and made them into blue men. Then, with other stones, she made some men with goats' heads. Thus, there were four great troops of armed men before Muirchertach on the Brug plain.[44] Muirchertach then took up his weapons and his armor and rushed at them, as swift and angry as a bull. He killed and wounded many of them, but each man that he killed rose up again behind him. And he did this until the day became night.

The king abandons the battlefield and, completely exhausted, returns to the fortress of Cletch. Sin welcomes him and, pretending to comfort him, makes him drink magic wine. He sleeps soundly during the night. The next day he begins to fight the blue men and headless men again, still under the same circumstances.

That's when three clerics arrive, sent by Cairnech, who is nervous about the king's fate. "The men of the Church met him on the Brug where he was striking stones, branches, and hillocks." The situation is perfectly grotesque, but the clerics realize the king is bewitched and perform an exorcism. Muirchertach regains consciousness of reality, becomes very repentant, confesses, and takes communion. As for the clerics, they dig the foundations for a chapel on the slope facing the fortress, and the king promises to build the rest of it. Muirchertach manifests ardent faith in Christ and the Virgin Mary.

But as soon as he reenters the fortress, he falls back under Sin's "spell." She makes a great speech to demonstrate to him the ignorance and incompetence of the clerics, and then she completely muddles his mind. During the night, he has a strange dream, perceiving an army of demons and red flames over the fortress, and hearing the cries of enemy troops, in this case the members of the clan of Niall. He wakes up, rushes out of the fortress to rejoin the clerics, who are camping near the chapel foundations, and complains to them of his nightmare and his frailty. The clerics give him advice. The king returns to Cletech and addresses Sin: "Cursed is the tempest of this night, for the clerics in their camp. They cannot sleep because of this *tempest* of the night!"

Of course, he has just involuntarily spoken the name of Sin, and she reproaches him in no uncertain terms, prophesying that he will soon die. Nevertheless, she gives him something to drink and he sleeps soundly, haunted by another dream. "He found himself in a boat on the sea, and the boat sank, and a griffin with powerful claws came toward him, lifted him onto its back, and carried him down an endless drop while he felt the griffin's back burning him terribly." The king wakes up and cannot rest until he has gone to tell his dream to one of his companions, who is the son of a druid. His companion says to him:

> The boat is your realm on the ocean of life, and you, you are the pilot. The boat is sinking. You are carried off and your life comes to its end. The griffin with the powerful claws who carries you on its back is the woman who is in your company, who intoxicates you, who takes you into bed with her and who keeps you in your Cletech fortress so that it will burn down around you. The griffin fell with you, which means that this woman will die because of you. That is the meaning of this vision.

More and more exhausted, Muirchertach falls back asleep. "While he slept, Sin arose and arranged the warriors' swords and javelins before the doors, the points turned toward the interior. By magic she conjured large crowds around the fortress. She herself reentered the fortress and threw fire throughout, on the ramparts and on the house. Then she went back to bed." It is then that the king awakes, frightened by the tumult. Sin claims that his enemies are there, ready to avenge themselves on him for the Battle of Granard.[45] Muirchertach rises hastily, looks for his weapons, but cannot find them. Sin bounds out of the house and the king follows her, completely distraught. He encounters the warriors, who strike him violently and turn him back toward his bed. But the fire crackles on the roof. He looks for a way out and can't find one. "He caught up a helmet full of wine and threw it over his head to protect himself from the fire. But the fire fell on him: five feet of his body were burned and the wine protected the rest."

The next morning the clerics discover the half-burnt body of Muirchertach. They inform Cairnech, and the latter, grief-stricken, carries the cadaver himself to Tuilen. There Queen Duiabsech dies of grief when she sees this sad sight. Cairnech has the queen buried in a tomb, and the king is buried "near the church on the north side," that is, in the spot reserved for infidels and the excommunicated. That doesn't keep Cairnech from composing a prayer to ask God to pardon the sins that Muirchertach committed, and to honor the past actions of the king.

However, "when the clerics had finally buried him, they saw coming towards them a beautiful, radiant woman, all alone, wrapped in a great cloak trimmed with gold fringes, and over her skin, a rich silk blouse. She reached the spot where the clerics were standing and greeted them. They, too, greeted her. They saw that she had a sad and helpless air about her, and they recognized her to be the girl who had led the king to his downfall." Cairnech then asks her who she is and why she acted as she did. The girl gives him her name and explains that she wanted to avenge her father's death, as well as her mother's and her sister's, all killed by Muirchertach in the Battle of Cerb, on the Boyne, as well as the loss of many relatives and friends. But she displays her grief in a moving song of lament:

> *I myself will die of sadness because of him,*
> *the noble king of the western world*
> *under the weight of the great suffering*
> *that I caused for Ireland's sovereign.*

Alas, I have mixed up a poison for him
that has poisoned the king of the noble troops . . .

She has Cairnech hear her confession, and "there, immediately, she died of grief for the king." Cairnech orders his monks to dig a tomb for Sin and to cover it with turf. And this is how Sin disappears, this strange figure with the evocative name, the magician who is heir to ancient druidic practices, but who is reconciled to the Christian God after carrying out the vengeance that fate had in store for Muirchertach, despite her love for him.

Suibhne's Folly

Particularly moving in and of itself and probably one of the master-pieces of Gaelic literature, *Suibhne's Folly*[46] poses certain problems that are difficult to resolve. In it we discover the primitive framework of a the well-known story of Merlin, at least in its earliest version, the one in which the hero appears under the name of Lailoken among the Bretons of the north, also called the realm of Strathclyde, in the area of Glasgow.[47] Did the northern Bretons influence the Irish Gaels or was there Gaelic influence in the Britonic legend of Merlin? The narrative involving Suibhne originates with a very precise historical reference, the Battle of Moira in 637, which involves the Irish king and some Gaelic contingents coming to recently Christianized, Gaelicized, Scotland. But the hagiographic *Life of Saint Kentigern*, which deals with Lailoken, as well as the *Vita Merlini* by Geoffery of Monmouth, the first version of the Merlin legend, allude to some historical events that took place at the end of the sixth century among those called the Bretons of the North. It is difficult to determine which tradition pre-dates the other. Furthermore, *Suibhne's Folly*, to the same extent as the early legend of Merlin, brings into view certain conflicts between the Christian clergy and the chiefs still very much influenced by the dru-idic religion.

Suibhne (*Sweeney* is the English transcription) is king of Dal n'Araide (Dal Riada), a territory that corresponds to the modern-day counties of Antrim and Down, in Ulster. One day he learns that Saint Ronan, the same figure who will later appear in Brittany's Armorican tradition, is about to establish a church in his realm. He becomes furiously angry, grabs the psalter from the holy man, throws it into a lake, and mounts an attack to keep the Christians from constructing this church. At this stage in the story it is quite clear that Suibhne is not disposed toward admitting Christianity into his domain, which is contrary to the actual history, because northeastern Ireland had been Christianized some time previously. This is the same territory of Down where Saint Patrick, Ireland's evangelizer, had laid his earliest foundations. Must we view Suibhne's fury as a resurgence of druidism? Perhaps. At least, we must not see this as a banal power struggle between royal and ecclesiastical forces. Whatever the case, open war is declared between King Suibhne and the abbot-bishop Ronan.

But Celtic Christianity sometimes takes on very strange characteristics; in the hagiographical accounts the Irish saints, Patrick especially, often use magic methods they seem to have inherited from the ancient druids. Thus it happens that an otter returns Ronan's psalter to him, and the saint pronounces a curse against Suibhne. Then he tries to intervene and prevent the battle that is brewing. Becoming more and more furious, Suibhne kills one of Ronan's clerics with one throw of his javelin, and throws a second javelin at the saint himself. He succeeds only in breaking the bell he is carrying. Then Ronan pronounces a terrible curse against Suibhne, which strongly resembles a geis from the pagan period: Suibhne will fly into the air like the wood of the javelin, and later he will die from a blow from the same weapon he used to kill the cleric.

The battle begins, but in the middle of the tumult Suibhne is overcome by a terrible panic. His weapons fall out of his hands and he flees, his feet never touching the ground, across all of Ireland, until he comes, exhausted but somewhat calmer, to a pleasant and fertile valley, far from all habitation. Here he feeds himself on wild fruits, talks to the animals, and sleeps in a tree. One day he meets his grandson, to whom he sings of his life as a man of the woods: "I am in great distress this evening. The bitter wind pierces my body, my feet are sore, my cheeks are pale. . . . I have endured so much suffering that my body has grown feathers."

We cannot help but compare this story with the legend of Merlin, another king who goes mad during a battle and seeks refuge in a forest, where he makes prophecies and talks to the animals. We cannot help but notice a relationship between the feathers that Suibhne claims are growing on his body and the "shamanic flight," as well as the "language of birds," and again, the mysterious "plumed Merlin" to which certain Continental versions allude. By all evidence, like Merlin (and his model, Lailoken), under the power of a magical curse, King Suibhne has become the Madman of the Woods who returns to the domain of the former druids, the clearing in the forest, the nemeton where rituals are carried out that allow communication to be established between the visible and the invisible. And neither can we ignore the Welsh poems (actually, of the "Northern Bretons") attributed to Myrddin, that is to say, the historical Merlin. In any case the shadow of shamanism hovers over this out-of-the-ordinary situation.

Despite the pressing invitations of his grandson, Suibhne refuses to return to "civilized" life. He learns that his former wife is sharing a bed with a pretender to the throne, but that doesn't seem to upset him at all—no more than Merlin is upset when his wife Gwendolyn remarries, at least in Geoffrey of Monmouth's version. In any case he agrees to see her. Both of them recall their memories with much feeling, but Suibhne lets her leave with the man she has chosen. As for him, he makes the rounds throughout Ireland, and then establishes his residence in a yew tree. By using trickery—and probably magic—his grandson succeeds in bringing him back to his senses. Suibhne agrees to take his place again in community life and becomes king once more.

But one day someone mentions his past madness to him. Immediately, Suibhne climbs a tree and begins to become delirious, evoking the trees of the forest where he lived, the stags and the does that were his companions, and the privations he endured. This gives him the opportunity to chant some admirable poems:

> Last night, I was on the mountain of Moune. The rain
> and cold bit me cruelly. This evening, all the limbs of
> my body are broken on the fork of this tree I'm in. . . .
> I haven't rested in my wandering. . . . How hard it is to
> pass the night without feathers in a tree, at the top of a
> tree full of leaves, hearing no voices, no speech. . . . And
> I run wildly toward the mountain peak. Yet, when I
> was active, nothing vanquished me. Alas! I am stripped
> of all my goods.

And Suibhne once again flees to the forests where he continues to lead a miserable life.

However, his madness is healed by this contact with nature, and he himself decides to return to his realm. But Saint Ronan prays to God that Suibhne never be forgiven during his life on earth. Suibhne is seized by an extraordinary delirium. Bodies without heads and heads without bodies appear to him and follow him all over Ireland. He then arrives, exhausted, at the monastery of Saint Moling. Saint Moling welcomes him with kindness. The monastery cook prepares a vat full of milk for him to drink and take comfort in. But the swineherd, who is the cook's husband, is jealous of his wife's feelings for the unfortunate one. He strikes him with a javelin—the same one, of course, that Suibhne used to kill the cleric. Suibhne dies, but before dying, he receives communion and reconciles himself with God.

Thus ends *Suibhne's Folly*. But the questions this narrative poses are far from being answered, even if the link with the Merlin legend is clear. Renegade, apostate, druid, or shaman—which is Suibhne's real identity? Surely, he is the Fool of the Woods, with all the connotations of this "function"—because it is one—might have. And it makes for a very beautiful story.

The Voyage of Maelduin

This narrative[48] falls within the framework of *Imrama*, that is, those marvelous voyages heroes take to paradisical lands. This is one of the themes that has most engaged the medieval Celtic imagination. Founded on an archaic base that also gave us *The Voyage of Bran, Son of Febal*, it obviously belongs to the same tradition as the *Odyssey* or the *Argonauts*. But it is not at all clear that this is an adaptation, or even an imitation of the Greek model. We are always too willing to think that everything comes from the eastern Mediterranean; we forget that during the Middle Ages, as with antiquity, commercial and cultural exchanges occurred in both directions. In any case why not admit a common Indo-European base, translated according to the temperament of each culture?

But *The Voyage of Maelduin* contains no lack of surprises. First, despite a light Christian flavor, it has retained its clearly pagan character. Again, we must emphasize that its Christian elements are somewhat strange: Maelduin is the son of a nun (like Merlin the magician), and when he meets hermits on some islands, they more closely resemble cyclops and sorcerers than Christian monks. On the other hand, this story was so popular that someone later decided it would be good to make it entirely Christian. In the ninth century it became the *Navigatio Sancti Brandani*, a Latin narrative devoted to the marvelous pilgrimage of a certain Brendan who is searching for paradise, a work that was distributed throughout Europe and translated and adapted into many Anglo-Norman languages. It is this work that Renan considered "one of the most astonishing creations of the human mind and perhaps the most complete expression of the Celtic ideal."[49]

Now, the historical existence of Saint Brendan, who was supposedly the abbot of Clonfert, born in Ireland in 484, has not been very well established. Especially at issue here is a double by the name of Bran, and it is very curious to note that this is a Christianization of the well-known theme of the *quest* to reach the Land of the Fairies, the Celtic paradise, a quest carried out by a pagan hero, Bran, who became Saint Brendan (because heroes are always saints or demons in Celtic Christianity, which has never been able to get rid of some ancient beliefs), and filled with episodes borrowed from *Maelduin*.

But if Bran left to find the Land of the Fairies, Maelduin is content to hunt for his father's assassins. On the advice of a druid—and here we see the mix of paganism and Christianity—he embarks aboard a ship that he has built, accompanied by seventeen men. Now, at the time of departure his three foster brothers throw themselves into the water from the shore, in an effort to join him. It is an ill omen for them, and a kind of broken taboo, because it has been said that the boat must only carry sixteen men in addition to Maelduin.

The ship comes into the proximity of two bare islands. Maelduin hears a voice bragging of having killed his father, but just as he wants to land, a great wind carries the boat out to sea. That's when the fantastic voyage begins. First, they discover the Island of Birds, then a large island where "a beast resembling a horse was found. It had the legs of a dog, bristly hair, sharp claws, and great was its joy at seeing them, because it wanted to devour them, them and their boat." The voyagers barely escape this danger to run into another on an island where demon horses gallop about. Then they come to a very high island where a house stands. There is no one home, but Maelduin discovers nourishing food there, and excellent drink.

The next island is reminiscent of Emain, the Land of the Fairies. In fact, there is a thick forest covering the whole surface of the island, and Maelduin cuts a small branch from it. "Three days and three nights the branch remained in his hand . . . , and the fourth night, he had a cluster of three apples at the end of the branch. For forty days, each of these apples was enough for them to eat." What we have here, of course, is the "branch from the Emain apple tree" of *The Voyage of Bran*, a branch from those apple trees that grow on the island of Avalon *(Insula Pomorum)*, which bear the food of immortality.

The voyagers pursue their travels, landing in a country where the ground is heated by the feet of strange beasts that hide away in caves during the night (an image of volcanic earth), and where they gather magic apples (probably equivalent to the golden apples of the garden of the Hesperides). On another they enter a fortress. There is no one there except a cat that jumps from one pillar to another. Filled with wonder, the voyagers discover a treasure consisting of brooches, necklaces, and swords, and then a feast that seems to have been prepared for them. One of Maelduin's companions seizes a bracelet. Immediately, the cat rushes at him and reduces him completely to ashes. This was one of Maelduin's brothers, one of those who were not supposed to take part in the expedition.

Then the strangest and most significant episode in the narrative takes place:

> They notice a new island with a barbed stockade which divides the island in two. There were many sheep there, a black herd on one side of the fence, and a white herd on the other. And they saw a large man who was separating the sheep. When he threw a white sheep over the fence . . . , it immediately became black. Likewise, when he threw a black sheep over the fence, it immediately turned white.

We need to compare this episode with a passage in the Welsh narrative *Peredur*, which is also a *quest*, in fact, the archetype of the quest for the Grail, since Peredur is the same figure as Perceval.

On one bank, there was a herd of white sheep, and on the other, a herd of black sheep. Each time that a black sheep bleated, a white sheep crossed the water and became black. On the shore of the river stood a tall tree: one half of the tree was burning from the roots to the top branches; the other half was green with foliage.[50]

Here we are at the boundary between the two worlds. As much in *Maelduin* as in *Peredur*, it is a matter of a symbolic representation of the border zone where exchanges between the world of the living and the world of the dead take place. The tree that is burning on one side and green on the other is nothing other than the image of life that is also death, just as the Celtic god Teutas-Dispater is both the one who gives life and the one who gives death.[51] Moreover, Maelduin suspects something and so he tries an experiment: He throws a black branch onto the side of the white sheep and the branch becomes white; he throws a white one onto the black sheep's side and it becomes black. Terrified of the results of this experiment, and *afraid of changing color themselves*, the voyagers leave the island.

They come to an island that a large river runs through. German, one of Maelduin's companions, plunges his sword into it, and half of it is consumed as though it had been burned by fire. Then they come to the Island of Weepers. One of Maelduin's surviving brothers gets mixed up with a group of people who never stop lamenting, and he himself begins to weep. All efforts to bring him back to the ship are in vain.

Another island is divided into four parts by four enclosures made of gold, silver, bronze, and crystal.[52] A very beautiful girl receives the travelers, and gives them food and drink that make them sleep for three days and three nights. When they wake up again, they are on their ship, out at sea. After that, they come to an island with a bronze fortress on top of it that can be reached only by crossing a glass bridge. A woman bids them welcome and serves them a food "which resembled cheese, or curdled milk. Each of them found the taste and the flavor to be what he wanted."

Here we come very close to the feast of the Grail in Corbenic, where, when Saint Vase appears, the guests find themselves served all the dishes they like best. Maelduin's men think that the woman would make a perfect wife for their chief, and suggest that she sleep with him. She then serves them a drink that puts them to sleep, and they once again find themselves on their ship, sailing away from this mysterious island.

After various adventures, notably on the Island of the Wild Blacksmiths, where a cyclopean figure analogous to Polyphemus of the *Odyssey* throws a mass of red iron at their boat, they sail "on a sea which looks like green glass. So clear was it that they could see the pebbles at the bottom of the sea." From there, they cross a "sea similar to a cloud, and they didn't believe it could support their boat. Then they looked under the sea: there were the roofs of a fortress and a beautiful country." Of course, this is the Drowned City, or more precisely, the Underwater Country, so common in literature with Celtic origins.

Around another island, the waves form an impassable wall of water. A woman literally bombards them with large nuts. On an island nearby the sight is no less strange. A column of water rises from one side of the island to fall onto the other side, in such a way that the voyagers can pass under this arc without getting wet. Then they discover an immense column of silver in the middle of the ocean, and a voice coming from the top of the column addresses them in an unknown language.

Farther on they come to an island on a pedestal. They look for some way to gain access to it, but in vain. There are people on this island, but these people don't say a single word to them, which recalls the *silent ones* of Latin and Greek poetry. Finally, they come to a magnificent land where they are received by a queen and her seventeen daughters. The queen, a new Circe, or rather, an new aspect of Circe, makes them remain there for the three months of winter, "and it seemed to them that those three months lasted three years." Maelduin becomes the queen's husband, while his companions marry the seventeen daughters.[53] They are all homesick, however, and ask Maelduin to return to sea. Taking advantage of the queen's absence, they embark and raise the anchor. But at that moment, the queen appears and "threw a ball of string at the boat. Maelduin caught it and it stuck to his hand. The queen only had to pull on the string to make the boat return to shore."[54]

Thus the voyagers remain on the mysterious island for nine months. Finally, Maelduin's companions hold council, decide to embark, and take precautions to keep their chief from catching the ball of string if the queen should throw it toward them. This is what happens: One of the crew catches the ball, which sticks to his hand. Immediately, Diuran the Poet cuts off the hand, and the boat, freed, regains the open sea. "Then the queen began to lament and to cry out in such a way that the whole earth was nothing but cries, wails, and despair."

This doesn't mean the adventures are over, however. The voyagers discover an island of intoxicating fruits and make a visit to a hermit, one of Brendan's last companions—according to the text—that is to say, in fact, one of the companions of Bran, son of Febal. They witness a battle between two eagles after which the wounded, losing bird plunges into a fountain and regains all its strength. None of the travelers dares to bathe in this fountain except Diuran the Poet, and that is why, until his death, he suffers from no pain or disease. Here we can recognize the famous Fountain of Health of the Tuatha de Danann, which Diancecht filled with all the healing herbs and which is described in *The Battle of Mag Tured*.

After that, the voyagers come to the Island of Laughers, where one of them, Maelduin's third brother, gets mixed up with the inhabitants, begins to laugh like them, and cannot return. This episode is exactly identical to the one in the *Voyage of Bran*. After having come up beside a rampart of fire (yet another reminder of volcanoes), they meet a hermit who tells them his story, reveals to them where the murderer of Maelduin's father is to be found, asks Maelduin to pardon this crime, and shows them the way to follow to return to Ireland. They take leave of the hermit and, like the ancient Gauls who emigrated by following the flights of birds, follow a falcon to find themselves once again in sight of the Irish shores.

With its many unexpected reversals, this *Voyage of Maelduin* is clearly of interest for studying Celtic beliefs. But we must not forget the part that dream and poetry play here, which is what makes this narrative a masterpiece. As we have said, Renan considered *The Voyage of Saint Brendan* to be "the most complete expression of the Celtic ideal"—and he had before him only a pale copy, altered and watered down by a somewhat dull-witted Christianity. What would he have said if he had read *Maelduin*, that is, the original? There is no possible comparison between *The Voyage of Saint Brendan*, a minor work, placating and edifying, meant for the use of young boarding students in convents, and *The Voyage of Maelduin*, a work of poetry, strong and full of color.

Nevertheless, this tradition has not been lost to everyone. Rabelais rediscovered in Celtic folklore those things he so often used without even knowing they were Celtic. Beneath their satire, the adventures of the *Fourth Book* and *Fifth Book* are in the same vein and of the same inspiration. When will someone, then, decide to read Rabelais, forgetting that he was a devout Hellenist, and reveal to us the true sources of *Gargantua* and *Pantagruel*?

Another writer who remains largely unknown and unappreciated within the academy (although that may be an honor), a writer from the beginning of the twentieth century, Alfred Jarry, has nevertheless gotten *Bran*'s and *Maelduin*'s message. And he has truly gotten it, because he read the French translation of *Maelduin* by d'Arbois de Jubainville and the English translation of *Bran* by Kuno Meyer. This can be proven by the details found in his work scorned by *serious* readers, the *Gestes et opinions du docteur Faustroll*, which includes a typically Celtic voyage and in which Bran's name is even cited, directly or through word play (the Baron Hildebrand on the sea of Abundes). But of course Alfred Jarry is, above all, the author of *Ubu Roi*, which the programmers *(sic)* of our academic *(sic)* culture believe is dishonorable to recommend. It is true that humor is dangerous, especially when it is black. And that is perhaps what so many "serious" people find disconcerting about Celtic literature. At no time does it depart from poetry (which is not serious anymore) or humor, and it is a grating humor—which does harm, which is corrosive, which knocks the lid off a pot already cracked and full of holes, the pot of classical logic that assured the tranquillity of minds.

But in our world—which is looking for an identity, which has lost contact with human nature because of abstract will, because of the desire to classify by category—can there be any remedy more marvelous than a *Voyage* into dream and imagination? Finally, the solution to our problems is found in man and in man alone, whenever he comes to understand that he must travel through the islands of his thought and his desires.

⊃ote

INTRODUCTION

1. Michel Bréal, *Mélanges de mythologie et de linguistique* (1877), 155.

2. Here are the names of the most important manuscripts for the epic literature of ancient Ireland: *Leabhar na h'Uidre (L.U.)*, that is, the *Book of the Brown Cow* (an allusion to the binding), the oldest (1100), for which the copyist was a certain Maelmuire Mac Ceilechair, and which is kept in the Royal Irish Academy of Dublin; *The Book of Leinster (L.L.)*, dating from about 1150 and kept at Trinity College in Dublin; the Rawlinson B 502, comprised of twelve folios from the eleventh century and seventy folios from the twelfth century, kept in the Bodleian Library of Oxford; the *Yellow Book of Lecan (Y.B.L)* and the *Book of Ballymote*, both from the fourteenth century and kept at the Royal Irish Academy in Dublin; the Harleian 5280 and the Egerton 1782, both from the fifteenth century; the mss. *X.L.* of the Law Library of Edinburgh, the ms. of Leyde, and the *Book of the Lismore Deanship*, all three from the sixteenth century; and the Additional 18747, from the eighteenth century. The library of the Royal Irish Academy in Dublin, just by itself, contains thirteen hundred manuscripts from the twelfth through the nineteenth centuries. For information on this subject, see H. d'Arbois de Jubainville's *Essai d'un catalogue de la littérature épique de l'Irlande* (Paris: 1883), with a supplement in the *Revue celtique* XXXIII: 1–40.

3. George Dottin, trans., *L'Épopé irlandaise*, new ed. presented by J. Markale (Paris: les Presses d'Aujourd'hui, 1981).

4. In the following study only a small part of the whole incredible collection of very diverse narratives can be found. Because this literature is so rich, it is impossible to comment on all of it. Moreover, I have systematically excluded all narratives inspired or too heavily marked by Christianity, not because they are of any lesser interest (which is

206

not at all true), but because I wanted to limit myself to Celtic civilization in its most archaic and thus most original state.

CHAPTER 1

1. Rawlinson B 502 ms. English translation by Kuno Meyer, *Voyage of Bran* (London: David Nutt, 1895). French translation by d'Arbois de Jubainville, *L'Epopée celtique en Irlande* (Paris: 1892).

2. According to Meyer and d'Arbois de Jubainville.

3. Harleian 5280 ms. Text and English translation by Withley Stokes, *Revue celtique* XIII: 52, 306. French translation by d'Arbois de Jubainville, *L'Epopée celtique en Irlande*, 403. Extracts, Georges Dottin, *L'Epopée irlandaise*, 37.

4. On this subject see Jean Markale, *The Celts* (Rochester, Vt.: Inner Traditions, 1993), 106–108.

5. This First Battle of Mag Tured we know in detail through Keating's *History of Ireland,* a vast compilation from the seventeenth century.

6. In the Welsh tradition it is not Nudd but Lludd Llaw-Ereint (golden hand) who goes by this nickname.

7. In the *Song of Roland,* see the episode concerning King Marsile, who, having lost his right arm, flees and is forced to give his power over to the emir Baligant.

8. This dialogue between Lugh and the porter, who answers that there is already someone with that talent at the gathering each time Lugh declares a skill, has an identical counterpart in the Welsh narrative of *Kulhwch and Olwen,* with Gwalchami-Gauvain for its hero. A Welsh poem from the *Black Book of Carmarthen* treats the same subject.

9. See Markale, *The Celts,* 231–34, 276; *L'Epopée celtique en Bretagne* (Paris: Payot, 1971), 44, 199.

10. Eugene O'Curry text, *Atlantis* IV: 220. English translation by Tom Peete Cross and Clark Harris Slover, *Ancient Irish Tales* (New York: Henry Holt, 1936), 49. French translation by R. Chauviré, *Contes ossianiques* (Paris: 1947) and Ch. J. Guyonvarc'h, in *Ogam* XVI: 233.

11. Text from various mss. by Kuno Meyer, English translation, *The Voyage of Bran.* French translation by Dottin, *L'Epopée irlandaise,* 55.

12. *L.L.* and Egerton 1782 ms. Published by E.Windisch, *Irische Texte* III (Leipzig: 1880–1909), 230; French translation by d'Arbois de

Jubainville, *Les Druides* and *Les Dieux à forme d'animaux*, and Ch. J. Guyonvarc'h, *Ogam*, XII: 73.

13. When the Tuatha de Danann took refuge in the mounds, they elected Mananann Mac Lir for their king, and he lavished his pigs upon them for the feast of immortality that the blacksmith Goibniu held. In Welsh literature the swineherd and the swine share the same sacred character, as becomes clear from the episode in "Mabinogi of Math" telling how Gwyddyon seizes the swine of Pryderi.

14. Ch. J. Guyonvarc'h trans., *Texts mythologiques irlandais* (Rennes: Éditions Ouest-France, 1980).

15. Guyonvarc'h translation. The three quotes that follow also come from this translation.

16. See Markale, *The Celts*, 234.

17. See Mircea Eliade, *Le Chamanisme*, new ed. (Paris: Payot, 1992).

18. *L.U.* ms., text transcribed by Maelmuire Mac Ceilechair, who died in 1106. Published with English translation by J. O'Beirne Crowe, *Kilkenny Archaeological Journal* (1870): 1. English translation by P. W. Joyce, *Old Celtic Romances* (London: David Nutt, 1879), 94.

19. I have translated this poem in *Cahiers du Sud* 319: 383. For all these matters, see Markale, *The Celts*, the chapter entitled "The Submerged Town or the Celtic Myth of Origins," 21-36, and especially 24-25.

20. Hersart de Villemarque, *Barzaz-breiz chants populaires de la Bra* (Paris: Perrin, 1987), 39-46. This poem may not be as apocryphal as is generally assumed. It seems to be made up of scattered and very fragmentary elements surrounding the legend, badly assembled. Basically, all Villemarqué did was to follow the example set by numerous Irish and Welsh authors.

21. A text from the *Dindshenchas* (Rennes mss., published with an English translation by Stokes, *Revue celtique* XV: 481) relates the same adventure with Oengus, happening not to Ecca, but to Rib; it is Mider, the adoptive father of Oengus who gives him the horse, and the horse begins to urinate so much that Rib has to build a house around him. Thirty years later the urine overflows and the whole country is drowned under a lake. We must note that in the Razzia de Cualngé, the queen Medb urinates for such a long time that she creates an actual lake, which is called Fual Medb (Medb's urine) ever after.

22. Gwyddno Garanhir: "Great cries of madness overwhelm me this night."

23. Gwyddno Garanhir: "Cursed be the young woman who has freed, after having groaned, this guardian of the fountain, the formidable sea."

24. *Y.B.L.* ms., and for the second part, Egerton ms. 1782. Fragments in *L.U.* text in Ernst Windisch and Whitley Stokes, *Irische Texte* (Leipzig: 1880), 127. Text and English translation by R. I. Best and Osborn Bergin in *Eriu* XII: 142.

25. The same story is told in a different way in *The House of the Two Cups.* (*Livre de Fermoy* mss. Text and English translation by L. Duncan in *Eriu* XI: 186 and Dobbs and Van Hamel, *Zeitschrift für Celtische Philologie* XVIII: 190) Oengus is the adopted son of Elcmar, and it is Mananann, the head chief of the Tuatha de Danann, who suggests to Mac Oc a way to seize the Brug: "Throw upon him a geis of destruction of some kind so that he cannot enter the house again until the earth and sky, sun and moon are joined." Oengus obeys and Elcmar leaves the Brug with all his own. Then Oengus feels remorse and invites his adoptive father to stay, since the power of the geis is such that he cannot, in any case, enter his old residence again.

26. There is historical significance to these three demands. These are the Tuatha de Danann, that is, the megalithic populations who were the first to clear Irish lands, drain the marshes and the peat bogs, and use gold and silver.

27. According to the other texts, this is Oengus's ritual gesture of protection. See "Diarmaid and Grainne" in this volume.

28. See the commentaries that this theme inspires in "The Adventures of Art, Son of Conn" in this volume.

29. See Markale, *The Celts,* 229-230; *L'Epopée celtique en Bretagne,* 94-108.

30. This description is given almost word for word in the text of *The Destruction of the Inn of Da Derga,* with regard to the same Etaine.

31. Egerton 1782 ms., Best and Bergin translation.

32. Which is only found in Egerton 1782 ms., Best and Bergin translation.

33. It must be admitted that Racine's Hippolytus does not shine with intelligence or character. He is truly spineless, and by virtue of Racinian Jansenism it is right that he receives no pardon, that he is condemned.

34. The *Deo Medru* of the Strasbourg museum (inventory 30377) bears a lance in his left hand, is dressed in a sort of cloak, and rests his right hand on the head of a bull.

35. This is one of the similarities between Eochaid and King Arthur, whose name may also come from the root *ar*, "plowman." The second similarity is going to be the abduction of Etaine, which can be compared to the kidnapping of Guinevere by Meleagant. The nickname *Aireainn* seems more related to the tradition according to which Eochaid razes the Irish burial mounds; more on this subject to follow.

36. There is a kind of epilogue. Eochaid attacks all the sidh unrelentingly, razing them from top to bottom to find Etaine. In the end, to calm him down, Mider gives him the so-called Etaine, who is, in reality, the daughter of Eochaid and Etaine. When Eochaid realizes that he has slept with his own daughter, his shame is so great that he ceases to attack the mounds. As to the child that he has by his own daughter, he tries to get rid of her, but she lives and becomes the mother of Conaire the Great. See "The Destruction of the Inn of Da Derga" in this volume, which is the continuation of "The Courtship of Etaine."

37. Egerton 1782 ms. *Revue celtique* III: 344. Complete French translation by Guyonvarc'h, *Textes mythologiques irlandais*, 233-235.

38. "The Food of the House of the Two Cups," a narrative included in the manuscript entitled the *Book of Fermoy* (fifteenth century), Guyonvarc'h translation, *Textes mythological irlandais*, 258. Emain Ablach, the "isle of the apples or the apple trees," where Bran, son of Febal goes, is the equivalent of the isle of Avalon from Arthurian legend.

39. Guyonvar'ch translation. Fingen the doctor appears in many narratives from the Ulster cycle. He is the perfect example of the druid-doctor.

40. In fact, Boann is the Boyne River deified. This name comes from *Bovinda*, the "white cow." According to the *Frâech and Finnabair* narrative, her sister is named Be Finn—that is, "beautiful woman," or "white woman"—which cannot help but evoke the "white ladies" of popular tradition. In reality, Be Finn and Boann are two names for the same divine figure of the sweet waters, of whom, in all likelihood, the fairy Vivian of Arthurian tales is the exact replica, on both the mythological and the linguistic levels.

41. Guyonvarc'h translation.

42. Guyonvarc'h translation.

43. *X.L.* ms. from the Law Library of Edinburgh. *Revue celtique* XVII: 127–153. Complete French translation in Dottin, *L'Epopée irlandaise,* 76–90.

44. The Gaelic name *Finnabair* is identical to the Welsh name *Gwenhwyfar* (white ghost), which is also the name of the queen Guinevere of Arthurian legend.

45. In fact, Be Finn is the double of Boann, who goes by the name of Eithne as well. Divine figures in Irish mythology are often presented in triads, and we often hear of the "triple Brigid," goddess of poetry and technical skills, but who can also be presented under the names of Bobdh, Macha, or Morrigan.

46. Dottin translation.

47. To boil food in. The cauldron is found in almost the center of the house, on the hearth, under the opening of the roof that allows smoke to escape.

48. Dottin translation.

49. Ibid.

50. Here an interpolation slips in: "Unless he comes to help us in the Cattle Raid of Cualngé," which links this narrative to the Cualngé cycle. But this connection is absolutely artificial, even if Frâech is one of the warriors killed during one of the battles of the raid.

CHAPTER 2

1. I have omitted from the Ulster cycle all the narratives involving Cuchulainn, the importance of this figure warranting a special chapter.

2. *L.L.* and Harleian 5280 mss. Text in Windisch, *Irische Texte.* French translation by d'Arbois de Jubainville, *L'Epopée celtique en Irlande,* 320.

3. See "The Birth of Cuchulainn" in this volume.

4. *Y.B.L.* ms. Text and English translation by Meyer, *Revue celtique* VI: 173. French translation by Dottin, *L'Epopée irlandaise,* 64.

5. The same text also presents another version. Ness sees the druid Cathbad pass and asks him, "What is this moment good for?" The druid answers, "To make a king with a queen." Ness invites him to come close, "then Ness became pregnant and the child was in her womb three years and three months."

6. *L.L.* ms. Text and English translation by Stokes in *Eriu* IV: 18. French

translation by Guyonvarc'h in *Ogam* XI: 56 (under the title *Naissance de Conchobar*).

7. Here we can recognize the *jus primae noctis*, the famous sexual rights of the lords of the Middle Ages.

8. Except Fergus, who cannot be satisfied with a single helping. Indeed, Fergus is inordinately large. It takes seven pigs and seven beef cattle to feed him, and even seven women to satisfy his sexual needs.

9. *L.L.* and Harleian 5280 mss. Text and English translation by Stokes, *Revue celtique* VIII: 48.

10. This is Conall's deformity. The other deformed Ulates were Cuscraid the Stutterer and Cuchulainn the One Eyed. All the women who fall in love with these heroes take on the same deformity. See "Cuchulainn's Childhood" in this volume.

11. This curious custom of mixing brains with earth to make a weapon seems very ancient. But outside of this text, there are no other details on the subject. This detail is very important, moreover, for *The Death of Conchobar*. As to the ritual of cutting off of heads, see Markale, *The Celts*, 61–62, 79–80.

12. *L.L.* ms. Text and English translation by O'Curry, *Atlantis* III: 377. French translation by d'Arbois de Jubainville, *L'Epopée celtique en Irlande*, 220. Dottin, *L'Epopée irlandaise*, 76 ("L'Exil des fils d'Usnech").

13. This image is found again just like this in the Welsh narrative *Peredur*. The hero, seeing a crow drink the blood of a duck on the snow, thinks of the woman he loves, who also bears these three colors.

14. See "Diarmaid and Grainne" in this volume, and the parallels between the geis thrown by an amorous woman and the love potion of Tristan and Iseult. Also see Markale, *L'Epopée celtique en Bretagne*, 215–223.

15. Y.B.L. ms. and *Book of Ballymote*. Text and English translation by Stokes, *Revue celtique* XXIV: 272.

16. The author is careful to specify that there were four Manananns. The first, son of Allot, lived on the isle of Arran and became Emain Ablach, thus the true Tuatha de Danann. The second was the son of Cerp, king of Man; the third, son of Lir, a famous merchant; and the fourth, son of Athgno. It is, in fact, a matter of all the same figure, but the author or the copyist, shocked by the disturbing paganism hidden in this mythic figure, divine and immortal, preferred to make four mortals out of him, from four different periods.

17. *L.L.* ms. Eugene O'Curry, *Lectures on the Manuscript Materials of Ancient Irish History* (Dublin: W. A. Hinch/P. Traynor, 1879), 637. French translation by d'Arbois de Jubainville, *L'Epopée celtique en Irlande,* 368.

18. O'Curry, *Lectures,* 643.

19. *X.L.* ms. Text and English translation by Kuno Meyer, *The Death Tales of the Ulster Heroes* (Dublin: Hodges Figgis, 1937), 36.

20. We can recognize here the theme of switched hats from the story of Tom Thumb.

21. Harleian 5280 ms. Text and English translation by Bergin, in *Eriu* VII: 242.

22. Egerton 1782 ms., Edited by Rudolph Thurneyson, *Die irische Helden und Königssage bis zum siebzehnten Jahrhundert* (Halle: Verlag von Max Niemayer, 1921), 311–317.

23. On the night of Samhain the mounds are opened, and there is communication between the world of the living and that of the dead. This belief has persisted in all Celtic countries, and notably in Armorican Brittany.

24. This is clearly a matter of a symbolic object and not an actual weapon.

25. Formerly at the Copenhagen musuem, not at the Aarhus museum (Denmark), with a copy at the National Museum of Antiquities in Saint-Germain-en-Laye.

26. Here I've used the French version that I mention in *Les Cahiers d'histoire et de folklore* 6 (1957): 65–72.

27. *X.L.* ms. Text and English translation by Meyer, *The Death Tales,* 32.

28. A more detailed account of the main events involving Fergus, Medb, and Ailill will follow.

29. We can see here that Ailill's idea of entertainment is worthy of Nero or Caligula.

CHAPTER 3

1. *L.U.* and Egerton 1782 mss. Text: Windisch, *Irische texte,* I 131–145. Alternate version: Egerton 1782 and Stowe D. 4.2 ms., edited by Meyer, *Zeitschrift für Celtische Philologie* V: 500. Duvau French translation in d'Arbois de Jubainville, *L'Epopée celtique en Irlande,* 22; by Guyonvarc'h, *Ogam* XVII: 366.

2. Her name comes from *epos,* the Britonic word for horse. Compare this to *equus* in Latin and *hippos* in Greek.

3. Inserted into *The Raid of Cualngé. L.L.* and *L.U.* mss. French translation by d'Arbois de Jubainville, *L'Enlevement des Vaches de Cooley,* 63–83. Partial translation in Dottin, *L'Epopée irlandaise,* 113–117.

4. The word is Britonic. It seems that an argument can be made for Breton origins for this hero. He might have been part of a tribe coming from the British isle, the tribe of Setantii belonging to the Brigantes who originally settled in Yorkshire and along the coast of the Irish sea. *Setana* is the Gaelic pronunciation of *Setantios.* We must not forget that Ireland was a mosaic of Gaelic and Britonic peoples, a mosaic in which the Gaelic element prevailed.

5. Exodus 34:29–35.

6. We are clearly dealing with a magic ritual here for achieving a state of trance. Here druidism seems related to shamanism as well.

7. The *Cuchulainn's Malady* narrative affirms this claim.

8. Dottin translation.

9. *Cu-Chulainn,* the "dog of Culann." *Chulainn* is the genitive of *Culann.*

10. It is all the more true that Cuchulainn's absolute geis (ban) will be against eating dog flesh, which makes perfect sense since the dog is, in some way, his totemic animal. Now, it is in violating this geis that Cuchulainn meets his death (see "The Death of Cuchulainn" in this volume). Thus, Cuchulainn's destiny is implicitly contained in his name, and his destiny is nothing other than his relative existence.

11. Compare this to adopting the veil among religious Christians, the use of monastic names among monks and religious figures, the adoption of the cassock among priests, the pontifical name of the pope, and so forth. The list is endless.

12. And not automatically inherited from the Greeks, because what evidence could be given for direct Greek influence? We must rid ourselves for good of our uterine complex with regard to the Greek and Latin worlds, a complex resulting from a stupid education that has endured for centuries and that has us look only toward the Mediterranean. Things are not so simple.

13. The same theme is found in the *Mabinogi of Owein* and the *Chevalier au Lion* of Chrétien de Troyes. Yvain kills the Black Knight, guardian of the fountain of Barenton (door to the Other World); but in marry-

ing the knight's widow, he himself becomes the guardian of the fountain. See Markale, *L'Epopée celtique en Bretagne*, 166–175.

14. I do not think we need to cite Vivien here, from *Aliscans* and the *Song of Guillaume*, or Roland, from the *Song of Roland*, who fight alone against one hundred thousand pagans. Those are cases involving the desperate resistance of men who know themselves to be condemned and who want to die heroically.

15. d'Arbois de Jubanville translation.

16. Egerton 106 ms. (eighteenth century). Text and English translation by Stokes, *Revue celtique* XXXI: 110. This entire narrative is compared with the *Courtise d'Emer* (Rawlinson B 512 and Harleian 32 mss.), text and English translation by Meyer, *Revue celtique* XI: 442. French translation by Guyonvarc'h, in *Ogam* XI: 44.

17. Let us remember that the term *Scot* originally referred to the Irish. It is with the founding of the Dal Riada realm, and then the founding of the Iona monastery by Saint Colom-Cil, that the Irish in northern Britain gave their name to the country.

18. *Courtship of Emer:* In the company of Loegaire and Conchobar; Arriving at the sorceress Scatach's, they have a vision of Emain Macha, and Cuchulainn is separated from his companions. It is not clear why Conchobar is there, because he is Cuchulainn's uncle and very old. Conall is the hero's foster brother and his usual companion, even if he is also much older.

19. *Courtship of Emer:* It is Domnall who teaches the tricks, which are perfectly ridiculous and very much suited to "freshmen": blowing into square bellows until their feet turn black or green, that is, until they run out of breath.

20. *Courtship of Emer:* Dordmair, who is called Dornoll, falls in love with Cuchulainn: "Great were her knees; she had heels in front, feet behind, she was hideous. Cuchulainn did not want her and she promised to get revenge" (Guyonvarc'h translation).

21. No doubt this is Forgall Manach (the Great Gallic Wily One), Emer's father in the *Courtship*, who, wishing to keep Cuchulainn away from his daughter, sends him to Scotland to get rid of him.

22. In the Irish texts there is an ongoing play of words between *Scotie*, that is, Scotland, and *Scythie*. Scatach's name means "the one who causes fear," or "the one who protects," which indicates the ambiguous nature of this figure, a being both divine and infernal.

23. *Courtship of Emer:* Uatach, taking on the aspect of a servant, enters Cuchulainn's bedchamber. Cuchulainn breaks her finger. The girl lets out a cry, which wakes the champion Cochor Crufe, who comes to do combat with Cuchulainn and succumbs to his blows. Three days later Uatach gives Cuchulainn the means of obtaining three wishes: a faultless education, marriage with Uatach, and the ability to foresee the future.

24. In the *Tain Bô Cualngé* Queen Medb offers "the friendship of her haunch" to the possessor of the divine bull.

25. One could speak of tantrism here, but we must be aware that all comparisons of this kind are coincidental. Moreover, the many forms that tantrism takes—Buddhist and Brahmanic—require us to be even more careful.

26. There is much more to say about this initiation by Celtic women warriors, especially about their relationship to shamanism, and about the fact that there are many woman-shamans.

27. *Courtship of Emer:* Scatach is at war with Aife and sends Cuchulainn against her rival. Cuchulainn fights Aife and spares her life, but only in return for three wishes: peace with Scatach, sleeping with him that night, and bearing him a son.

28. A narrative in the *Y.B.L.* is devoted to the son Conlea's arrival in Ireland, where he searches for Cuchulainn. But as two of his taboos are not to make himself known and not to refuse combat, he is killed by his own father with a stroke of the *gai bolga* because his father doesn't recognize him.

29. *Courtship of Emer:* Cuchulainn has killed Ess Enchenn's three sons, and she wants to get revenge.

30. That is why, in the *Tain Bô Cualngé*, Cuchulainn can come in at Ferdead's end and kill him with a stroke of *gai bolga*.

31. This story bears a strange resemblance to the *Romance of Tristan* (and also the legend of Theseus and the Minotaur). The Cornouaille owes a tribute of young men and women to the Morholt, the Irish giant. Tristan kills the Morholt, and since he is wounded, he roams the sea before being healed by Iseult, whose love he wins even if he himself remains indifferent. See "Diarmaid and Grainne" in this volume.

32. The manuscript breaks off here. *The Courtship of Emer* relates that, upon his return to Ireland, Cuchulainn goes to abduct Emer and her foster sister at the fortress of Forgall Manach.

33. *L.U.* ms.—incomplete version—*L.L.* and *Y.B.L.* Text in Stokes and Windisch, *Irische Texte.* German translation by Windisch. English translation by St-O'Grady in E. Hull, *The Cuchullin Saga,* L.W. Faraday, *The Cattle Raid of Cualngé,* J. Dunn, *Tain Bô Cualngé.* French translation by d'Arbois de Jubainville, *L'Enlèvement des Vaches de Cooley,* Dottin (fragments) in *L'Epopée irlandaise,* and Guyonvarc'h in *Ogam* XV, XVI.

34. The system of separation of goods existed in Celtic law.

35. See "The Two Swineherds" in this volume.

36. See "The Two Swineherds" in this volume.

37. See "The Malady of the Ulates" in this volume.

38. This scene with the bird and the bull is quite frequently represented on Gallic coins and is a favorite theme of the Osismi engravers. What's more, one of the sculptures on the Nautes altar in the Cluny museum in Paris, the famous *Taureau aux trois grues* [Bull with Three Cranes], seems to be an illustration of the same theme.

39. d'Arbois de Jubainville translation.

40. The theme of the sword appears again, but as proof of chastity, in the Tristan romance, when Mark surprises the two lovers sleeping in the woods but separated by the sword that Tristan has stuck into the ground. The king takes Tristan's sword and replaces it with his own. Let us also note the role of the sword in the legend of Phaedra, which Racine understood very well, since Phaedra, not being able to make Hippolytus love her, tries to get herself pierced with his sword; because he does not want to raise his weapon, she rips it away from him as a sign of castration, or simply out of fetishism. The meaning is simple: The sword is the phallic symbol *par excellence,* but when it is stuck in the ground, it is harmless; thus there can be no actual sexual act.

41. d'Arbois de Jubainville translation. This fantastic description has something to appeal to any lover of modern poetry. It is proto-surrealism, with true verbal alchemy, an incantation whereby the entire being participates in the metamorphosis that results. Just imagine that this literature dates back to the first centuries of the Christian era; that it comes from a country considered "barbaric" up till now; and that this theme of transformations is found represented earlier still, in the engravings on Gallic coins, notably from Great Britain, and also in certain petroglyphs on megalithic documents from Ireland and Brittany dating from the beginning of the second millennium B.C.

42. This chariot armed with scythes seems to be a Celtic practice because it is mentioned by the authors of antiquity: Lucien, Pomponius Mela, and Frontin. The Galatians will use it against Antiochus Soter in 272 B.C. In any case this description proves the archaic nature of the Irish civilization. While the Gauls and the Bretons are fighting from horseback, the Irish Gaels are still using the battle cart pulled by two horses, with a driver and a warrior. An extraordinary illustration of these battles from battle carts is found engraved on the pedestal of the famous *Cross of the Scriptures*, at the monastic site of Clonmacnoise (where the *Raid* narrative was recorded as well), in central Ireland.

43. See "The Death of Cuchulainn" in this volume.

44. See "Cuchulainn's Education " in this volume.

45. See "Cuchulainn's Education" in this volume.

46. The sword of Arthur—*Excalibur* in the French and English romances—is called *Caledfwlch* in Welsh, a name sometimes translated as "strong cutting edge" but that also comes from the Indo-European root meaning "lightning." *Caladbolg, Caledfwlch,* and *Excalibur:* these three terms designate a formidable weapon, the symbol of power and sovereignty, the "Violent Lightning," which is in keeping with the magic or divine origin of the sword. According to certain traditions, the sword Caladbolg would have been the sword of Nuada, one of the Tuatha de Danann. In any case, a bit later it is called the "sword of Lete, coming from the country of the gods." It is a magic and divine sword. We must note that Fergus plays an important role in the Ulster cycle, but probably diminished in relation to the role he must have played in the primitive tradition. The name of Fergus (perhaps *ferg* means "anger") bears some relationship to the name for man *(fer)* and to the Indo-European root from which come the Welsh *gwr* (man) and *guor,* a prefix corresponding to the Gallic *ver,* and the Latin *vir, virtus.* There is a certain relationship between *Fergus* and *virga* (the rod or penis) and *virgo* (the virgin).

47. Dottin translation.

48. Ibid.

49. This is a professor of letters speaking.

50. *L.L.* and Trinity College H3.18 mss. Text and English translation by Carl Marstrander, in *Eriu* V: 208.

51. In principle, Scandinavia. But the time might indicate the mythic country of the Fomor, which seems to be the case here, given the fairy

aspect the two young girls take on. See "Cuchulainn's Malady" in this volume.

52. Celtic societies are exogamic. All copulation within a clan is incest. Now, Cuchulainn has sucked the blood of Derbforgaille, which establishes a family tie between them, a blood tie.

53. Marstrander translation.

54. Text ed. by Windisch, *Irische Texte* I, 254. French translation by d'Arbois de Jubainville, *L'Epopée celtique*, 81.

55. See Markale, *The Celts*, 61–62, 79.

56. Ibid., 29.

57. *Mesca Ulad. L.U., L.L.* mss. Ed. by J. Carmichael Watson, Dublin 1941; W. M. Hennessy, *Todd Lectures Series* I, 1889. English translation by Cross and Slover, *Ancient Irish Tales*, 213. French translation by Guyonvarc'h, in *Ogam* XII, XIII.

58. This is the reputation all Celts had among the authors of antiquity.

59. See Markale, *The Celts*, 265.

60. Guyonvarc'h translation.

61. Guyonvarc'h translation.

62. In fact, only the men leave on this expedition.

63. See Markale, *The Celts*, 29, 237–51.

64. Guyonvarc'h translation. The well-known theme of the warrior's ardor. When Cuchulainn is filled with this ardor, he must be plunged into at least three vats of cold water, one after the other, to return him to normal.

65. For further explanation of this divine function, see Markale, *The Celts*, 276–78.

66. Guyonvarc'h translation.

67. In fact, we are dealing with an ancient rite that is part of the Samhain festival and that we find mentioned in other Celtic texts, in particular, *The Adventures of Nera* and the Welsh *Mabinogi of Branwen*, quoted in Markale's *The Celts*, 232–33: "When they knew they were drunk, they began to build a fire of coal around the house and use the bellows on it until everything was white hot. . . . The heat becoming intolerable, he threw his shoulder against the wall and flinging it open, got out, followed by his wife."

68. Here we see that the figure of Gargantua, a character from folklore who owes nothing to Rabelais, is the remnant of an ancient Celtic hero something like Cuchulainn. The same holds true in *The Cattle Raid of Cualngé*, when Cuchulainn takes on the whole Irish army alone.

69. See the role of Medb in the *Raid* and also Ailill's compliance with regard to the affair between Medb and Fergus the Exile.

70. *L.U.* and Trinity College H4.22 mss. Text in O'Curry, *Atlantis* I; Windisch, *Irische Texte* I. English translation by O'Curry, *Atlantis* II; Myles Dillon, *Scottish Gaelic Studies* VII. German translation by R. Thurneysen, *Sagen aus dem Alten Irland,* (Berlin: 1901). French translation by d'Arbois de Jubainville, *L'Epopée celtique en Irlande*; Dottin, *L'Epopée irlandaise*; Guyonvarc'h, in *Ogam*.

71. In the second part of the narrative, which is probably the end of a different text, his wife is called Emer, as in the other narratives in the same cycle. But it is not impossible that Ethne is a "wife for a year," that is, a concubine.

72. Birds are often fairy creatures (see The Birth of Cuchulainn" in this volume), or even humans transformed into birds by magic.

73. Though menhirs and other megaliths are not Celtic, they neverthe-less play an important role in Celtic beliefs. Perhaps in this act of leaning against a menhir, we must recognize a ritual for entering into contact with the Other World, otherwise known as a medita-tion ritual.

74. Two interpolations, no doubt coming from another text, interrupt the narrative. First, a general survey on the election of the high king of Tara and the festival of the bull. See "The Destruction of the Inn of Da Derga" in this volume. Then some curious precepts, spoken by Cuchulainn, on the role of the king. And finally, we find the manu-script repeating what comes before, with Emer in the place of Ethne Ingube, which proves that two ancient narratives were put together by the *L.U.* copyist.

75. Dottin translation.

76. The idea of chastity among the Celts has nothing in common with our Christian notion. For the man, it is a matter of keeping his word to a woman. For the woman, it is a matter of granting exclusivity to a man. Let us not forget that after being betrothed to Emer, Cuchulainn entered into at least two "annual marriages" in Scotland, without count-ing Scatach's "friendship of the thighs."

77. A poetic cliché: Mananann rides over the flowering plains of the sea. Mananann is the son of Lir, that is, the waves. See "The Voyage of Bran" in this volume.

78. Dottin translation.

79. *Y.B.L.* ms. Text and English translation by Best, in *Eriu* II.

80. Markale, *Les Grandes Bardes gallois* (Paris: Picollec, 1956), 90.

81. Ibid., 83.

82. Joseph Loth, *Mabinogian* I, 119. See Markale, *L'Epopée celtique en Bretagne*, 42–53.

83. See Markale, *The Celts*, 47–48.

84. Ibid., 30.

85. Blathnait's treason and her punishment recall the story of Tarpeia who, according to certain traditions, delivered Rome to the Sabins, according to others, to the Gauls, and who was crushed under the conquerors' shields to pay for her treason. Ibid., 55–56.

86. *L.L.* and National Library of Scotland XIV manuscripts. Text in Van Hamel, *Compert Con Culaind*, 69. French translation by d'Arbois de Jubainville, *L'Epopée celtique en Irlande*, 332; Dottin, *L'Epopée irlandaise*, 147; Guyonvarc'h, in *Celticum* VII and in *Ogam* XVIII.

87. See *Cad Goddeu*, "The Battle of the Trees" in Markale, *The Celts*, 237–251.

88. In the Edinburgh manuscript the sorceress throws the spit that wounds Cuchulainn. The poison cuts his strength in half.

89. Guyonvar'h translation.

90. Dottin translation.

91. Guyonvarc'h translation.

92. Dottin translation.

93. Guyonvarc'h translation.

CHAPTER 4

1. See Markale, *The Celts*, 258.

2. Text and English translation in *Revue celtique* V: 197, and by Meyer in *Eriu* I: 180.

NOTES

3. A narrative in the *L.U.* (French translation by d'Arbois de Jubainville, *L'Epopée celtique en Irlande*, 379) gives in detail the causes of the Battle of Cnuch. Nuada was the druid of Cathair Mor, king of Tara (perhaps we should recognize in this Nuada a vestige of the Nuada of the Silver Hand, one of the Tuatha de Danann). In payment for his services, Cathair gave him the fortress of Almu. His son Tagd, who was a druid as well, had a marvelously beautiful daughter, Muirne. Cumall, son of Trenmor, asked for her hand in marriage. Tagd refused and Cumall stole the girl. Tagd complained to King Conn of the Hundred Battles, who sent an expedition out against Cumall led by three chiefs: Urgrui, son of the king of Luagne; Daire the Red, also called Morna Wryneck; and his son Aed. That is how the Battle of Cnuch comes about. Cumall was killed in it and his men massacred, but Aed lost an eye and was called Goll (the One Eyed) from then on.

4. According to the *L.U.* text, Bodbmall, the Strong Woman, was the wife of Fiacail and the sister of Cumall. The Gray One of Luachair, who is not named in the *L.U.*, is one of those sorceresses or women warriors found so often in Irish texts.

5. This is still the case today among certain African peoples: The blacksmiths constitute their own class, with their own customs and a half-benevolent, half-threatening character. Lochan, whose name goes back to Loch, "the lake," recalls the blacksmith Trébuchet in Chrétien's *Perceval* and the Perzival of Wolfram. Trébuchet lives near the Lac source (Wolfram), or near Lake Cotoacre (Chrétien).

6. At the risk of seeming obsessed with Freud, let us note that the instincts of destruction are repressed within the unconscious, and thus the metaphor is very clear. The forger who represents both Thanatos and unmentionable Eros is driven back into Hell (the unconscious) by Zeus or any other divinity representing the clear and organized consciousness, that is, the superego.

7. This episode must be compared to Setana's initiation by the blacksmith Culann and the granting of his permanent nickname, Cuchulainn.

8. *Cruithnig*, "the Picts," is a word that, through the transformation of the ancient Indo-European Q (retained in Gaelic and Latin) into P (characteristic of the Britonic languages), we get *Pretannoi*, from which come *Britanni* and *Britannia* (the Welsh *Prydein*).

9. In fact, many other factors argue in favor of this hypothesis. The hatred between the clans of Morna and O'Baicsne—that is, Finn's ancestor—goes back to rivalries in Britain. The narrative *The Little Inn*

of Allen, which is quite recent, dating from the eighteenth century
(French translation in Dottin, *L'Epopée irlandaise,* 164–173), has Goll
say, "I went to Britain, I took possession of the country, I killed the
king and massacred his men; but Cumall drove me out."

10. The Finn cycle is marked by these magic wild boars: in addition to
this sow there is the wild boar of Ben Gulbain in the story of Diarmaid,
and the swine of Formael in *The Hunt of the Sidh of the Beautiful Women.*

11. The *Tucait Fhaghbala in fesa Do Finn inso* text (Stowe 992 mss., edited
with English translation by Meyer, *Revue celtique* XIV: 245) gives a
different explanation of how Finn obtained knowledge: Finn is already old. Each morning someone in his house is responsible for boil-
ing a pig. It is Oisin's turn. Now, *something* seizes the pig out from
under Oisin's nose and runs off with it. Oisin pursues *the thing,* to the
top of the Femn sidh, where it disappears inside. The next day the
same thing happens to Cailte. The third day Finn cooks the pig himself and *the thing* seizes the pig. Finn stabs the back of *the thing* with
his lance, and *the thing* flees, abandoning its prey. Finn pursues it and
breaks its back at the moment it enters the sidh. Finn puts out his
hand to hold the sidh door open, but the door closes on his thumb.
He then puts his thumb in his mouth and hears the lamentations of
the people of the sidh.

12. These three things seem to have been practiced by the druids and the
fili. The *teinn laida* requires the use of a wand, which was placed on the
object or the person about which the question was posed. To practice
the *imbas forosna,* one had to chew a piece of red pig, cat, or dog, and
sing an incantation to the divinities before falling into a magic sleep
lasting nine days; it was during this sleep that one learned what he wanted
to know. As for the *dichetul dichenniab,* that consisted of the improvisation of a quatrain. All three are analogous to shamanic rituals.

13. Markale, *The Celts,* 228–29; *L'Epopée celtique en Bretagne,* 96.

14. These famous *Paps of Anu* are found in the barony of Magunihy, County
Kerry. This is a vestige of Ana or Dana, ancestor of the Tuatha de
Danann, goddess-mother whose Welsh equivalent is Don and whom
we can recognize in the Latin Anna Parenna, the Indian Anna Purna,
and even the Greco-Scythian Diana. On the subject of this goddess-
mother, see Markale, *The Celts,* 278–86.

15. Manuscript of Leyde, sixteenth century. Text and French translation
by L. C. Stern, *Revue celtique* XIII: 12–17, reproduced in part in Dottin,
L'Epopée irlandaise, 157.

16. Ms. 24 B 28. Text and English translation by Joyce, *Old Celtic Romances* (1879), 223. Abridged French translation by A. H. Krappe, *Revue celtique* XL: 96.

17. Fragmentary texts: *Y.B.L.* and Harleian 5280, edited with English translation by Meyer, *Zeitschrift für Celtische Philologie* I: 458, and *Revue celtique* XI: 125. French translation by Dottin, *L'Epopée Irlandaise*, 160. *Book of Lismore*, English translation in *Revue celtique* XXXIII: 52, and Manuscript of the Law Library, Edinburgh; *Duanaire Finn*, edited with English translation by Eoin Mac Neill, 149, 197. Other fragments in Edinburgh Gaelic ms. XLVIII (*Revue celtique* XXX: 168). *Dindshenchas*, Rennes manuscript (*Revue celtique* XV: 447). Oral version discovered in 1774 by Campbell, *Leabhar na Feinne* (1872). Another complete version compiled in the eighteenth century, published by Standish O'Grady, *Transactions of the Ossianic Society* IV, translated into English by Cross and Slover, *Ancient Irish Tales*, 370.

18. Note the importance given to the potion both in the Irish legend and in the Britonic legend of Tristan.

19. Acccording to other texts, Diarmaid has a beauty spot that makes him irresistible to women. A popular Gaelic tale collected in the nineteenth century by Douglas Hyde presents an adventure that involves Oisin, Cailte, and Diarmaid spending the night with a peasant and his daughter. Each of them tries to climb into the daughter's bed to win her favors. To each of them she declares that she is Youth, and that she has already belonged to them and can no longer belong to them henceforth. But as a consolation, she gives Diarmaid the gift of being loved by all women.

20. Eighteenth-century version. See the episode of the geis in "The Story of Deirdre" in this volume.

21. In Celtic and Germanic languages the moon is masculine in gender and the sun is feminine. In certain traditions coming from northern Europe, and notably in the myth of the Scythian Diana, there is opposition between the moon god and the sun goddess. Also consider the story of the solar goddess Amaterasu in Japanese mythology, and the role of the moon god Sîn among the Assyrians.

22. Compare this with the role of queen Medb, who possesses sovereign power that she doles out not only to her husband but also to her lovers. The same is true for Guinevere, Arthur's wife, whose lover, Lancelot, is given a share of the royal power.

23. Modern commentators and adapters of the legend have generally understood nothing of this, Wagner in particular. In his opera he is content to season a few elements of the story with a Buddhist flavor all the more suspect because Schopenhauer spiced it up first. The praise for annihilation in the waves wished for by Tristan and Isolde seems to me less an aspiration for nirvana than a sadomasochistic belch from the being who is powerless to live for a "marvelous" destruction. The Wagnerian *liebentodt* finds its direct source in the Germanic mythology that produced Wagner and exalts in catastrophe and suffering, a beautiful prefiguration of Naziism. In fact, Wagner's *Tristan and Isolde* (and let us not speak of its incontestable musical genius) contains nothing either Buddhist or Celtic. It is Germanic in the worst sense of the word, with the foul smell of crematory ovens. At the opposite extreme, Jean Cocteau is the only one who has truly understood the myth's meaning and its schema. In his endlessly beautiful film, *L'Eternal Retour*, when Patrice requests the hand of Nathalie for Marc, Nathalie at first thinks he is going to ask for himself, and her expression reveals an intense mix of emotions because of this hope that she considers too beautiful to be true. And when she comprehends Patrice's indifference, she flees, slamming the door behind her. In another sequence, on a boat that carries Patrice and Nathalie to Marc, Patrice, seized by who knows what unconscious leap, says dreamily, "When I asked for you in marriage, I was foolish enough to think that you believed I was asking for myself." And Nathalie, tears in her eyes, answers him, "You have five years," which is an obvious allusion to his nonpuberty, thus to his lack of masculine power. In *L'Eternal Retour*, the love potion no longer plays a magical role, but takes a more important one on the psychological level. It is the object that serves to make Patrice aware of what has happened within Nathalie, and, unconsciously, within himself.

24. See Markale, *The Celts*, 228–230.

25. I believe that the meaning sometimes given to the name *Eve*, "water," must be taken very seriously, as we must insist upon the ambiguity of the name *Maria*, which means both "Mary" and "the seas [les mers]." But these interpretations only apply to the Latin, and we must remember that the Hebrew name for Eve is *Hava*, which means "life." But the name *Hava* is given to the woman—by Adam, no less—only after the fall and the banishment from Paradise. Up until then, if we are to believe the Biblical text, she was named Isha.

26. Do not forget the double meaning of *secunda,* "second" and "favorable."

27. Yahne le Toumelin, radio interview with Markale, *Lumière des Celtes,* ORTF (Paris), 1970. See "Cuchulainn's Education" in this volume.

28. *Y.B.L.* fragment, Dottin, 162–163.

29. Oengus has already gathered Etaine, changed into an insect, under his mantle. See "The Courtship of Etaine" in this volume.

30. Eighteenth-century version.

31. The Edinburgh Law Library manuscript, English translation in the *Revue celtique* XXXIII: 54.

32. R.I.A. 2 B 8 ms. *Revue celtique* XXXIII: 46.

33. R.I.A. ms. This assumes that Grainne had not yet been the wife of Finn.

34. *Duanaire Finn,* Eoin Mac Neill, ed., 197. The expression *son of O'Duibhne* means "son of the clan of Duibhne."

35. *Dindshenchas,* Rennes mss., *Revue celtique* XV: 447. Once more we can note an element that the Tristan legend shares, since there we find pieces of bark thrown into the current by Tristan to signal a rendezvous with Iseult. An oral version recorded by Campbell says that these are scraps thrown by Diarmaid into the current to show Finn the way to the cave.

36. Edinburgh Gaelic 48 ms. *Revue celtique* XXXIII: 168.

37. *Book of Lismore* R.C. XXXIII, 165. According to oral versions, Diarmaid's only vulnerable spot is his right heel, a clear echo of Achilles.

38. Eighteenth-century version.

39. Eighteenth-century version.

40. Edinburgh Gaelic ms. 48.

41. Eighteenth-century version.

42. On the subject of the legend of Tristan and its relationship to *Diarmaid and Grainne,* see the work of Michel Cazenave, *La Subversion de l'âme, mythanalyse de Tristan et Iseult* (Paris: Seghers, 1981). Also see Markale, *Women of the Celts,* (Rochester, Vt.: Inner Traditions, 1986) and *L'Amour courtois, ou le couple infernal,* new ed. (Paris: Imago, 1993).

43. Egerton 1782 ms. Text and English translation by Meyer, *Fianaigecht* (Dublin: 1910), 52. Partial French translation by Dottin, *L'Epopée*

irlandaise, 173. Fragments of the Bodleian Codex Laud 610 and Egerton 92 published by Meyer, *Zeitschrift für Celtische Philologie,* 464.

44. This is the Egerton 1782 version. The Bodleian version is very different: "Old age came to Finn . . . his men made him acknowledge it and he did not deny it. 'Why don't you go to the Irish king,' they said, 'and we will gather around you?' 'I am very satisfied,' he said. Nine men went with him. But in the morning, one of them went back to rejoin the Fiana. Then another left, and thus it went."

45. Meyer translation.

46. Which, coincidentally, seems to be the sequel to the fragment found in the Bodleian that has already been cited.

47. *Book of Fermoy* ms.; Nutt and Meyer, *The Voyage of Bran,* (1895), 42.

48. Egerton 88 ms. This short account seems to have been constructed just to prove the identity between Mongan and Finn.

49. The Gaelic word *finn,* which means "blonde, white, beautiful, and of good lineage," gives rise to many symbolic references. Thus, in this narrative, there will be continual and meaningful opposition between *finn* and *dubh,* which means "black."

50. See this entire account in "La naissance du roi Arthur" in Markale, *Le Cycle du Graal,* première époque (Paris: Pygmalion, 1992).

51. Mananann's cloak is a magic object, like Oengus's: It can contain innumerable objects and has the gift of making one invisible or causing a memory lapse.

52. This is one of the names of the Other World, but more specifically reserved for the mysterious realm over which Mananann Mac Lir is king.

CHAPTER 5

1. *Baile en Scail,* Harleian 5280 ms.

2. It is also claimed, in certain close circles of Scottish masons, that this is the "Stone of Jacob." But the antiquity of the stone of Tara needs no further proof: "It is the Tuatha de Danann who will bring with them the great Fal, that is, the Stone of Knowledge which was at Tara. . . . The one under whom it cried was king of Ireland" *(Book of Conquests).* But the same narrative, a synthesis of various ancient Irish traditions, adds this curious detail: "That is how it was until Cuchulainn struck the stone, because it hadn't cried under him or under his adopted son,

Lugaid." But the text adds, "Since then, this stone no longer cried except under Conn of Tara." That says something about the importance given to Conn of the Hundred Battles.

3. Actually, the daughter of Balor, the strange chief of the Fomor whose eye can strike down his adversaries, and whom Lugh kills with a slingshot during the Second Battle of Mag Tured. But Tigernmas is a nickname that means "great lord."

4. This will not always be the case, but this narrative was designed to give back to the ancient sanctuary of Tara, the absolute religious and political center of pagan Ireland, the prominence it lost with the introduction of Christianity. We know that in the fourth century, according to his legend, Saint Patrick lit the first Pascal fires on the hill of Slane, not far from Tara, a few moments before the king of Ireland lit the pagan fire of Beltane on the hill of Tara, in a year in which Beltane coincided with the Christian holiday of Easter. That is when the decline of Tara, a prehistoric, megalithic, and druidic site, as well as the theoretic capital of Ireland's high king, began.

5. The title of a series of broadcasts that I did for France-Culture radio in 1972.

6. *L.U., Y.B.L., Book of Fermoy*, and Egerton 1782 mss. Edited with English translation by Stokes, *Revue celtique* XXII. English translation by Cross and Slover, *Ancient Irish Tales*, 93.

7. Philippe Lavastine, radio interview with Markale, *Lumière des Celtes*, ORTF (Paris), 1970.

8. Ibid.

9. Ibid.

10. This is the meaning of the root of *regere*.

11. In fact, this curse is only explained in the third part of *The Courtship of Etaine* and in the *Dindshenchas*, a collection of stories about well-known places in Ireland (Rennes mss., ed. by Stokes, *Revue celtique* XV: 290). As a result of one of Mider's ruses, when he was supposed to return Etaine to King Eochaid, it was Esa, Eochaid and Etaine's own daughter, whom he brought back to the king. And the king had a daughter by her, Mess Buachalla. Thus Mess is both daughter and granddaughter of King Eochaid.

12. *The Race of Conaire the Great* text (*Y.B.L.* and *Book of Ballymote* mss., edited with English translation by Lucius Gwynn, in *Eriu* VI: 133)

presents the choice and crowning of the king very differently. "There was a royal chariot at Tara. To this chariot were harnessed two chargers of the same color who had never before seen a harness. . . . A man who was destined to the Tara monarchy could not master them. . . . There was a royal cloak in the chariot: for anyone who was not to be granted sovereignty over Tara, the cloak was too big. There were two stones at Tara, Blocc and Bluigme . . . which opened so that the chariot passed through . . . but they did not open before a man who could not be the monarch of Tara, and their usual position was thus: only the hand of a man could pass between the two of them. . . . And there was the Stone of Fal, the stone-penis, in front of a racing cart. When a man was to have the Tara monarchy, it cried out . . . in such a way that all the world could hear it." In this same text, it is Mess Buachalla, Conaire's mother, who shows her son the way to obtain the throne, and who, as a precaution, secures for him the assistance of a large army—which is none other than the army of the sidh of Bri-Leith, the mound where Etaine lived with the god Mider. All this is supposed to have taken place around A.D. 40 to 50.

13. Because there is the risk of killing the men of his race, who often take on the form of birds, as we have seen in the Cuchulainn cycle and in *The Courtship of Etaine.*

14. Literally: "You will not go around the city of Tara by the right or the plain of Breg by the left." Among all the Celts, Gaels, and Britons, the east is in front, the west behind, the north to the left (the cold and *sinister* side), and the south to the right.

15. A historical allusion to the incessant raids Irish pirates made along the western coast of the British isle.

16. In *The Sons of Conaire* text, he is called Ingcel Caech, the Breton. *Caech* (in Breton, Kaer) may mean "beautiful." A historic figure behind this name has never been identified.

17. If Fer Rogain and his brothers represent the negative forces of the unconscious, Ingcel the One Eyed, with his unquestionably cyclopean nature, represents the subterranean forces, otherwise known as natural catastrophes, earthquakes, volcanoes, storms. Thus, this is a pact between all destructive forces, material and psychological.

18. The king was required to keep open house for his subjects. As a result, not being able to meet his obligations, he delegated his powers to a head-host who, as a beneficiary of many gifts and taxes, took on this role as an administrative function. See Markale, *The Celts,* 111.

19. This detail reappears in many descriptions of Cuchulainn, which allows us to consider the Ulate hero a sort of divine woodsman, a sacred land-clearer, as d'Arbois de Jubainville observed in comparing him to a bas-relief representation found in the Cluny museum. Compare this to the description of the rustic in "The Feast of Bricriu" in this volume.

20. The mark of belonging to the Other World is this pig, which is the magic food of the Tuatha de Danann (the pigs of Mananann).

21. Stokes translation.

22. It is not surprising that he comes through almost alone, since, as a cyclops, he represents the disruptive elements of nature put into motion by the psychic will of Fer Rogain and his brothers. Once the latter disappear (that is, the destructive cause), the effects persist and spread throughout the world.

23. The narrative *The Sons of Conaire* (*L.L.* m., ed. with English translation by Gwynn, in *Eriu* VI: 144) recounts the vengeance of Conaire's three sons, who discover Ingcel Caech in the house of Nemed Mac Scrobcind and organize an expedition during which the Breton pirate is killed.

24. Twelfth-century ms., *Romania* XXVIII (1898), 558.

25. Dottin translation, *Les Littératures celtique* (Paris: Payot, 1924), 101.

26. Of course, this is Saint Patrick.

27. This is the name of the mound where a fairy king of the isle of women is supposed to reign.

28. See Markale, *La Tradition en Bretagne armoricaine* (Paris: Payot, 1975), 30–32. The hagiographical narrative was published by Arthur de la Borderie in the *Trois vies latines de saint Tugdual* (Rennes: 1887), 43.

29. *Book of Fermoy* ms., Text and English translation by Best, in *Eriu* II.

30. This detail proves that the measure of feminine beauty among the Celts, and particularly the Irish, was that artificial blonde obtained by dying, and not natural blondeness, which was quite rare among these people. Moreover, it is likely that men colored their hair themselves in certain tribes.

31. This is the well-known theme of the child who must be sacrificed so that his blood, that is, his new strength, can strengthen a fortress or a royal power. It is the theme developed in the legend of the child Merlin. We must notice the relationship here to the sacrifice of the first-

born among certain Semitic peoples (Isaac) and also to the role of Christ.

32. Let us mention in passing that the infamous Judge Lynch was Irish.

33. Although this is a Christian interpolation made by an author who has forgotten the very meaning of such a sacrifice.

34. Best translation.

35. This geis turns up again in the Welsh *Mabinogi of Math,* in which Arianrhod proclaims the following taboo for his son Lleu Llaw Gyffes: He can be loved by no daughter of men. That is why his uncle, the magician Gwyddyon, will use his incantations to create a woman out of flowers, Bloddeuwedd, in order to get around the taboo. See Markale, *L'Epopée celtique en Bretagne,* 71.

36. Compare this to Cyrano de Bergerac's journey toward the sun by means of a geodesic crystal chamber in which the convergence of the sun's rays produced incredible heat and made the chamber into a veritable reactor.

37. *Y.B.L.* ms. Text and German translation by K. Muller-Lisowski, *Zeithschrift für Celtische Philologie* XIV: 145. Text and French translation by M. L. Sjoestedt, *Revue celtique* XLIII: 8.

38. Sjoestedt translation.

39. *Y.B.L.,* fourteenth-century ms. Stokes, *Revue celtique* XXIII: 396.

40. On this topic see Markale, *Le Christianisme celtique,* new ed. (Paris: Imago, 1993).

41. See the translation of the *Kat Goddeu* in Markale, *Les Grandes Bardes gallois,* 74–81; commentaries in Markale, *The Druids* (Rochester, Vt.: Inner Traditions, 1999), 134–35.

42. Loth, *Les Mabinogion,* new ed., (Paris: Slatkine, 1979), 59–81; commentaries in Markale, *L'Epopée celtique en Bretagne,* 59–76.

43. See Markale, *Histoire secrète de la Bretagne,* new ed., (Paris: Albin Michel, 1992), 138–147.

44. The Gaelic name for the Boyne valley where the most beautiful megalithic monuments in all of Ireland are found. See, in particular, "The Courtship of Etaine" and "The Dream of Oengus" in this volume.

45. Which took place in 480, according to the *Annals of the Four Masters.*

46. Ms. from 1175, which includes a narrative and poems from at least the tenth century.

47. See Markale, *Merlin: Priest of Nature* (Rochester, Vt.: Inner Traditions, 1995), 41–42, 58–63.

48. Text in Meyer, *Zeitschrift für Celtische Philologie* XII: 149. French translation by d'Arbois de Jubainville, *L'Epopée celtique*, 455.

49. Ernest Renan, *Essais de morale et de critique.*

50. Loth, in *Mabinogion* II, 95.

51. See Markale, *The Celts*, 247–49, 276–77.

52. Which recalls Kaer Padryfan, the quadrangular citadel in a Welsh poem attributed to Taliesin. See Markale, *Les Grands Bardes gallois,* 84.

53. The same adventure happens to Bran, son of Febal. It is likely that the original version ended here, since the goal, that is, the Blessed Land, has been reached.

54. The same anecdote is found in *The Voyage of Bran.*

INDEX